It Happened on Washington Square

CENTER BOOKS ON SPACE, PLACE, AND TIME
George F. Thompson, Series Founder and Director

Published in cooperation with the Center for American Places
SANTA FE, NEW MEXICO, AND HARRISONBURG, VIRGINIA

It Happened on Washington Square

EMILY KIES FOLPE

The Johns Hopkins University Press   Baltimore and London

To Herb
and the memory of Pauline and Arthur Bardack

Frontispiece: View of New York from Washington Square to Central Park.
Photograph, ca. 1934; detail. New York University Archives

This book was made possible by the generous support of Furthermore, the
publication program of the J. M. Kaplan Fund.

The Johns Hopkins University Press
2715 North Charles Street
Baltimore, Maryland 21218-4363
www.press.jhu.edu

Library of Congress Cataloging-in-Publication Data

Folpe, Emily Kies
  It happened on Washington Square / Emily Kies Folpe.
    p.   cm. — (Center books on space, place, and time)
Includes bibliographical references and index.
  ISBN 0-8018-7088-7 (acid-free paper)
    1. Washington Square Park (New York, N.Y.)—History.   2. Washington
Square (New York, N.Y.)—History.   3. New York (N.Y.)—History.   4. City
and town life—New York (State)—New York—History.   I. Title.   II. Series.
  F128.65.W3 F65 2002
  974.7'1—dc21

2002000598

A catalog record for this book is available from the British Library.

Contents

Preface and Acknowledgments

Upon moving to Washington Square several years ago, I would look out the window each morning and observe tourists spilling from tour buses and descending on the park, cameras ready. They would take photographs of the Square and the Arch and each other, sometimes stopping traffic to dart out into street for the perfect shot. Back at home in Tokyo or Madrid or Kansas City, these pictures would be prized mementos of their New York experience. What draws them here? I wondered. What gives Washington Square and its Arch such a special place in the world's view of New York?

My curiosity about the Square's past grew as I became involved in community activities on behalf of the park. Trolling the shelves of libraries and bookstores, I found an abundance of books on Greenwich Village, with many references to Washington Square. Yet I could find no single book focusing exclusively on the Square. The subject's potential became more obvious to me upon reading *Around the Square, 1830–1890,* a slim volume of essays on the history of Greenwich Village published in 1982 by members of the New York University community. Dwelling on a number of issues related to the Square, the essays were republished in 1993 as part of *Greenwich Village: Culture and Counterculture,* edited by Rick Beard and Leslie Cohen Berlo-

witz, which included additional chapters on the twentieth-century subjects. What impressed me from these readings was how many events
of local and national importance had taken place on the Square; how
many colorful characters had lived there or were involved with it in
some way; and how its architecture of two centuries had survived, or
been lost. The pull of the material with its accompanying stories was
irresistible. And so I embarked on writing a comprehensive narrative
of Washington Square.

x

For a traditionally trained art historian, urban history was new territory, but I was fortunate in finding many guides. One of my first stops
was the Greenwich Village Society for Historic Preservation, where
Vicki Weiner, and later Kimberly Stahlman Kearns, opened files and
offered valuable advice. From beginning to end, Nancy Cricco, director of the New York University Archives, offered her expertise with extraordinary collegiality as did her assistants. George A. Thompson, reference librarian at NYU's Bobst Library, generously shared his
knowledge of New York history and early periodicals. Staff at the New-
York Historical Society, the Museum of the City of New York, the Metropolitan Museum of Art, Columbia University's Butler and Avery Libraries, New York City's Municipal Archives, and the New York Public
Library helped me locate prime sources and original documents, rare
books, prints, photographs, and drawings in their collections.

Many individuals in the Greenwich Village community contributed
immeasurably to this book. Anthony Dapolito, longtime leader of community organizations and currently chair of Community Board 2 Parks
Committee, offered his unique perspective on a half-century of park
history in a long interview and graciously answered questions any time
I popped in to his bakery with a new query. George Moody, senior
minister emeritus of Judson Memorial Church, contributed his reminiscences of Judson in the 1950s and 1960s. Conversations with other
members of Community Board 2, notably Arnold Gorn, Verna Small,
Diane Whelton, and board members of the Washington Square Asso-

ciation, particularly Regina Kellerman and others who had intimate knowledge of the Village in previous decades, contributed to my understanding. I have also to thank my readers, Gerald Barry, Susan De-Vries, and Anthony Wood, for their thorough reviews of earlier drafts of the manuscript.

In addition, I wish to thank the many others who offered assistance in a variety of ways: Barbara Cohen and Judith Stonehill of New York Bound Bookstore; Robert Cohen of New York University's Department of Community Relations; Christopher M. Crowley, landscape architect, New York City Parks and Recreation; Linda Stone Davidoff; Peggy Friedman of the Washington Square Music Festival; Roberta Gratz; Carol Greitzer; Madeline Kent of the Seymour B. Durst Old York Library at the City University of New York Graduate Center; Jonathan Kuhn, director of Art and Antiquities at the New York City Department of Parks and Recreation, Christopher Moore, Chris Neville, Kate Burns Ottavino, partner in A. Ottavino Corp.; Steven Pearson and family; Steven Rizick of the New York City Parks and Recreation Map File; K. C. Sahl and William K. Tai, park managers of Washington Square; plus the many unnamed who clarified information, enriched my knowledge, patiently answered questions, and helped me on my way.

This book could not have happened without the Center for American Places and specifically George F. Thompson, president, and Randall Jones, editor, who believed in the project and wisely guided me through the writing and publishing process. With their backing and that of the Washington Square Association, led by Anne-Marie Weimer-Sumner, and the Friends of Washington Square under Arrial Cogan, I was able to obtain grants from Furthermore, the Publication Program of the J. M. Kaplan Fund, which enabled me to bring this book to completion.

My heartfelt thanks to Daniel Walkowitz for his thorough review and thoughtful suggestions for refining the manuscript. And to Peter

xi

Dreyer my profound appreciation for his scrupulous editing of the final text.

To family and friends who expressed enthusiasm and encouragement or read drafts of the manuscript, I owe a debt of gratitude. Most of all, I offer loving thanks to Herb, who for five years listened, questioned, read and reread my words, and never wavered in his conviction that this book would surely be born.

Introduction
It Happened on Washington Square

Washington Square Park, situated in Greenwich Village in lower Manhattan, is a small park with a long history. Its 9.75 acres are bordered on the north by the finest surviving row of Greek Revival houses in New York, dating from the 1830s. Judson Memorial Church, built in the 1890s by Stanford White, faces the south side of the park. New York University, located on the Square since the 1830s, occupies the late nineteenth-century buildings on the east, as well as structures of more recent vintage on the south. (Construction of the latest NYU additions on the south side began in 2000.) Apartment buildings from the 1920s line the west side. The Washington Arch by Stanford White, completed in 1895, commands the northern edge of the park. There is no mistaking where we are: from the base of the Arch looking up the length of Fifth Avenue, a visitor can see the Empire State Building a mile and a half to the north. Before September 11, 2001, the two towers of the World Trade Center were in clear view an equal distance to the south.

While embellished with the attributes of a park, Washington Square makes no pretense at being bucolic. It defies easy categorization, and critics have complained that it is neither a park, a tranquil green, nor a town square. No sheep were intended to graze on its grounds, as they

did on the commons of old New England towns, nor were any introduced later for pastoral effect, as they were at Central Park. The
Square is leafier than most European plazas or piazzas, but like many
public places of such older cities, it resembles a great outdoor room
whose walls are formed by the buildings around it. It is one of the few
open spaces for many blocks around—a magnet and major destination
point in the neighborhood—and often serves as a forum for public
events. Fourteen narrow streets converge on it (including one that was
converted to a pedestrian walk between NYU buildings), carrying
thousands of people to and from its grounds every day. This is no ordinary park, to be sure. Through nearly two centuries, the Square has
been a place to linger, to play, to declaim; to celebrate, demonstrate,
and mourn. (For the past quarter-century, it has also been a place to
buy illicit drugs, but that subject falls beyond the limits of this book.)
It functions as a campus green, a crossroads, and a top spot for people-
watching. Washington Square is a place not to escape from city life but
to enter into it.

It is fair to say that the Square's appeal over the years owes less to
the park's landscaping than to the people who have lived on it and the
buildings surrounding it. Yet elements of the landscape contribute to
the park's layered history. At the center is a large fountain and basin,
set in place in 1871, encircled by a wide ring of pavement and low concrete benches installed in a 1970 renovation. Radiating out from the
fountain are paved walkways, which lead visitors past mature shade
trees and curving sections of lawns to the edges of the ground. A mon-
umental arch, two new playgrounds, two nineteenth-century pieces of
sculpture, a dog run, and hundreds of benches punctuate the landscape.

In his novel *Washington Square,* written more than one hundred
twenty years ago, Henry James described the Square of his childhood
as having a "riper, richer more honorable look" than other parts of the
city—"the look of having had something of a social history." His words

are quoted in nearly every related book or guide, because they capture a lingering quality of the place. Washington Square remains a palimpsest; the past has never been fully erased. Although much has changed since James's youth, still embedded in the earth of the park and in the brick and stone of the buildings around it are clues that yield a remarkably full picture of the past. By examining this cityscape, we gain a greater appreciation for a neighborhood's legacy and a deeper understanding of our urban and national heritage.

As a witness to previous centuries, Washington Square is unusually blessed. Documents referring to the location date back to the period of Dutch settlement more than three hundred fifty years ago. Over the past two hundred years, while its functions have shifted, the site has remained a public space. Because of this unusual longevity, the activity swirling around it, and the availability of documentation, the Square provides a unique platform for observing the ebb and flow of history over a long period of time. In addition to archival material and the usual sources, such as books, articles, diaries, and letters, I have sifted through period newspapers and magazines seeking contemporaneous views and voices, and quoted them wherever possible. More than might be expected—or in my case, hoped for—the Square made the news. Given all the enticing material about Greenwich Village and the city, keeping the focus on the park and its immediate surroundings for this book has been a challenge. But to my delight, mining the narrow shaft of Washington Square's past has yielded a precious lode of urban and American history, with rich veins that extend out in many directions.

The driving idea behind this book is how Washington Square's story converges with New York's and the nation's history; how events on and around the park site have mirrored aspirations, accomplishments, and difficulties of urban American life. The Square came to prominence in the years immediately following the opening of the Erie Canal in 1825. By the mid nineteenth century, New York was the country's largest metropolis—its cultural and commercial capital, major entry port for immigrants, and gateway to and from the world. Gotham's meteoric growth and new wealth directly contributed to the site's development as an elite enclave in the 1830s. But the influx of new money and power simultaneously had the less salutary effect of widening the gap between the privileged and the poor. Closely entwined with the city's fortunes, Washington Square displayed ample evidence of both the promise of the American dream and the problems of American life. Principles of democracy and capitalism shaped the Square by enabling upward mobility, personal liberty, and accumulation of wealth. But so did social ills: ethnic and racial strife, extreme economic disparity, abusive labor practices, corrupt politics, and urban decay. Washington Square's success as an urban public space is a tribute to pragmatism, civic activism, the interplay of public and private interests —and the city's resiliency. Through the centuries, the site has adapted to changing conditions, regenerated, and survived anew.

While the Square's story is unique, it may provide a model for discussing urban spaces around the country. Whether conceived deliberately or created by happenstance, small parks, town squares, and other city places often carry memories of bygone times and contribute to a city's identity and sense of itself—think of Rittenhouse Square in Philadelphia, Pioneer Square in Seattle, or the old Plaza in Santa Fe. Their condition and use are a gauge of the city's health and viability. With American cities experiencing reinvigoration at the beginning of the twenty-first century, it is instructive to ask how these special urban places have fared. Why have they survived? What meaning do they hold for their local populations? How can they be improved?

The three chapters of this book follow Washington Square's evolution chronologically, beginning in the early 1600s and concluding with the closing of the park to traffic in 1958; the epilogue sketches in some of the issues and events of the past half-century. Three themes weave through the text. The first is the Square's emergence as an iconic place in the city's and country's development. In the early nineteenth century, the park site was the scene of patriotic celebrations and demonstrations. At the same time, it formed the nucleus of an upscale community of wealthy, enterprising New Yorkers. Its reputation as a locus of genteel society was burnished in the writings of Henry James and Edith Wharton. Construction of the Washington Arch boosted the Square's visibility in the expanded metropolis and made it a fixture in the city's public life.

The second theme is Washington Square's long association with the arts. The Square in the nineteenth century was an incubator for American art and architecture. Local citizens patronized local artists, commissioned noteworthy buildings, founded art institutions, and built the Arch. At the beginning of the twentieth century, the Square became the heart of Greenwich Village's thriving bohemian community, a haven for artists, writers, radicals, and political dissidents and a favored subject for painters and photographers. Washington Square was identified so closely with Greenwich Village as to become a stand-in for it; the Arch, too, has come to signify not only the park, but the Village as a whole.

The third theme is the ongoing struggle between well-heeled bourgeoisie and working-class ethnic New Yorkers over the character and use of the park. Population on and around the Square was more diverse than its early image as a bastion of wealth and propriety might suggest. In the twentieth century, the battle was joined by New York University and powerful New York politicians. Whenever city leaders interceded, the advantage generally went to the well-to-do or the university, not the poor or unempowered. A corollary to this theme is the continuous activism and civic involvement that has characterized the Square's community through the better part of two centuries.

Chapter 1, "From Potter's Field to Parade Ground," begins with the period of Dutch occupation in the 1600s and continues up to the Civil War in the 1860s. The chapter discusses each of the site's transformations, as well as the Square's evolving social and cultural life. The marshy ground that would become Washington Square Park was located a few miles north of the small trading post of New Amsterdam, established in the 1620s by the Dutch West India Company. In 1643, the director of New Amsterdam freed a few African-born slaves of the settlement and granted them plots of land to farm in return for a portion of their crops. Some of the land grants overlapped the site of the future Washington Square. Under English rule in the early eighteenth century, the free black farmers lost the right to own land and were banished from their property. They remained in the area, but their farms were incorporated into large estates owned by English and Dutch landholders.

After the Revolutionary War, the city fathers of New York acquired a few acres of this ground for use as a public burial place in which the poor and indigent, mostly victims of yellow fever, were laid to rest. The need for this kind of burial ground, known as a potter's field, to supplement the church cemeteries in the city reflects just how primitive conditions were in early New York, especially for those living in poverty. After more than twenty years of use, the potter's field was filled, and city development was fast approaching the site. Practical-minded members of New York's Common Council determined that the former cemetery would be a good place for a much-needed drilling ground for the city's volunteer militia companies. On July 4, 1826, the old potter's field was therefore officially declared the Washington Parade Ground, named after the country's first president. Leveled and landscaped by the city, the new parade ground conferred a status to the area and helped elevate the value of surrounding real estate. Within a few years, affluent New Yorkers had created a prime residential neighborhood around it. Elegant houses ringed three sides of the Square, and on the east stood the new Gothic Revival edifice of New York University, where Samuel Morse perfected his telegraph and in later years Winslow Homer could be found painting on the rooftop. Not only was Washington Square, as it came to be known, esteemed for its patriotic associations and genteel society; it was recognized as a place that fostered intellectual and artistic development.

The apparent harmony of the district was frequently shattered when the tensions of the city intruded. A labor riot erupted on the Square when stonecutters protested the university's use of prison labor. Ethnic enmities exploded in violent rioting at the nearby Astor Place Opera House, and the volunteer regiment that usually drilled on Washington Square was called in to quell it. Dozens on both sides died or were seriously wounded. During the Civil War, racial hatred and fear fueled the draft riots of 1863, resulting in the bloodiest urban conflict in American history. Troops summoned from Gettysburg camped out on the Square to ensure peace in the vicinity.

Chapter 2, "A New City Park Takes Shape," begins in 1870, when Tammany "Boss" William M. Tweed transformed the shabby parade ground into a stylishly landscaped park. Despite improvements to the park, the neighborhood was slipping. Tenements packed with poor immigrant families were pressing in on the south side of the park; commercial loft buildings for light manufacturing were going up on streets to the east. While many wealthy families moved uptown, some of the "old-New-York" arbiters of society described by Edith Wharton maintained their homes on the north side of the Square. As conditions deteriorated, tension between these affluent residents on the north and the more needy population to the south increased, resulting in a north-south split that continued well into the next century.

In 1889, one well-connected resident of Washington Square North, William Rhinelander Stewart, was determined to bring positive attention to the neighborhood. He persuaded friends and neighbors to contribute to the cost of erecting a temporary structure to be part of the celebration honoring the centenary of George Washington's inauguration. The papier-mâché and plaster arch, designed by the architect Stanford White, did indeed bring the centennial festivities to the

Square. So successful was White's temporary monument that the architect was commissioned to design a permanent version in marble to be set in the park. With the permanent Arch in place at the foot of Fifth Avenue, the Square was assured a spot on every parade route and a prominent role in civic life for years to come. Both Arches were funded entirely by private donations and built on public land under Stewart's close surveillance.

The civic involvement that brought about the Arch was typical of New York then—and still is. The privileged were expected to contribute to the public welfare. Residents of the Square participated in many philanthropic projects and committed considerable time and money toward ameliorating New York's social problems. Yet they could be blind to the grim conditions existing only yards from their doorsteps. Rarely were the city's contrasts more painfully apparent than at the time of the Triangle Fire in 1911. The Triangle Shirtwaist Company was a notorious sweatshop located in a loft steps away from the east side of the park. When the fire broke out on the building's top floors, more than 146 workers, mostly young women immigrants, jumped to their deaths to escape the blaze. A week later, an immense line of mourners passed through the Arch in a citywide funeral procession. For years after the tragic fire, labor organizations staged demonstrations and marched through the Arch at Washington Square.

Some of the very conditions that had contributed to the Square's downfall as an upper-crust neighborhood in the late nineteenth century were, oddly enough, responsible for its remarkable reincarnation and new identity as America's bohemian haven in the years just before World War I. Chapter 3, "Radicals and Real Estate," opens with a discussion of the youthful generation of artists, writers, and radicals then arriving in New York from all over the country. These talented and defiant newcomers discovered that lodging was cheap in the boarding houses around the Square. They found the immigrants on local streets to be tolerant, and the neighborhood's diversity full of character and vaguely European. World War I and the Red Scare that followed brought most of their impassioned activities to a halt. Soon afterward, with the beginning of Prohibition, the Village's rebellious reputation took on a more frivolous coloration.

A roster of those who lived on Washington Square and the streets of Greenwich Village just before, during, and after World War I is an impressive listing of American cultural heroes and heroines of the early twentieth century. Since their accomplishments and capers have been fully covered in many publications on Greenwich Village, I have attempted to limit the discussion as much as possible to those directly linked to Washington Square. This is not always easy, because distinctions between "the Village" and "the Square" are blurred, and in popular parlance the two are often used interchangeably. By the 1920s and the era of Prohibition, the fame of "the Village"—and the Square— had spread throughout the country and acquired mythic proportions. Washington Square, once considered a separate entity from Greenwich Village, becomes its synechdochic stand-in.

In 1921, at a Ziegfield Midnight Frolic at the New Amsterdam Theatre on Forty-second Street, the popular singer and comedienne Fanny Brice (subject of the 1964 musical *Funny Girl* and 1968 film version starring Barbra Streisand) introduced a song that would become one of the hits of the year—"Rose of Washington Square," written by Ballard Macdonald with music by James F. Hanley. "I'm Rosie the queen of the models / I used to live up in the Bronx / But I wandered from there down to Washington Square and Bohemian Honky Tonks." With a "Roman nose" that pleased "artistic people," she had plenty of beaux "with second-hand clothes and nice long hair. . . ."

For many Americans, Rosie of Washington Square epitomized the unconventional life-style closely identified with Greenwich Village. After World War II, a new generation of rebels—"beatniks," folksingers, hippies, and others of countercultural persuasion—flocked to the Village and gathered in the Square. Their activities recharged the

9

park's reputation as a place where people were free to recite poetry, stage a revolution, and behave—or misbehave—in any way they wished. The Square's identification with both personal liberty and Greenwich Village accounts for a good part of the appeal it holds for visitors from all over the world.

The final section of the third chapter traces the heroic efforts by neighborhood groups to protect their turf from the triple threat of real estate developers, Robert Moses and other city officials, and New York University. As real estate values escalated in the 1920s, developers homed in on property around the Square, replacing many of the hundred-year-old houses with high-rise apartment buildings. A few years later, the Parks Department planned to renovate the park and run a highway through its center. For nearly three decades, resistant Villagers jousted with the invincible "power broker" Robert Moses and an array of city planners and officials, finally achieving victory and a park free of cars in 1958. But the neighborhood's struggle against NYU's expansion on the park was less successful. Steamrolling local opposition, the university tore down old housing on the south and displaced some of the area's working-class residents—an uncomfortable parallel to the English removing black landholders from the site three centuries earlier. NYU now owns most of the property around the Square and continues to build. In confronting both public and private entities, community members wrestled with fundamental and sensitive issues concerning the nature and use of public space. Whose park is it anyhow? Who makes the decisions? And how are those decisions made? These questions still circulate around the park.

In thinking about Washington Square, a curious paradox surfaces. On the one hand, as I have argued, the Square is closely associated with many aspects of New York's development and history. In the minds of many people, however, the Square, along with the rest of Greenwich Village, possesses a spirit that separates it from the rest of the city. Writing in 1915, the anarchist writer, publisher, and Village personality Hippolyte Havel called Greenwich Village "a spiritual zone of mind." It is no mere coincidence that the Village preserves a physical separateness as well, although not as obvious now as in former years. The original hamlet of Greenwich lay close to the banks of the Hudson River. The Greenwich Village of today takes in all the blocks east to Broadway, south to Houston Street and north to Fourteenth Street. On any map of New York, the crooked streets of the west Village—the early village—are easily distinguished from the relentless right angles governing the rest of Manhattan's grid plan. Only the city's southernmost streets, laid out by the early Dutch and English inhabitants, exhibit similar irregularities.

A map dating from before World War I would supply another reason for the neighborhood's singular identity. Until Sixth and Seventh Avenues were extended in the twentieth century, there were no major north-south avenues running through the area. As a result, traffic between uptown and down generally avoided the Village's oddly angled streets, isolating the neighborhood and unintentionally protecting it as a unique community. In 1967, the New York City Landmarks Commission designated Greenwich Village as a historic district, which limited future development. Washington Square Park falls within the district, but the streets along its south and east sides are excluded.

If location is everything, as New Yorkers frequently say of real estate, then Washington Square—and by extension the Village—provides an interesting example of the axiom's flexibility. At first, while the city was beginning to grow northward after the Revolutionary War, the Square's site was remote enough, but still convenient for use as a public cemetery. It was not long before development neared the site, and the Washington Square Parade Ground at the city's northern fringe became *the* place to live. By the time of the Civil War, the Square was close to what was then New York's geographic center, within walking distance or a short carriage ride south to the old parts of the city and the business district—or north to the newer quarter approaching Fortieth Street. (The less populated, mostly rural outlying boroughs of Brooklyn, Queens, the Bronx, and Staten Island did not become a part of New York until the consolidation of 1898). Toward the end of the 1800s, major commerce and industry bypassed the area and so did many of the wealthier citizens. A few years later, after bohemians discovered the Square, the bourgeoisie returned, driving up the rents. And so it goes. In spite of the vicissitudes of the economy and real estate market, the Washington Square neighborhood survives as one of New York's most vital and distinctive districts.

NOTE: Some caveats about word usage in the text. In general, I have referred to "the Square" to indicate the area of the park and its perimeter and usually intend that term to include the inhabitants as well. By "the park," I generally mean the specific landscaped ground. And although I have used the word "community" to describe a group of residents involved in one action or another, there are in fact many communities in the Village. Some are determined by location—more than thirty active block associations exist in an area that can be crossed in a fifteen-minute walk! Others are defined by common interests, ethnicity, politics and life-style. Villagers get involved. Individuals and organizations will join together in support of a cause, and committees readily spring up to combat any perceived challenge. Regarded by municipal authorities, or anyone trying to accomplish a large-scale project here, as one of the most contentious neighborhoods in the city, the Village prides itself as a place of activism and dissent.

And now back to where it all began.

Detail from *Plan for the City of New York, in North America: Surveyed in the years 1766 and 1777. Bernard Ratzer, cartographer* (London, 1776). Map Division, The New York Public Library, Astor, Lenox and Tilden Foundations

When the British were fighting the French in the New World before the American Revolution, they needed an accurate map of Manhattan in case the area became a battleground. Ratzer, a skilled military engineer, was recruited by the British and sent to America to survey New York. His map, perhaps the finest of an American city in the eighteenth century, extended from the southern tip of Manhattan up to today's 50th Street and included all major roads north of the city, shown and named for the first time. This detail of the map, centered on what today would be SoHo, Greenwich Village, and Washington Square, indicates farms and estates, tree-lined roads and country lanes. The road to Greenwich on the left, west along the river, passes Lady Warren's property at the upper left. Bowery Lane on the east leads to Sand Hill, which would later define the northern edge of the Square. Sand Hill road connects to Monument Lane by way of a small bridge over Minetta Stream, called here Bestavers Rivulet: the Square would eventually lie immediately south of that junction. Property of Herring, Bayard, Delancey, Stuyvesant, and others is clearly indicated, as is a farm owned by A. Elliot Esquire north of Sand Hill. Elliot's land was acquired by Thomas Randall and eventually became the source of wealth for Sailors' Snug Harbor, which leased lots to the builders of the Row on Washington Square North.

Map of Greenwich Village with overlay of old roads and property lines. Collection of the New-York Historical Society (# 20955)

The potter's field extended approximately from Margaret Street to Minetta Brook, which formed the boundary between the Warren and Herring properties. The burial ground of the Scotch Presbyterian Church at the northeast corner of the field bordering Margaret Street, upper right, was closed when the parade ground was formed. After the parade ground was completed, the north side of Washington Square corresponding to Sixth Street was called Washington Square North, and the extension of the street to the east and west was named Waverly Place in honor of Sir Walter Scott's "Waverley" novels, written 1814–19. (The street name omits the second *e*.) Scott's romances about Scottish life were very popular among American readers at the time.

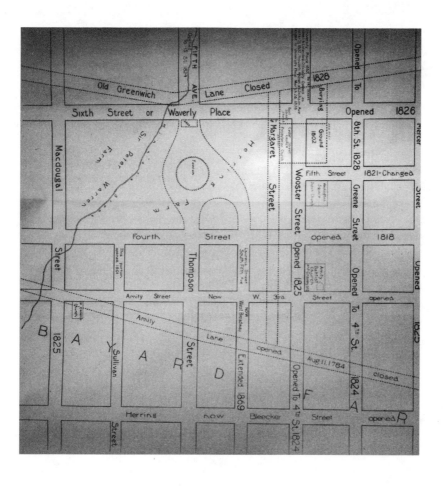

17

Map of lower Manhattan, 2001, detail. Courtesy AAA map of New York City, 2001–2 edition

Following the directive of Mayor DeWitt Clinton in 1804 to plan for the city's future growth, a commission of three men projected a metropolis of equal-sized blocks and lots extending over 11,000 acres, or 2,000 blocks. Their plan, known as the Commissioners' Plan of 1811, tamed Manhattan's naturally hilly terrain with long avenues and cross streets meeting at perfect right angles running up to 155th Street. Residents of Greenwich Village complained that the plan obliterated Manhattan's natural beauty and balked at the city imposing its arbitrary geometry on their old streets. If the existing block-and-lot divisions were invalidated, property owners would stand to lose a lot of money and have to pay for street improvements as well. Finally, the city agreed not to extend the grid past Sixth Avenue, and the Village kept its crooked streets and many of its old street names. The result of this successful demonstration of civic activism is still evident on any map or walk through the Village, particularly at the baffling intersections where West Fourth meets West Tenth and West Twelfth Streets.

Baroness Hyde de Neuville, *Bridewell and Charity School, Broadway opposite Chambers Street, Manhattan, Feb. 1808*. Wash drawing. I. N. Phelps Stokes Collection, Miriam and Ira D. Wallach Division of Art, Prints and Photographs, The New York Public Library, Astor, Lenox and Tilden Foundation

At the center of this drawing stands the Charity School. Behind it looms Bridewell, the city's prison, and in back on the left is the new City Hall, then still under construction. In the foreground on the right is the Board of Health. Visitors from abroad, like the woman who recorded this scene, were amazed at the sight of farm animals roaming freely in New York's streets. Charles Dickens, after visiting the United States in 1842, wrote in *American Notes for General Circulation* of having seen "two portly sows . . . and a select part of half a dozen gentlemen hogs" on Broadway and a solitary swine who was "in every respect a republican pig, going wherever he pleases, and mingling with the best of society, on an equal, if not superior footing." Here in this drawing from the early 1800s, a pig and cow boldly graze within feet of the office of the Board of Health. The board had little authority to carry out its regulations, including a prohibition against animals running free, but it did start keeping records of births, marriages, hospital admissions, and deaths. Mayor James Harper, elected in 1844, finally banished pigs from the streets and prohibited citizens from driving cattle below Fourteenth Street.

Baroness Hyde de Neuville made many drawings depicting early city life. She and her husband had fled France when Napoleon came to power and settled in New York in 1807. After the monarchy was restored in 1814, the baron became France's minister to the United States.

The Row on Washington Square North. Photograph, 1970s. New York University Archives

The Greek Revival houses that comprise the Row have lined the northern side of the Square since the 1830s. When Sailors' Snug Harbor converted the houses into apartments in the 1930s, the cornice line was altered and some architectural details were lost, but the original unity of the street front has for the most part been preserved. In contrast to more modest Greek Revival houses with plain stone trim, homes on the Row employed marble for the broad front steps, carved balustrades and fluted Doric and Ionic columns framing deeply recessed doorways. The white marble at the entranceways and on the lintels above the windows provides a pleasing contrast to the red-brick walls set in Flemish bond. A decorative wrought-iron railing running the length of the block separates the private front gardens from the public walk and contributes to the Row's unified appearance. One exception is No. 3, visible at the right. In 1879, the owner added extra floors and converted the house into artists' studios. Edward Hopper was a tenant in the building from 1913 to 1966.

Washington Square North, west side of Fifth Avenue. Photograph, 1922. Collection of the New-York Historical Society (# 33338)

When Henry James visited New York in 1904–5 after an absence of twenty years, he wrote that coming upon the streets of lower Fifth Avenue and the Square "was as if the wine of life had been poured for you, in advance, into some pleasant old punch-bowl." No. 14 Washington Square North at the corner of Fifth Avenue belonged to William C. Rhinelander and his wife, Mary Rogers Rhinelander. Their two unmarried daughters, Julia and Serena, lived in the house all their lives; Serena Rhinelander survived until 1914. The Rhinelanders' grandson, William Rhinelander Stewart—the man responsible for the Washington Arch—lived three doors away at No. 17 in the house with the bay window on the second floor. Next door at No. 18 was the home of James's maternal grandmother, Elizabeth Walsh. The author's parents were married in the house.

Nowadays these homes continue to impart an old-fashioned atmosphere to the Square, but early residents would have considered themselves to be very modern. Living at the city's outskirts, they adapted a new "suburban" lifestyle, which required that they relinquish some habitual patterns of upper-class daily life. It had been customary for male heads of households to return home from their nearby places of business for dinner at midday. Once businessmen started commuting to work, they preferred to eat lunch at restaurants or to buy it from street vendors downtown and take the main meal of the day with their families in the evening after returning home. Menus and mealtimes were adjusted accordingly.

PHOTO TAKEN
FEB. 24, 1922

Berenice Abbott, Washington Square North, nos. 21–25 . Photograph, Aug. 12, 1936. Museum of the City of New York, Federal Art Project: Changing New York

During the Depression, Berenice Abbott set about photographing New York City with support from the Federal Art Project, a relief agency for artists under the Works Project Administration. Her project, which she entitled "Changing New York," featured many views of Greenwich Village, including this stretch of six Greek Revival homes along the northwest side of the park.

From right to left, the three houses at 21, 22, and 23 Washington Square North were built for one owner and display many distinctive features of the period: high stoops, tall French windows, and decorative ironwork with Greek-inspired motifs on the railings, gates, and balconies. The three houses beyond, built between 1837 and 1839, bear similar decorative elements. Currently, 22 Washington Square functions as NYU's Admissions Center. The other five houses were renovated in the 1940s and divided into residential apartments.

Otto Boetticher, *The Seventh Regiment on the Washington Square Parade Ground,* 1851. Museum of the City of New York / J. Clarence Davies Collection

In this unique view of the parade ground in use, the artist has exaggerated the park's open space and eliminated the trees and crosswalks in order to emphasize the impressive showing of the Seventh Regiment in full dress uniform. (Members of the regiment designed and paid for their own uniforms.) Looking back, the towers of the university and the Dutch Reformed Church rise on the east side of the park; to the right are the fine homes lining the Square's south side. In the foreground, elegantly dressed families from the neighborhood gather to enjoy the colorful review. A few months after the painting was completed, the fountain was installed at the center of the park, reducing the space for such parades and altering the look of the parade ground (see pages 39 and 41).

The socially prestigious Seventh Regiment, known as the Twenty-seventh before 1847, developed from military companies formed before the War of 1812 to protect New York from a British invasion. A kind of national guard, it was called on to squelch civil uprisings such as the Stonecutters' riot of 1834 and the riot at the Astor Place Opera House in 1849. The regiment was one of many companies that trained at the Square. In *A Glance at Old New York,* written in 1837, Asa Greene described the parade ground at that time: "There the militia display their skills with fine uniforms and equipment. There also the 'slabs,' in their dress of all sorts, with their arms and accouterments of all kinds, are dragged on winter days, to share the glory of the volunteers." Reminiscing in the *Tribune,* June 20, 1920, the ninety-one-year-old John Voorhis, a native of the Village, told how squads of twenty-five to thirty men in working clothes, some bearing broomsticks to substitute for weapons, would gather for their mandatory drilling. On parade day, the men were formed into companies and pronounced soldiers. "It was an occasion when almost every man got drunk," he recalled.

New-York University Building and Reformed Dutch Church. Anstice and Co., *New-York Views* (1850). New York University Archives

Gothic Revival architecture, a romanticized amalgam of medieval styles, was just beginning to gain popularity when the university and the church were constructed on the east side of the Square. "The grey and more or less 'hallowed' University building—wasn't it somehow, with a desperate bravery, both castellated and gabled?" Henry James wrote in *The American Scene* (1907). James was born in 1843 in a house on Washington Place, the street that runs between the two buildings. His home was on the left, just beyond the university.

When New York University first opened, it rented space to a few institutions, including the University Grammar School, located on the ground floor. Two hundred boys attended classes, one hundred in the Primary Division, and another hundred in the First Department. D. Maitland Armstrong was a student at the school in the 1840s. A lawyer, diplomat, and later in life a stained-glass artist who worked with Stanford White, Armstrong wrote in his memoirs how he would sometimes play hookey and go off down the hall to paint in the studio of his teacher, Mr. Coe.

A. J. Davis, *New York University Chapel, interior.* Watercolor, 1835. Collection of the New-York Historical Society (# 30013)

Davis was an expert watercolorist who often conveyed his architectural ideas through elaborate drawings that verged on the fantastic. This watercolor of the University Chapel on Washington Square, for example, suggests the atmosphere he wished to create as much as the structural elements. After designing the chapel, Davis assumed responsibility for overseeing the entire construction of the school's Gothic Revival building. In later years, he became widely known through publications for his work in the "picturesque" style, which featured bracketed woodwork and other details associated with American architecture of the Victorian era. His designs, often in collaboration with Andrew Jackson Downing's landscaping plans, were adapted for villas and cottages across the country.

33

Asbury Methodist Church (originally New Dutch South Reformed Church). Photograph by George C. Dodd, ca. 1890–95. Collection of the New-York Historical Society (# 48258)

American architects in the nineteenth century frequently turned to Europe for inspiration and drew on examples known to them from architectural drawings reproduced in books. In building the Gothic Revival Church on the Square, for example, Minard LaFever adapted one of his own designs he had published in his 1829 book, *Young Builder's General Instructor.* His plans for this model church closely resemble the National Scotch Church built in London, 1824–27, a structure Lafever knew only from reproductions in books. The London church was in turn inspired by the façade of the medieval York Minster. Such borrowing of architectural ideas was widely practiced and approved.

Toward the end of the century, when this photograph was taken, commercial development was advancing on the east side of the Square. The pseudoclassical loft building with its advertising sign pressing on the rear of the Gothic-inspired structure captures the incongruous architectural mix east of the Square in the 1890s. By 1895, the congregation was too small to maintain its house of worship, and this splendid example of Gothic Revival architecture was torn down, to be replaced by a warehouse.

The Tenth Street Studio Building. Photograph, ca. 1858. Avery Architectural and Fine Arts Library, Columbia University in the City of New York

The Tenth Street Studio Building designed by Richard Morris Hunt for James Boorman Johnston was the first structure of its kind with space tailored for making, showing, and selling art. Eager patrons flocked to the Tenth Street building to visit artists in their studios or attend special exhibitions held in the more formal exhibition space. Several Studio tenants were associated with the Hudson River School or later with American Impressionism, and included many of America's most accomplished nineteenth-century artists: Albert Bierstadt, Frederick Church, Sanford Gifford, Martin Johnson Heade, John La Farge, Emanuel Leutz, John Ferguson Weir, J. Alden Weir, Thomas Worthington Whittredge, and at least one woman, Anna Mary Freeman, a poet and painter of miniatures. When Church displayed *The Heart of the Andes* in 1859, twelve thousand people lined up around the block and paid twenty-five cents a piece to see his colossal painting of the tropics. In the 1870s and 1880s, the figure most closely associated with the Studio Building was the American Impressionist William Merritt Chase, whose commodious studio, artfully decorated with eclectic furnishings, fulfilled the public's fantasy of the artistic life.

Silas A. Holmes, *Washington Square Park Fountain with Pedestrians.* Salted paper print from glass negative, ca. 1855. J. Paul Getty Museum, Los Angeles

Most photographers of the mid nineteenth century earned their living through portraiture, but some like Holmes seem to have been captivated by the urban landscape. This picture, the earliest known photograph of Washington Square, was made from a glass negative, which accounts for the extraordinary clarity of its multilayered subject. Water in the fountain's one-hundred-foot basin provides a smooth reflective surface in the foreground, while on the far side of the pool, well-dressed people promenade. Behind the fountain, narrow diagonal paths crisscross the grassy areas of the parade ground and a broad walk leads out to the arched wrought-iron gate on Washington Square East. Beyond, through the thinly leafed trees, rise the majestic towers of the University Building on the left and the Dutch Reformed Church on the right. In *The Columbia Historical Portrait of New York History: An Essay in Graphic History* (New York, 1972), John Kouwenhoven notes that the city was changing so rapidly in the 1850s that an evident nostalgia began to appear in pictures of older parts of it. Images like this one seem to reflect that phenomenon.

James Smillie, *Mount Washington Collegiate Institute Washington Square*. Etching, 1856. Miriam and Ira D. Wallach Division of Art, Prints and Photography, The New York Public Library, Astor, Lenox and Tilden Foundations

Beneath grand sweeps of sky, human activity is precisely rendered, orderly and tranquil in this bird's-eye view of the park as a pleasure garden, observed from the southwest corner. Groups stroll the grounds and children play at the edges—one child rolls a hoop in the corner on the right. To the east, in back, are the towers of the University and the Dutch Reformed Church. Horses and carriages pass on Washington Square West in the foreground, and midway on the right, we see the fine homes lining Washington Square South.

In 1863, Dr. George W. Clarke purchased the corner house at 40 Washington Square South, shown on the right, for $9,500 and converted it into a school named the Mount Washington Collegiate Institute. Dr. Clarke earned the gratitude of his students—according to Edward Mitchell, an alumnus, who was editor of the *Sun* after Charles Dana—for his high standards and "judiciously administered discipline of the rattan stick." Clarke won the gratitude of his neighbors, too, for leading a successful protest against the routing of the Sixth Avenue elevated train along Washington Square South. The "el" was erected along West Third Street instead.

Hooking a Victim. Lithograph, Serrell and Perkins, ca. 1850. Museum of the City of New York/gift of Karl Schmidt

One block east of the park, sandwiched between Broadway and the Square, was Greene Street, New York's prime red light district, extending from Canal Street up to Eighth Street. Higher prices prevailed in the brothels that were closer to Washington Square. Young women earned their living by entertaining clients nightly—and at lunch hour, too—in brick houses distinguished by colored lamps and signs over the doors. By midcentury, they could frequently be seen in Washington Square in the evening, when "proper" women would not be out alone.

Hanging a Negro in Clarkson Street.
Harper's Weekly, August 1, 1863

"The Town is taken by its rats. . . .
All civil charms . . . these like a
dream dissolve, / And man rebounds
whole aeons back in nature." These
lines from Herman Melville's poem
"The House-Top: A Night Piece,"
written at the time of the Civil War
draft riots, convey the savage de-
struction that overtook the city.
Some of the bloodiest fighting took
place south and west of Washington
Square in the Minettas and along
Bleecker and Carmine Streets,
where the long-established black
community defended their homes.

The hanging vividly rendered in this
illustration took place on Clarkson
Street, a continuation of Carmine
Street, located in the southwest part
of the Village. Following the riots,
many blacks were unable to reclaim
their former jobs or follow their normal routines. White longshoreman
kept black labor off the waterfront;
white omnibus drivers and passengers prevented blacks from using
public transportation, and beatings
by gangs of white boys continued
through the summer. "A large number of colored families have left the
city with the intention of never returning to it again," the *Tribune* reported on August 3, 1863.

Military Encamping in Washington Square. Frank Leslie's Illustrated Magazine, September 5, 1863

In response to the draft riots, Lincoln did not impose martial law on the city, but instead sent 6,000 troops from Gettysburg to help New York keep order. Many of the Union soldiers were assigned to Washington Square, among them Mason Whiting Tyler of the Thirty-seventh Massachusetts. "Everything was as quiet and orderly as a New England Sabbath," he wrote in his memoirs, *Recollections of the Civil War* (New York, 1912). "No disturbance occurred anywhere, and in the evening the various details gathered again in the park and we slept with our guards and our pickets thrown out as if we were in the enemy's country." The second round of drafting, begun in Greenwich Village in August, came to a peaceful conclusion.

MILITARY ENCAMPING IN WASHINGTON SQUARE

ONE

From Potter's Field to Parade Ground

*F*rom the 1600s to the 1860s, Washington Square's site evolved in response to the needs of the burgeoning city of New York. After being farmed by freed slaves under Dutch rule, the site of the future Square was first designated a public burying place following the American Revolution and then converted into a military parade ground. The landscaped green attracted successful businessmen, who moved their families from the crowded downtown streets to what would soon become New York's preferred residential section. Graced by prominent residents, a university on one side, and artists and writers living nearby, Washington Square became esteemed for its genteel society and cultivated ambience. Nevertheless, this elite quarter felt the reverberations of ethnic, racial, and class hostilities, which intensified over the years and exploded during the Civil War.

Before Washington Square

Manhattan is a long skinny island,[1] built on layers of bedrock formed many millions of years ago. The bedrock rears up as impressive bluffs at the island's northern tip and inclines down to the south, breaking through the earth as boulders of mica schist in Central Park. It then disappears underground to provide a secure base for the two stalagmite-like clusters of skyscrapers that characterize the New York sky-line—the towering buildings of midtown and those of the financial district a few miles to the south. The rock is never far below the surface. But midway between the skyscrapers, near the base of Fifth Avenue at Washington Square, the bedrock plunges sharply before rising again to support the towering structures at the southern end of the island.

In the hollowed-out rock basin below today's Washington Square, prehistoric glaciers deposited boulders and gravel, sand, soil, and vegetation. American Indians knew the area as a marshy place abundant in waterfowl, bordered on the north by a prominent sandy ridge about fifty to one hundred feet high. Bubbling through the marsh was a fine trout stream they called Minetta, which the Dutch named Bestaver Kill (Bestawerkil). Formed from the confluence of two springs to the north near what is now Twelfth Street, the stream bisected the area of the cross streets between Fifth and Sixth Avenues and ran through the western half of the future Square to empty into the Hudson at a point further south. Although buried, it still flows. Vigorous trees along its route attest to the water's presence, most notably the great English elm in the northwest corner of Washington Square, believed to be hundreds of years old. Further evidence of Minetta may be seen at Two Fifth Avenue, on the north side of the park, where water from the stream bubbles up in a narrow glass cylinder set into the outside corner of the lobby.

The American Indians who lived in the vicinity of Greenwich Village called themselves Lenape (meaning "men" or "people"). Moving among seasonal camps in small groups, they settled near shores in spring and summer and inland in the fall and winter. A web of trails connected their planting fields and campsites. Branching off from their main north-south route was a trail that ran from what is now Eighth Street near Astor Place to their encampment of Sapokanikan, located approximately where Twelfth Street meets the Hudson River. The Lenape trail followed along the prominent ridge on the north side of the marsh and crossed Minetta Brook. The east-west route along the marsh, named the Strand by Dutch settlers and Sand Hill Road by the English, developed into Waverly Place and Greenwich Avenue. The portion of Sand Hill Road along the end of the marsh ultimately became the northern boundary of Washington Square.

Dutch Settlers and African Slaves

While some of the New World's colonies were born of struggles for religious or political freedom, New York's settlement was rooted firmly in commerce. In 1624, a small group of settlers sponsored by the Dutch West India Company established the trading outpost of New Amsterdam at the southern tip of Manhattan island. Eager to engage in the profitable fur trade, this rag-tag band of multinational fortune-seekers demonstrated little enthusiasm for building a fort or tending to the crops or animals necessary for the colony's survival. In 1626, a month after Peter Minuit had concluded his legendary purchase of Manhattan from the Lenape for sixty guilders' worth of trinkets, the Dutch company sent over eleven African slaves, all men, who were put to work improving the post. More slaves followed, including the first three African women, who arrived in 1628. A few years later, there were pastures and planted fields as far north as the vicinity of Greenwich Village, which the Dutch referred to as Noortwyck. There Wouter van Twiller, director of the colony from 1633 to 1638, built himself a large farm. His farmhouse stood about a block from what is now the northwest corner of Washington Square. Van Twiller prospered, growing tobacco in the fertile soil of the area and acquiring vast landholdings for himself. More interested in personal gain than in the colony's welfare or profits for the Dutch West India Company, he enjoyed only a brief tenure on his acres near the Square. The company recalled him to the Netherlands, annulled his land purchases, and sent over a new administrator, Willem Kieft.

When Kieft arrived in 1638, he found the outpost of 400 people in chaos, its buildings in disrepair, farms vacant and decaying, and conflicts with the Lenape escalating. In response to Dutch assaults on their encampments, the formerly peaceable Lenape were burning farms, destroying crops and cattle, and killing settlers as far away as Connecticut. By the summer of 1643, farmers in the employ of the Dutch West India Company had fled for safety behind New Amsterdam's palisade at the tip of Manhattan, and the fields and pastures a few miles north had become virtually a no-man's-land. To revive the farms and bolster the dwindling food supply—and to provide an early warning system against Lenape attacks—Kieft devised a pragmatic solution. He granted some of the Africans their liberty and parceled out the abandoned land for them to farm. This granting of land and liberty was not impelled by a moral repugnance of slavery but was a practical way to improve the vulnerable colony's chances of survival.

Documents relate that African men and their wives who had been slaves in service of the Dutch West India Company for seventeen or eighteen years were granted freedom, to be on an equal footing with other free people in New Netherlands. But there were certain conditions. Males were set free for life provided they made annual payments of a portion of their crops: twenty-two bushels of any two crops grown—corn, wheat, peas, beans—plus one fat hog. Failure to comply meant a return to servitude. And children of the former slaves, even those yet to be born, would remain slaves of the company.

The first recorded grant went to Catelina Anthony, a widower, who received eight acres around present-day Canal Street and Broadway in July 1643. Manuel Trumpeter (Trompeter) received eighteen acres to the north on December 12, 1643. Two years later, a grant dated September 5, 1645, conveys to Anthony Portuguese "a piece of land . . . on a Cripplebush" (an archaic term for swamp or marsh, from the Dutch *kreupelbos*) bordering Minetta Brook. From the description, his plot would have covered a good part of what is now Washington Square. Anthony Portuguese, one of the original slaves in the colony, must have been working the site for a few years, because the earlier grant to Manuel Trompeter refers to his farm and mentions other Africans in the vicinity as well: "A certain piece of land stretching on the east side of Anthony Portuguese land to Cossin Gerrits waggon path . . . going into the woods S, SW—next to the land of Groot Manuel." Property to the northwest was granted to Paolo Dangola and later held by his widow. The names of these freed blacks reflect their origins: Portuguese slave traders had originally brought them from Angola, in West Africa, then a Portuguese colony. Fifty years later, Susannah Anthony Roberts, described as a "free negress" and probably a descendant of Anthony Portuguese, was recorded in 1694 as the owner of a tract of land across Minetta. As a result of these land grants, blacks were farming about 300 acres in lower Manhattan through the end of the seventeenth century.[2]

To protect their land and livestock, the black landholders were summoned on March 31, 1644, to participate in the communal building of a fence along the edge of the marsh: "Everyone who owns cattle to come on Mon. morning April 4 at 7 o'clock to aid in constructing the fence. . . . a palisade running west along the old highway . . . in the vicinity of Paolo Dangola's plot as far as Minetta Water, where the bridge crosses the road to Sappokanican." The fence built over the old Lenape path followed approximately along what is now Washington Square North.

Not long after, the inhabitants of New Amsterdam concluded a peace treaty with the Lenape and, in September 1645, celebrated Thanksgiving with them. Yet the settlement never flourished. Peter Stuyvesant, appointed director general two years later by the Dutch West India Company, imposed order on the unruly colony and improved the harbor to facilitate shipping. Within a few years, a number of wealthy merchants from Holland settled in New Amsterdam, establishing an elite class there for the first time. Descendants of these families—van Rensselaer, Philipse (or Vlypse), Schuyler, Beekman and

Bayard, among others—were active in city life and formed the core of New York society.

New Amsterdam held on until 1664, when James Stewart, Duke of York, dispatched Colonel Robert Nicholls with an English fleet of four frigates and 2,000 men to take over the Dutch post. The colony's population then numbered about 1,500, of whom perhaps 250 were men capable of bearing arms; there was neither the means nor the spirit for withstanding an assault. Stuyvesant wanted to resist, but ninety-three of the most prominent men in the settlement—including his own son—urged him to accept the peaceable terms offered by the English. The director general capitulated, the Dutch colors came down, and Nicholls renamed New Amsterdam in honor of his patron, the duke of York. Stuyvesant retired to his Manhattan farm, which stretched from the East River over to what is now Fourth Avenue and from Fifth to Seventeenth Streets. He was buried in 1672 beneath the chapel of his manor house, now the site of Saint Mark's Church in the Bowery, about half a mile east of Washington Square. Although the Dutch briefly regained control of their colony in 1673–74, New Amsterdam soon yielded completely to English rule.

In the century before the United States won its independence from Britain, issues of race were already scarring New York. During Stuyvesant's tenure, slaves numbered some three hundred—20 percent of the population (Stuyvesant himself owned forty). Under the English, slavery was institutionalized and the city became a port for ships engaged in the slave trade. A slave market was established at the foot of Wall Street in 1709. Many of New York's prosperous and later socially prominent families first grew rich from businesses that depended on slave labor or trade. City ordinances prohibited black residents from owning land, and by 1716, all the property granted to the freed Africans and their descendants had passed to Dutch or English landholders. Left without homes or land, blacks found employment as domestic servants, agricultural workers, artisans, and tradesmen. Many gravitated to a section south of the Square around the "Negroes' causy," or causeway, which skirted the edge of the marsh around Minetta Brook, corresponding to today's cluster of Minetta Street, Place, and Lane, located near the southwest corner of the Square. Following the abolition of slavery in New York State on July 4, 1827, the census of 1830 indicated that there were 14,083 free blacks living in the city. As late as the 1880s, according to the African American history scholar James Weldon Johnson, a major portion of that population was still living in "Little Africa" as it was called, on the streets south and west of the Square. Italian immigrants later displaced most of these African Americans, who then moved to the area south of Times Square called the Tenderloin. But according to Johnson, vestiges of the historic black community near Washington Square persisted through 1930, the year he published his definitive study *Black Manhattan*.

The Potter's Field

A good part of what is now Greenwich Village, stretching from Washington Square to the Hudson River, was owned in the mid eighteenth century by Sir Peter Warren, an admiral of the British navy. As a young commander stationed in New York, Warren had gained considerable wealth from the sale of booty captured from French and Spanish vessels bound for the West Indies. With this fortune from privateering, he purchased 300 acres of land bordering Minetta Brook for a country seat, the first of many summer homes developed in Greenwich, as the English called it. For most of the year, Warren and his family lived in a townhouse in lower Manhattan, but summers were spent in their country house several blocks northwest of the present Washington Square. Before he left for England in 1748, Warren divided his Greenwich property among his three daughters, who subsequently sold most of the estate. By the late 1700s, land in the area had been subdivided into blocks and lots to facilitate the growing real estate trade.

Affluent New Yorkers, attracted by the rural atmosphere, clean air, and cool breezes of the area, bought up parcels of Warren's former property and built themselves country retreats in Greenwich Village after the Revolutionary War. But in 1797, to their consternation, New York's city fathers decided to establish a public burial ground close to their homes. The previous cemetery (located on the site of today's Madison Square at Twenty-third Street) was full, and the city required space away from the densely populated center to bury deceased paupers, prisoners, and indigents. Public cemeteries of this type were commonly called potter's fields, a term derived from the Gospel of St. Matthew, 27:7. After Judas repented for betraying Jesus, he gave his reward of thirty pieces of silver to the priests who "bought with them the potter's field, to bury strangers in."

The need for a new potter's field was particularly urgent, because yellow fever had afflicted the city, first in 1795 and again in 1797. Death rates soared, and whole neighborhoods were decimated. In an era in which little was known about the transmittal of disease, the filthy and overcrowded port of New York was particularly at risk. The yellow fever virus was carried by mosquitoes, which slipped aboard vessels in the West Indies bound for the docks on New York's East River. From there the virulent disease spread to the most deprived sections of town, preying on those who could not afford to flee from the fever's grip. Ignorant of the mosquitoes' role, and reluctant to discourage the profitable shipping trade, city officials and many of the well-to-do citizenry blamed the poor, whose unsanitary living conditions—water polluted by waste matter, open sewers, overflowing privies—certainly contributed to the problem. Despite the city's attempts to institute cleanup measures, the dying continued. Attacking in the summer heat and abating with the frost, epidemics of yellow fever plagued the metropolis for decades.

On April 10, 1797, the city's governing board, the Common Council, announced the purchase of land for a new potter's field: "A piece of Ground containing about 90 Lots, parcel of the Land of William S. Smith bounded on the road leading from the Bowery Lane at the two Mile Stone to Greenwich having been purchased at public Auction & offered to this Board as a proper Place for public buryal Ground, at the price of £1800."[3] This property, bounded on the West by Minetta, accounts for about two-thirds of the land that now makes up Washington Square.

The transaction was not quite so simple. The land was part of an estate that in 1755 had been conveyed by Hendrick Brevoort to Elbert Herring, a descendant of an early Dutch settler, Jan Pieterson Haring. At Herring's death in 1773, following instructions in his will to ensure the most equitable distribution, Herring's executors sold the farm and divided the proceeds among his ten children. But some of the siblings and their spouses (Cornelius Roosevelt, Samuel Jones, James De-Peyster, and Samuel Kip) traded among themselves and retained portions of the estate, which they later sold off in parcels to others, including Jacob Sebor. On August 1, 1795, Sebor sold his land to William Smith, a colonel in Washington's army, and granted him a large mortgage to enable the Revolutionary War veteran to purchase it. But Smith and his wife Abigail were unable to meet their payments to Sebor and sold their acreage to William Burrows (Burroughs). Since neither Burrows nor Smith had paid Sebor the balance of his principal and interest, due on February 13, 1797, Sebor filed a claim in court. James M. Hughes of the Court of Chancery arranged for a public auction, which, as the law specified, was announced weeks ahead in the daily papers. Real estate records for April 10, 1797, confirm that the state of New York paid £1,800 for land that was conveyed to "the Mayor, Alderman and Commonalty of the City of New York."[4] Contrary to the Common Council minutes, however, these records suggest that at the time of transfer, it was Burrows who owned the parcel that would become the potter's field, not Smith.

The owners of second residences in the vicinity, Alexander Hamilton among them, immediately objected to the city's establishing a public burial ground near their homes and fired off a letter of protest to the council, arguing that the proposed cemetery was " so near the City and contiguous to the publick roads leading from East to the West part of Town; also that the field lies in the neighborhood of a number of Citizens who have at great expense erected dwellings on the adjacent lots for the health and accommodation of their families during the summer season . . . that from the rapid Increase of Building that is daily taking place both in the suburbs of the City and the Ground surrounding the field alluded to, it is certain that in the course of a few years the aforementioned field will be drawn within a precinct of the City."[5] After reviewing the petition, a committee of aldermen reported back to the council on May 15. The petitioners, they said, were "prepared to make considerable Sacrifice" and had offered to buy another piece of land in exchange, an appropriate site with sandy soil and low brush located farther away from the city, council minutes record. But one major drawback was that hearses would have to travel on main roads to get there. The council's vote was split, requiring Mayor Samuel Varick to break the tie. And by his one vote, the potter's field— the future Washington Square—remained where it was.[6]

The controversy over the location of the potter's field reveals a great deal about New York two centuries ago. Then, as now, the city was sharply divided by wealth; it was a place in which a fortunate few could build summer homes "at great expense," while many others, barely subsisting, were unable to pay for burial. The gulf between rich and poor in New York had been widening since the Revolution. By the end of the eighteenth century, the richest one-fifth of the population owned four-fifths of the wealth, while the bottom *half* shared less than one-twentieth. Thousands of the very poor, most of them women, including those too old or too sick to work, sought shelter at the city's almshouse. When inmates of the almshouse died, the city interred them in the public burial ground.

58

The affluent petitioners protesting the cemetery's location were, like property owners everywhere, determined to block any changes that would adversely affect the value of their real estate and were willing to spend their money to do so. They objected to the potter's field because they believed it would disturb the area's bucolic atmosphere and contaminate its clean air. Yet, paradoxically, they recognized that the city's northward development would inevitably overtake their place of refuge. That, too, in their eyes, was good reason to locate the burial ground elsewhere. After a respectful hearing of complaints from some of the city's most prominent citizens, the city's governing body stood firm. By the end of the summer of 1798, yellow fever had claimed another 2,000 lives—almost 5 percent of the city's population. About a third of these were buried in the new potter's field.

After purchasing the land, the Common Council lost no time approving funds for preparing the new burial ground. Early in August, materials from the city's old almshouse were taken "for the purpose of putting the Ground. . . in order" and erecting a small house for the superintendent at the edge of the field. The superintendent's house, modified over the years, remained standing on the corner of Washington Square South and Thompson Place until 1948.[7] David Marshall, formerly gravedigger at the Madison Square potter's field, was appointed superintendent and paid a salary recorded at £16.12 and later £21, plus a few extra shillings for each burial. (One British pound was equal to about U.S.$2.55 then. By 1805, the keeper of the field was earning a dollar a day.) The council authorized a committee of aldermen to supervise the construction of a fence around "so much of the Ground used as the City public burying Ground . . . with good Posts and Rails" and "also the planting of trees in and about the said Ground as they shall think proper." After extra parcels of land were acquired in 1801, the council specified that a new tight board fence be erected to enclose the whole ground. And for the first time on record, the site is referred to as a "Park."[8]

FROM POTTER'S FIELD TO PARADE GROUND

New laws requiring yellow-fever victims to be buried apart from those who died of other causes intensified the demand for burial space, particularly since the small churchyard cemeteries in the city were filling up. Joshua Isaacs, president of the Jewish congregation Shearith Israel, petitioned the council on June 30, 1800, requesting a part of the field "inasmuch as a recent city ordinance deprives this congregation of the privilege of burying in their own cemetery the bodies of such of their dead as die of pestilential disorders."[9] Although this first Jewish cemetery, established in 1654, about a mile and a half south of the Washington Square site on today's Pearl Street in Chinatown, was nearly filled up, the request was denied. (In 1805, Shearith Israel founded a second cemetery, a remnant of which survives on West Eleventh Street near Sixth Avenue, four blocks north of Washington Square.) Another urgent request for burial space came from the African Zion Methodist Episcopal Church (later known as A.M.E. Zion) in August 1807. During the previous five years, more than seven hundred fifty bodies had been interred in a burial vault under the church. Investigating a complaint made by the health commissioner, City Inspector James Hardie found that when the vault door was opened, there emitted a "peculiarly offensive" smell, which, he feared, might produce "terrible consequences to the neighborhood." Burials in the vault were immediately suspended. A week later, in response to the congregation's plea, the council granted the church fifty square feet in the public ground.[10]

Ten years and thousands of burials took their toll on the cemetery formed from the soft soil of the Minetta basin. In September 1808, the Common Council directed the superintendent of repairs to "cause the high ground in Pottersfield to be drawn into the valley and leveled in such a manner as to render the same more suitable for the purposes of a cemetery."[11] Some of this activity may have been directed at controlling Minetta by filling in the stream or burying it. A new fence was installed a year later, and watchmen were stationed at the site beginning in 1810.

Duels and Hangings

The open space of the potter's field was often a stage where large themes of American history played out in small dramas. In 1803, William Coleman, editor of the *New York Evening Post,* and Captain Thompson, harbormaster of the port of New York, fought a duel there. Although the immediate provocation was a personal insult, the animosity arose from the political convictions of the two men involved, each of whom adhered to a fundamental but opposing philosophy of government. Alexander Hamilton, author of the *Federalist* and the nation's first secretary of the Treasury, was an advocate of strong centralized power and supported policies that were favorable to New York's growing business interests. In November 1801, he established the *Evening Post* to express the Federalists' point of view and enlisted Coleman, a lawyer from Boston, as editor. Hewing closely to Hamilton's line (and often incorporating Hamilton's own words), Coleman's sharp-tongued editorials in the *Post* riled political opponents to such a degree that two years later, the editor of the *American Citizen* challenged him to a duel for slander. The *American Citizen,* controlled by Aaron Burr, reflected Thomas Jefferson's belief in states' rights—that the federal government should concern itself mainly with foreign affairs and leave all other matters to state and local authorities.

Friends arranged for the two warring editors to cool off under a judicial order, but then along came harbormaster Thompson to rekindle the conflict. A combative Jeffersonian, Thompson asserted that although Coleman possessed a sharp pen, he had no fight in him and would readily turn the other cheek if attacked. After confirming Thompson's exact language, the *Post* editor challenged him to a duel. At eleven o'clock on a cold November night, Coleman and Thompson met at the potter's field, armed with pistols and accompanied by seconds and surgeons. Since it was snowing, the combatants agreed to fire at twelve yards. After the third shot, Captain Thompson fell. Before he died, he was able to tell the friends who were with him that responsibility for the duel was his and that he knew Coleman had not wanted to kill him. The following July, Hamilton and Burr themselves met for their infamous duel in Weehauken, New Jersey. Hamilton was mortally wounded, and Burr's political ambitions came to an end.[12]

Even as the area became more populated twenty years later, duels continued at the potter's field. "A disposition to dueling seems to have possessed the men of New York at this time. The pugnacious character of our citizens still continues," Henry Brevoort Jr. wrote in December 1827 to his close friend Washington Irving, then in Spain. (Brevoort owned a large tract of land north of the potter's field, which had been in his family's possession since 1714.) Barely a month later, on January 15, 1828, the *Evening Post* reported that a "pugilistic combat" had taken place on Washington Square. Two well-dressed men "came on the ground apparently friends with their seconds and after a number of furious rounds, which lasted about half an hour, both retired from the contest very much bruised. Such disgraceful scenes, in the heart of the city, should not be suffered to pass unnoticed. We hope the Police will examine the matter." Dueling was prohibited by state law three months later.

One of the most persistent myths about Washington Square concerns the so-called "Hanging Elm," a majestic tree in the northwest corner of the park. It was said that General Lafayette, while passing through New York, once saw twenty bodies hanging from its outstretched limbs, but there is no evidence to support the grisly tale. There were, however, gallows on the public burying ground, tended by the resident gravedigger, who conveniently doubled as hangman. Condemned inmates marched from Newgate Prison at Tenth Street near the river to meet their fate at the potter's field a short walk away.

The last known public hanging took place on July 8, 1819, when a young black woman named Rose Butler was hanged for setting fire to the house in which she worked. Daniel Megie, the last superintendent on the potter's field, would have officiated. *In Old New York*, written by Thomas Janvier in 1894, quotes an elderly gentleman who remembered looking from his front stoop east across unobstructed fields to the gallows in the Square at the time of Rose Butler's execution. Another witness recalled "stealing away from home to see the very hanging—and coming back so full of it that he could not keep his secret, and so was most righteously and roundly spanked." Rose's hanging had been delayed a few days, the *Evening Post* reported on July 10, "in hope that she would disclose some accomplice in wickedness." She never confessed to the crime, because in all likelihood the fire was accidental, as most were in that era of wooden houses, burning candles, and open cooking fires.

Bones below the Square

Burials became more problematic during the summer of 1822, when yellow fever made one of its most deadly attacks on the city and hundreds were hurriedly laid to rest in the potter's field. For the first time the disease appeared on the supposedly "safe" west side of town along the Hudson near the Battery, where many wealthier residents had built homes to escape the crush of city center. When the southern tip of Manhattan was declared an infected district, city dwellers fled to the safety of Greenwich Village, almost filling it overnight. To accommodate the yellow fever refugees, farmers cut down their cornfields and leased their land or sold lots to developers. Temporary wooden buildings, speedily erected, were fitted up as hotels, recalled a Glasgow businessman in the city then. "In this irregular and temporary city in the field, you might find in one groupe, banking houses, insurance offices, coffee-houses . . . grocery stores, milliners' shops. . . . business transacted here was prodigious."[13] With the arrival of frost, the epidemic abated, and most of the New Yorkers returned to their homes and businesses in town. But those who stayed, including the financial institutions for which Bank Street was named, transformed Greenwich Village into a thriving suburb of the city.

While the greatest flurry of real estate activity took place west of Sixth Avenue in Greenwich Village proper, the district around the potter's field was growing too. By 1823, there were houses and shops on the blocks immediately south of the cemetery; wells were dug, pumps installed, and streets regulated. In the course of the work, the city directed that surplus earth from those blocks be used to fill up the burial ground, which had sunken below the level of the adjacent streets. Observing the field's deterioration, people living in the immediate vicinity complained to authorities about burial practices that contravened health regulations: several bodies interred in one grave and corpses not fully covered over from one day to the next. They pleaded with the Common Council to establish a new public cemetery farther from the settled parts of the city. Repairs were ordered in the spring of 1824, but by then the potter's field was nearly full. The cemetery was officially closed, and burials were prohibited after May 1, 1825.[14]

To this day, the remains of more than 20,000 bodies rest under Washington Square. New Yorkers of a century ago told of a blue mist overhanging the park on hot summer mornings, said to be the vapors from the old bones below. From time to time, some of these old bones have resurfaced. A guide to the city published in 1848 mentions that the bones of the potter's field were collected in vast trenches on either side of the Square and planted over with trees.[15] Edward N. Tailer, who lived around the square all his life, recalled how the weight of heavy guns drawn over the ground broke through into trenches in which the dead were buried. Along the south side of the park near Thompson Street, he once saw an opened vault with a body still wrapped in the yellow sheet traditionally used for those who died of yellow fever. More evidence was uncovered in 1890, when workmen digging the foundation for the Arch came upon headstones with German inscriptions dating to 1803, thought to be from a private German graveyard at the north side of the field.

Bones came to light most recently in the summer of 1965, when Con Edison broke through a burial chamber while digging a twelve-foot shaft for a transformer to be installed in the northeast corner of the park. To the workers' astonishment, the excavation revealed the remains of about twenty-five skeletons jumbled together in a corner of an underground chamber measuring about fifteen by twenty by fourteen feet high. The domed roof of the whitewashed brick room was about five feet below street level; a stairway and wooden door sealed by earth led from the chamber to Washington Square above. After scholars briefly inspected the vault, Con Ed sealed the shaft and filled the hole.[16] There have been no new sightings recorded since then.

After closing the burial ground in 1825, the city directed its dead to a new potter's field at Fifth Avenue between Fortieth to Forty-second streets. About twenty years later that site, too, was converted into a park—now Bryant Park behind the New York Public Library—which in 1853 served as the location for the Crystal Palace, the first world's fair in the United States. Since 1869, New York's public burial ground has been on Hart Island, located in Long Island Sound offshore from the Bronx. Prisoners at Riker's Island act as gravediggers and access is restricted by a limited ferry.

The Washington Military Parade Ground

Washington Square's birth as a landscaped green is tied to the city's extraordinary economic boom in the second quarter of the nineteenth century. And that boom is due in great measure to the opening of the Erie Canal in November 1825. Envisioned eight years earlier by Governor DeWitt Clinton, the canal was a marvel of engineering that definitively set the course for the city's commercial supremacy. The 363-mile waterway audaciously cut across the western part of New York

State to link the Great Lakes with the Hudson River. By funneling the resources and agricultural riches of the Midwest to New York, the canal ensured the city's preeminence as the nation's chief port, soon to be its largest metropolis. Between 1790 and 1820, Gotham's population had nearly quadrupled from about 33,000 to 124,000. From 1820 to 1840, the number of New Yorkers more than doubled to over 312,000. The economy was booming and property values were soaring. The city was in a rush to build. With urban development pushing northward, lots on the former potter's field were worth many times what the city had paid for them, but the bones below made the site unsuitable for private or commercial use. How could the city best utilize the cemetery acreage?

Enterprising New Yorkers eyeing the felicitous development of London's West End in the 1810s to 1820s were aware that squares like London's Bloomsbury, Tavistock, Woburn, and the recently completed Belgrave Square anchored upscale residential development and conveyed prestige to a neighborhood. While open land itself would not yield any revenue, an attractively landscaped green in New York could be expected to lure wealthy householders, increase property values, and ultimately bring in higher tax payments from adjacent properties. Additionally, the city could levy special assessments on lots in the vicinity to help cover the costs of improving the field. Taking note of these considerations, the Common Council, under the leadership of Mayor Philip Hone, devised a plan for the defunct potter's field.

Hone, a Whig, was elected mayor of New York by members of the Common Council on January 3, 1826, after eight rounds of balloting. (New York's mayor was not directly elected until 1834). A self-made Yankee with little formal schooling, as a teenager he had joined his brothers in an auction business and made enough money—the then considerable fortune of $100,000—to retire in 1821 at age forty. Involving himself in municipal affairs, Hone rapidly assumed a position of leadership alongside the upper-class Knickerbocker offspring of old

Dutch and English families. His place in posterity is firmly assured above all because of his diary, begun after he left office in 1828, in which he recorded his activities as well as the goings-on and gossip of the city.

On his first day as mayor on January 16, Hone was presiding over a meeting of the Common Council when Alderman Abraham Valentine introduced a resolution that the old potter's field be appropriated for use as a military parade ground. Six weeks later, on February 27, 1826, the Common Council's Committee on Lands and Places formally gave its approval. "Having been so lately used as a public burial ground on an extensive Scale, it is presumed by your Committee that this Corporation do not intend to use these grounds for private purposes, under some years to come . . . Committee can see no objection to the Military being allowed to use these grounds . . . for Military purposes."[17]

Parade grounds were specified public spaces within the city where voluntary militia companies could train. In the years before the federal government established a standing army, the country's defense rested with a voluntary militia of citizen-soldiers, who were expected to show up for drilling and reviews led by appointed officers. Training sessions were also held in rented drill rooms where arms were stored on racks called "armories." With the exception of the Battery and City Hall Park, there were few open places in the old parts of the city. The Commissioner's Plan of 1811, which plotted Manhattan's grid of evenly spaced streets and avenues north to 155th Street, had projected a military parade as part of a large "central park" to be located between 23rd and 34th Streets. But that large park had not yet been implemented—it never was. The recently filled potter's field presented a serendipitous alternative. Designating the field a parade ground would prevent the land from being divided into building lots, an unsavory proposition considering the bones below, and would preserve the open green space. With appropriate landscaping, the new military ground could fulfill its nominal purpose and at the same time function as a much needed public green.

On June 19, 1826, the Common Council announced plans to inaugurate the new Washington Military Parade Ground on July 4, a date coinciding with the fiftieth anniversary of the signing of the Declaration of Independence. (By a strange fate, two of the founding fathers, John Adams and Thomas Jefferson, died on that same Independence Day.) In the days leading up to the jubilee, newspapers published the schedule of events and informed the volunteer regiments of their duties. The line would form on the parade ground at seven in the morning, and troops would be "uniformed, armed and equipped," instructed the *Evening Post* on July 1, adding that each troop was to furnish a trumpeter. On the big day, Colonel Henry Arcularius fired a national salute at seven and then paraded his troops on horseback around City Hall and up to the parade ground, followed by a procession of dignitaries and more military groups.

After speeches and a reading of the Declaration of Independence, the parade ground was officially named and the festivities began. Immense awnings were set up over two long tables laden with food. Along the west side of the ground "a couple of oxen had been roasted whole and handsomely placed upon tables decorated with flowers and greens of various kind," reported the *Evening Post* the next day. There were 200 hams, with a carver at each, immense piles of bread, and innumerable barrels of beer. Mayor Hone invited the assembled citizens, estimated at "upwards of 10,000 to approach the tables and join the feast, which they did to a man, in good earnest; and before they separated, relieved the tables, which were spread 400 feet in length, of their ponderous loads." The mayor meanwhile had retreated with Governor Clinton and officials to dine "more sumptuously" at City Hall. Observers estimated that 50,000 people, about one-third of the city's population, visited the spot in the course of the day. The public life of Washington Square was off to a rollicking start.

Toward the end of 1826, the Committee on Lands and Places found that the parade ground's "very irregular" shape was not adequate for its intended military purpose. Based on a survey of 1825 indicating the steplike contour of the potter's field on the west, the committee recommended that the field be expanded to fill Fourth to Sixth Streets and Wooster on the east to MacDougal on the west. "The whole Square ought forever thereafter to be and remain a Public square." This would not present great difficulty, the committee assured the council, because more than half of this block was already city property and the adjoining "grounds are still unimproved."[18] Over time, the city paid thousands of dollars—the sum varies, according to the source, from $43,000 to $87,000—for parcels of land equivalent to dozens of building lots. Eventually, the rectangular parade ground came to possess the dimensions of today's Square.

Forming the new square required some tinkering with streets. Since there was no existing road along the eastern edge of the parade ground, the city wanted to extend Wooster Street to form what is now Washington Square East. Some of the land on that side was occupied by the fenced-in burial ground of the Scotch Presbyterian Church. The city compensated the church for its trouble—an inadequate sum, complained church elders—and the church reluctantly dug up the graves under the proposed street and reburied the remains in the potter's field. With the 20,000 bodies already buried in the public cemetery, the Common Council reassured the church that it would never sell the ground or any part of it. "It is not the intention of the Board to disturb any graves within the grounds nor will there be any absolute necessity for such a measure." Streets bordering the Square have remained fixed ever since, and Thompson Street and Fifth Street (later called Washington Place) were closed within park grounds in order to form "a Public Place."[19]

69

"The Fashionable End of Town"

Homes and businesses had quietly co-existed at the southern tip of Manhattan since New York's earliest days, but during the booming 1820s, commercial activity along the lower East River spilled over onto neighboring streets. When "the murmur of trade had become a mighty uproar," as Henry James wrote in his novel *Washington Square,* locations around Wall Street and Broadway became less hospitable to residential life. Wealthy families began moving away from the clamor and clogged streets of downtown and headed to new dwellings uptown on Bleecker Street, a few blocks south of the Square, and Jones and Bond Streets to the east.

By then the area around the newly declared parade ground was ripe for building. Within months of the July Fourth inaugural celebration, eight landowners constructed twelve homes on the park's southwest side, down the block from the old hangman's house at the corner of Thompson Street. Colonel James Boyles Murray, an international trader, built five of the twelve houses. Modeled after an English-style "terrace," the attached, four-story houses shared a uniform, classically inspired façade. Alfred S. Pell, one of the city's wealthiest men, owned property on the west side of the Square and acted as a realtor negotiating sales in the area. In 1829, a three-story house on Washington Square South was renting for $650 a year. By comparison, housemaids were paid $4 to $6 a month.[20]

The presence of these well-to-do families lent respectability to the new square. Over the next months, the city levied assessments to pay for improvements at the new "Public Place," soon referred to as "Washington Square." Plantings and walkways embellished the Square, and a Committee on Lamps was considering placing lamps within the enclosure. Common Council minutes of February 25, 1828, indicate that $9,641.23 was spent on filling in and grading the field. Some of these expenses were recouped from the owners of nearby property, who were taxed for such improvements. As the neighbor-hood began to thrive, more nearby streets were paved and sidewalks graveled.

An account of changes to the Square appeared in the *Evening Post* of May 10, 1828. "Workmen are busily employed in putting a hand-some fence around this spacious public square, by far the largest of any in this city. And laborers are busy leveling and preparing the ground to be laid down to green turf with neat gravel foot walks around the margin and across it from each extremity. When this work is com-pleted and proper shade trees and shrubbery are hopefully set out over the whole square, it will afford a most delightful morning promenade."

Neighbors swiftly became involved in improving the park's appear-ance. In April 1829, a group petitioned "to have the Washington Square closed until the Grass is grown." The following spring, John Ireland, a property owner on the south side, asked that the gates of the parade ground be kept closed in order to protect the trees and shrub-bery, probably to protect the plantings from scavenging animals.[21] Swine regularly ran loose in the streets and grazed even in the best areas of the city. To Ireland and his neighbors at the parade ground, the livestock belonging to poorer city dwellers were a reminder of the very elements they wished to exclude from their privileged commu-nity. Not until 1844 were pigs finally banished from the streets at Mayor James Harper's direction.

Celebrating a French Revolution

The former burial ground fully assumed its iconic stature as a public square in November 1830, when thirty thousand people congregated to celebrate somewhat belatedly the revolution that had taken place in France the previous July. In the course of that three-day revolt, the French middle class, strongly supported by the press, had managed to dethrone the ultraroyalist King Charles X and declare Louis-Philippe king by popular acclaim. Americans were captivated by the so-called

July Revolution, because it brought about the end of an era of absolute monarchy in Western Europe and resonated with their own liberation from Britain a generation earlier. Underscoring this connection, the celebration was scheduled for November 25, known as Evacuation Day, a popular holiday commemorating the date that British troops had left New York in 1783.

After heavy rains forced a one-day postponement, the procession on November 26 began at Canal Street, heading first downtown to Tammany Hall, then up Broadway to Washington Square. Shops were closed and tricolor flags hung everywhere along the route. Philip Hone, the former mayor, who was chair of the arrangements committee, described the event in his diary, and newspapers carried full details. The parade blended allusions to the French revolution with symbols of America's achievements and technological advances. Trade groups sponsored elaborate floats, fifteen hundred representatives of the Fire Department marched with "beautiful engines, badges and other decorations," followed by Columbia University students and "a steamboat with her steam up and machinery in motion." In tribute to the French press, great carts carrying printing presses proceeded through the streets, churning out and distributing to the crowd copies of an ode to be sung to the tune of the French national anthem, "La Marseillaise." At Washington Square, the ailing ex-President James Monroe presided over the official exercises. After the orations and French songs, crowds tore at the platform and in their frenzy leveled it to the ground, leaving timbers all over the Square. Military regiments, waiting on nearby streets because the park had been so packed, were of little use in keeping order. Despite the rowdy ending, celebrants deemed the pageant one of the most splendid the city had ever seen.

The fête honoring the July Revolution was not an isolated example of New York's francophilia. Five years earlier, in 1824–25, the marquis de Lafayette had made an extended tour of the United States and was received enthusiastically. New York honored the French general, who was warmly remembered for his help during the Revolutionary War, by staging triumphant parades and extravagant balls. There were many other homages as well. Hone arranged for Samuel Morse, an artist best known for inventing the telegraph, to paint a full-length portrait of Lafayette for City Hall. The commission helped secure the young artist's reputation. John Jacob Astor, a fur trader turned realtor, was developing a new street one block east of Broadway, which he named Lafayette Place in the Frenchman's honor. Astor later dubbed the nine grand houses there "LaGrange Terrace" after Lafayette's country home in France. Façades of four of the homes, with their imposing double-height colonnade, still survive on Lafayette Street south of Astor Place.

The Row

At the time of the French celebration, the northeast side of the parade ground was open farmland. A year later, construction was under way on the most enduring and endearing element of the Square—the red-brick Greek Revival houses known collectively as "the Row." That a block of such houses have survived in New York is rare. Rare, too, is the uniformity of their design. The land on which the Row stands was part of a tract of twenty-one acres known as the Minto farm, which belonged to Thomas Randall in the eighteenth century. Minto stretched north from today's Washington Square to Tenth Street and from Fifth Avenue east to Broadway. Years later, Randall's son, Robert Richard Randall, deeded the land to Sailors' Snug Harbor, a charitable organization of his creation, which held on to the increasingly valuable property well into the twentieth century.

Thomas Randall, the father, was a Scottish émigré who had made his fortune as a privateer before the Revolutionary War. In 1770, he joined a group of colonial merchants in founding the Marine Society, a charitable organization to improve marine knowledge and relieve indigent and distressed shipmasters and their widows and orphans. At his death twenty years later, his son Robert, also a privateer and member of the Marine Society, inherited his father's fortune and the Minto farm. When Robert Randall died in 1801, he left no direct heirs. His will, probably written by his lawyer and good friend Alexander Hamilton, directed that the bulk of the estate—$10,000 worth of stock and the family land—be used to establish a home for aged or debilitated sailors, to be called Sailors' Snug Harbor. The organization was incorporated in 1806, but lawsuits by Randall's relatives lingered on until a Supreme Court decision of 1830 found in Snug Harbor's favor. By then, the value of land around the parade ground made it more profitable for the new institution to lease out the land on the Square and build the sailors' home somewhere else, which turned out to be the north side of Staten Island. The Snug Harbor complex on Staten Island, designed by Minard Lafever in the Greek Revival style, was completed in 1833, just as the first houses on the Row were nearing completion.

Snug Harbor's success in fulfilling its mission was closely entwined with the future development of the potter's field, since whatever was done with the burial site would affect the value of the former farmland. As Randall's will required, the governing board of Sailors' Snug Harbor included some of the city's most powerful men: the chancellor of New York State; the mayor of New York City; president of the Chamber of Commerce; rectors of the city's most prestigious churches; and officers of the respected Marine Society, among others. For years, the well-connected men in these posts were happy to fulfill their obligation and act on the charity's behalf. One the trustees was Philip Hone. With his election as mayor in 1826, Hone automatically became president of Sailors' Snug Harbor's board. It may well be that Mayor Hone's interest in transforming the old potter's field into a more attractive green was motivated not only by his sense of what was best for the city but also by what was advantageous for the benevolent institution. Higher property values would benefit the city's future tax rolls and assure Snug Harbor a good return on its chief asset.[22]

In April 1831, John Johnston, a Scottish-born merchant living downtown on Greenwich Street, persuaded James Boorman, his business partner, and John Morrison to join him in leasing land from Snug Harbor to build a row of houses facing the newly developed parade ground at the northernmost edge of the city. Cows still grazed in the fields beyond. Johnston was convinced that given the unsettled living conditions downtown, the Washington Square area would grow in value. Snug Harbor offered the builders twenty-one-year leases, which listed conditions and restrictions that today would be covered by zoning laws, codes, or other municipal regulations not in existence then. The terms of the leases stipulated that neither any slaughterhouse, forge, furnace, brass foundry, brewery, or bakery nor any glass, starch, glue, varnish, vitriol, turpentine, or ink factory, or other manufactory, trade, or business that might be noxious or offensive to the neighbors, be established there. These restrictions ensured that the property would be developed for prime residential use.

The first leases specified that the lessee complete construction within two years on a "good and substantial dwelling house of the width of the said lot, three or more stories high, in brick or stone, covered with slate or metal" with the front twelve feet back and parallel to Sixth Street (Washington Square North). Stables could be built in the rear of the lots. Depending on the width of the lot, land leases ranged from $130 to $150 per year, plus taxes. Numbering of houses runs counterclockwise around the Square, beginning at the northeast corner. Nos. 1 through 6 are on lots measuring twenty-seven feet across, two feet wider than the city's usual plots. The next seven houses, Nos. 7 to 13, are slightly wider, because they were constructed on the equivalent of eight lots, merged before building began. Johnston reserved two contiguous plots for himself, taking five extra feet from No. 6 for his own large house at No. 7. The west half of the Row was begun in 1832; the six houses to the east were built in 1833.

Although no architect is named in the records, the architectural historian Sarah Bradford Landau presents persuasive evidence that Samuel Thomson designed and constructed the Row houses, building No. 4 for himself on speculation. Thomson was a professional builder, well able to carry out such a project. In 1831, his firm of Samuel Thomson & Son had already repaired some of Sailors' Snug Harbor's properties on Eighth Street. In the summer of 1832, he was superintending construction of the sailors' Greek Revival home on Staten Island.

Greek Revival had first caught on in Philadelphia in the 1820s and spread rapidly, its popularity stimulated in part by America's sympathy for the Greeks then fighting to gain their independence from the Ottoman Empire. With plain brick exteriors and spare classical elements, the modest design of Greek Revival houses was well suited to a young nation committed to democratic principles. It was practical, too, because the style could be executed by ordinary builders and adapted for all types of buildings. The homes on Washington Square North conform to the general layout and design of early Greek Revival houses, but their scale is grander, and details, such as the white marble trim, are more lavish, in keeping with the occupants' elevated social standing. Behind the homes were deep gardens leading to stables and carriage houses; the rear service road is now a cobbled alley called Washington Mews, lined with two-story studios

The Row's relatively restrained exterior barely hints at the splendor within: lofty ceilings, spiraling open staircases and extravagant moldings customized to the owners' wishes. Many of the houses boasted gilt and bronze chandeliers and marble mantles carved in Italy. Mahogany sliding doors separated the front and back parlors, dining rooms were toward the rear, and kitchens were located downstairs below the parlor floor. Bedrooms were upstairs, and the privy was in the back yard. The fourth floor was servants' quarters—most households employed five to seven. Only No. 5 still retains most of its original features. Restored by New York University in the 1930s to serve as the chancellor's residence, it currently holds the dean's offices for New

York University's Graduate School of Arts and Sciences. Nos. 7 through 13 were converted into multiple residences in 1939; houses Nos. 1–6 have been modified for use by the university. NYU leased the Row from Sailors' Snug Harbor in 1949 and in the 1970s purchased the entire block.

Who's Who on the Square

In the second quarter of the nineteenth century, the newly developed Washington Square was *the* place to be. Its roster of residents included some of New York's oldest families, as well as those of more recently arrived successful businessmen. Through the years, the Washington Square families could be said to correspond to the Boston families of Beacon Hill or their counterparts in Philadelphia's Rittenhouse Square. Bound by social, family, and business ties, they were a tight-knit group who had known one another as neighbors or as colleagues in commerce downtown. John Morrison of No. 9, a merchant of Irish descent, and Robert Kelly at No. 10 were business partners, as were John Johnston of No. 7 and James Boorman, who built No. 13. Boorman later founded the Hudson River Railroad and was president of the line after 1849. His former next-door neighbor downtown on Chambers Street was James Tallmadge, a lawyer who moved in to 5 Washington Square. Women on the Square were equally close, frequently calling on one another and serving on charitable committees together. As years passed and some of their husbands died, the women stayed on, causing Washington Square North to be nicknamed "Widow's Row." In several cases, sons and daughters on the Row intermarried, and houses frequently held extended families. Even when the social luster of the Square later dimmed, successive generations of some of the original families continued to live in the houses.

Johnston, like many of the Square's first residents, was a self-made man. An émigré who had arrived from Scotland with little in his pocket, he achieved a comfortable life in New York from his import-export business. While his new home on the Row was under construction, Johnston took his whole family on a journey to Europe, returning in November 1833, just in time to move in. A few years later his son, John Taylor, brought his bride, Frances Colles, to live in the house, and their daughter Emily was born there. In 1856, after John Johnston Sr. died, the young family moved around the corner to their new mansion on Fifth Avenue at Eighth Street. Years later, Emily, granddaughter of the first Johnston on the Row, returned to live in 7 Washington Square with her own family and inhabited the house until the lease from Sailors' Snug Harbor expired in 1935. Her husband, Robert De Forest, descended from a family that had lived in Manhattan under Dutch rule in the seventeenth century, was active in civic affairs and like his father-in-law, served as president of the Metropolitan Museum of Art. The De Forest's daughter Frances, great-granddaughter of the first Johnstons on the Row, married William A. Stewart and moved into No. 1, a few doors away from her parents, where she remained until 1935.

Howland relatives, able to trace their family tree back to the *Mayflower*, were also well represented on the Square. Samuel Howland purchased 12 Washington Square in 1837 and for a few years shared the house with his older brother Gardiner Greene Howland, with whom he managed a worldwide shipping business. Gardiner Howland then moved to a new house at 15 Washington Square on the far side of Fifth Avenue. Gardiner's sister and brother-in-law, Mr. and Mrs. Henry Chancey Jr. lived further along the street to the west, at No. 24. His niece (Samuel Howland's daughter) and her husband made their home next door, at No. 25.

Another family with an extended history on the Square were the Griswolds, who purchased No. 9 in 1844. George Griswold was a partner with his brother in the shipping firm N. L. & G. Griswold, which owned ships and cargoes and profited handsomely from the China trade. The firm's initials—NLGG—were said to stand for "No Loss and Great Gain." The Griswolds were closely connected to other Washington Square families by friendship as well as marriage. George Griswold Jr. married Lydia Alley of 6 Washington Square. Their daughter Sarah Griswold married John C. Green, formerly one of her father's employees. The young couple moved to 10 Washington Square, next door to her parents' home. Marital connections at Washington Square were typical of New York's elite: in 1856, 37 percent of the city's wealthiest were directly interrelated. Matches were not arranged exactly, but a well-born young woman's social life was carefully supervised and Cupid's arrow generally found a suitable mark.

The Row was also home to three New York mayors. The first was Stephen Allen, mayor from 1821 to 1824, who moved in to No. 1 in 1835. Second was Edward Cooper, an earnest reformer who won election in 1878 as a fusion candidate opposing Tammany Hall. Edward's father was Peter Cooper, the founder of Cooper Union for the Advancement of Science and Art, which provided a free education for talented working-class students. The third mayor to live on the Square was George B. McClellan, son and namesake of the Civil War general, who rented 10 Washington Square during his tenure as the Democratic mayor of New York, 1903 to 1909.

Development across Fifth Avenue

Across Fifth Avenue on the western half of Washington Square North, development followed a very different course, because the family that owned the land leased the lots individually over a period of twenty years. As a result, this stretch of Greek Revival homes exhibits more individuality than the unified Row to the east. Unfortunately, the block has suffered some changes and now makes a less impressive appearance than it did 150 years ago.

In 1796, a year before the potter's field was established, John Rogers purchased a four-acre tract that was formerly a part of the Warren estate. When Rogers died, his sizeable holding was divided among his three children—George Jr., John, and Mary, who married William C. Rhinelander. Over the years, the Rogers siblings constructed fine houses for themselves and leased lots for others to develop, but they always held on to their patrimony. As late as the mid twentieth century, the Rhinelander branch of the Rogers family still owned a considerable part of Washington Square North west of Fifth Avenue.

Preceding the Row by a few years, the first house to rise west of Fifth Avenue was a magnificent Federal-style town house, originally thirty-seven feet wide and three and a half stories high, at what is now 20 Washington Square, built in 1828–29 for George Rogers. When it stood alone on the north side of the parade ground, it would have looked like a country mansion set in private grounds, with a carriage-way along its west side leading to a stable in the rear. It was probably intended as a summer home, since George, a wealthy bachelor, and his married brother John were sharing a joint residence downtown at the time. Additions made to the house in 1859 extended the first floor to the full fifty feet of the lot. In 1880, the young architect Henry J. Hardenbergh remodeled 20 Washington Square into four ample apartments, described as "French flats," patterned after the Parisian practice of dividing one elegant building into spacious quarters for separate households. To convert the Rogers's home into multiple living units, Hardenbergh widened the entire house, built a fourth floor, and added cast-iron railings around the front garden. Hardenbergh's work on the Square preceded his better-known large-scale projects uptown, including the Dakota Apartments on Central Park West (1880–84) and the Plaza Hotel at 59th Street (completed in 1907). The house was used as a convent and parochial school. It is now owned by the Sisters of Charity and houses a senior center and offices of the Caring Community, a local social service organization.

In 1839–40, a decade after her brother's house went up, Mary Rogers Rhinelander and her husband William built a large home on the corner of Fifth Avenue at 14 Washington Square. A matching house was built next door at No. 15 for Gardiner Greene Howland, who had been living with his brother across the way on the Row. Each of the Greek-Revival houses was forty-two feet wide, considerably broader than the twenty-seven-foot width of the Row houses. They stood three and a half stories high, with an ornate iron balcony at parlor level. The corner house was occupied by two unmarried Rhinelander daughters until the last sister died in 1914. Immediately west of these two houses, George Rogers built another pair at 16 and 17 Washington Square. Rogers resided at No. 16 until his death in 1870. His grandnephew, Mary Rogers Rhinelander's grandson William Rhinelander Stewart, inhabited No. 17 toward the end of the century, when he was involved with building the Washington Arch.

Aside from the Rogers family, one of the first to build on this part of Washington Square was Henry James's grandmother, Elizabeth Walsh. In 1834, the widowed Mrs. Walsh leased a lot and built a brick Greek Revival house, which was completed the following year. James's parents were married in the house, and many years later, it became the model for Dr. Sloper's residence in James's novel *Washington Square:* "The ideal of quiet and genteel retirement, in 1835, was found in Washington Square where the doctor built himself a handsome, modern, wide-fronted house, with a big balcony before the drawing room windows, and a flight of marble steps ascending to a portal which was also faced with white marble." The house is real, but James's doctor is all fiction: there are no physicians listed as residents in the early days of Washington Square North. Unfortunately, after a hundred years, Mrs. Walsh's house at No. 18 and its neighbor, No. 17, had deteriorated badly, and they were demolished in 1947. For a few years, the double lot stood vacant, like the gaping hole left by a missing front tooth.

Of the eight Greek Revival dwellings that originally filled out the westernmost section of Washington Square North, six have survived. At the western end of the block, there once stood two additional Greek

Revival houses. Today, their site is dominated by "Richmond Hill," a seven-story apartment house built in 1898 for Mary (Rogers) Chisholm. Before Richmond Hill replaced the houses at the northwest corner, three sides of the Square—the north, west and south—would have been lined with stately townhouses, all roughly of the same height. Much of that original architecture is gone now, but the elegant remnants that have survived on the north side allow us to reimagine the atmosphere of harmony and beauty historically associated with the Square.

A Revolution in Urban Living

The flowering of exclusively residential neighborhoods around Washington Square constituted a revolution in urban living. For the first time, the mercantile elite were separating themselves from crowded commercial surroundings and poor segments of the population to create a protected and homogeneous environment. Daniel Walkowitz, a New York University professor of history, portrays the park of this period as a symbol of orderly progress and economic achievement, a place that clearly asserted the hegemony of bourgeois authority and power. The Square's development also spurred the beginning of transportation systems, because home and work were now more widely separated. Since the heads of most of the households continued to be involved with their businesses downtown, a familiar feature of modern life emerged—the daily commute.

Businessmen living around the Square could choose between using their private carriages or riding in the well-appointed Corporation coaches standing ready at a station directly across from the "grand south entrance" to the park. The coach stand must have been in place before May 1828, when a notice in the *Evening Post* objected to "the congregation of coaches" as detracting from the effect of the new parade ground. Residents around the Square might also have tried an alternative mode of public transportation a few block to the east on

Broadway, where brightly painted omnibuses made frequent trips to Wall Street and the Battery. Drawn by up to four horses, omnibuses would stop to pick up or discharge passengers anywhere along the route and could hold a dozen or more people. A one-way ride cost twelve and a half cents and was much cheaper than taking a licensed hackney carriage but still far beyond the means of laborers earning a dollar a day. Then, as now, the hurried commuters of Gotham complained. "The cabal, quarreling, swearing and abuse among the omnibus drivers every day is disgraceful to the city. . . . compel them to start every five minutes and to keep moving—reduce the fare to 6 cents, and abolish filthy tickets," read a letter in the *New York Morning Herald* on May 19, 1835. Since horses supplied the power for all these vehicles, one of the common nuisances in town was the mess from their droppings, routinely picked up on boots or shoes and the long hems of women's dresses.

By the mid 1830s, changes around the Square and on nearby streets amazed New Yorkers. "The most fashionable end of town is now decidedly Washington Square and the surrounding neighborhood. . . . The elegance and beauty of this section cannot be surpassed in the country," the *Morning Herald* declared on May 12, 1835. More praise appeared in the *Herald* a week later: "Ten or twelve years ago, we used to shoulder our twist-barrel gun and go robin-shooting, somewhere around the Washington parade ground. Had Rip Van Winkle himself risen from his centennial dream and whispered in our ear that we should so soon behold a great city built on our shooting ground, we should have scratched our head and laughed at his visionary prediction."[23] In a swanlike transformation, a desolate resting place for the poor had blossomed into a most desirable section of the city.

The Founding of New York University

In May of 1837, Washington Square displayed an impressive addition—a large Gothic Revival building housing the recently established

University of the City of New York. The founders of New York University (as it came to be known after 1896) believed that a great urban university was the proper means of organizing culture within the city and establishing the city's claim to national cultural leadership. Culture and commerce in New York were closely linked. When the University Building on Washington Square was dedicated on May 27, 1837, the chancellor neatly summed it up, saying: "We are among those who ascribe important social and moral effects to the successful cultivation of the arts in a great city. We think it promises well for the commercial emporium."

The concept of a city university was hatched on December 16, 1829, when a group of nine citizens, led by Albert Gallatin, secretary of the Treasury under Presidents Jefferson and Madison, gathered in the home of Reverend James Mathews, pastor of the Dutch Reformed Church, to formulate plans. Stimulated by the example of London University, established in London's West End in 1827, the founding committee believed that such a university would not only further New York's image as a great commercial metropolis, comparable to London, but would also be a vehicle for giving the American city a cultural distinction that had so far eluded it. Gallatin, reflecting the Jacksonian democracy of the era, proposed that the college should be accessible to the community at large and educate those who would be "merchants, mechanics, farmers, manufacturers, architects and civil engineers." To think of higher education in such comprehensive terms was unusual. There were at the time only two colleges in New York City: Columbia, founded as King's College in 1754, which offered a strictly classical education emphasizing Latin and Greek; and the College of Physicians and Surgeons, founded 1807, for training doctors. At the proposed city university, courses of study would emphasize science, modern languages, and political economy (economics)—subjects not included in the classical curriculum.

By the fall of 1830, 175 subscribers had invested in the new venture and elected a council of thirty-two members, with Gallatin as chairman. The following spring, in April 1831, just as Snug Harbor started leasing lots on the Square, the University of the City of New York received its charter from the state legislature. The petition for the charter stated that one of the university's "prominent and essential purposes" was "to afford all classes of the public the education best fitted to aid them in their pursuits, whether intended for the learned profession, commerce, or the mechanical and useful arts." Within the year, however, Gallatin's egalitarianism gave way to the more limited classical education favored by the university's first chancellor, Reverend Mathews, and his conservative supporters. Following Gallatin's resignation, James Tallmadge of 5 Washington Square became president of the council, and John Johnston of No. 7, vice-president.

Responding to course listings advertised in newspapers, the first group of students began classes in September 1832 at Clinton Hall, located a block south of City Hall. Tuition was $80 for the year. Opening ceremonies were subdued: the city was in the throes of a cholera epidemic that had claimed over five thousand lives that summer. The following spring there were 158 young men between the ages of fourteen and twenty-two enrolled in the university. One of the students, John L. Parsons, recorded in his diary that classes were of short duration—three weeks to cover U.S. history, for example—and students were tested by oral exams. Lectures were held in the mornings, afternoons were free, and evenings were devoted to social gatherings or study. Parsons also noted that the seven faculty members cut classes as much as their students did.

In late November of 1832, the university purchased property on the east side of Washington Square from Samuel Thomson for $40,000. Thomson may have been acting as agent for the school when he acquired the land earlier that fall for $33,005. (He also tried to sell the university some bricks he had been storing on the property, material perhaps left over from building the Row.) The university commissioned the architectural firm of Town, Davis & Dakin to design the building in the Gothic style specified by a faculty committee. Although Gothic was probably selected for its strong associations with the medieval English colleges of Oxford and Cambridge, James Dakin, the principal architect on the project, firmly disapproved of the choice. Town, Davis & Dakin were known primarily for their Greek Revival work. Writing to his young partner Alexander Jackson Davis, Dakin declared the preliminary design was "a half-barbarous thing" and "half savage." Dakin would have preferred a simpler Greek Revival design, and Davis duly submitted such a proposal to the university. But ultimately the architects acceded to the client's wishes and created one of the earliest models of "collegiate Gothic," a style later adapted by countless American colleges and universities.

The large building of light-colored stone was constructed on a symmetrical plan, 180 feet long by 100 feet deep, with a marble-paved entrance hall 20 feet high. Wings extending from the center led to towers at the four corners. A wide marble staircase brought visitors to the second-floor chapel, "probably the most beautiful room of its kind in America" proclaimed *Frances' New Guide to the Cities of New-York and Brooklyn* in 1854. The three-story chapel was the work of the thirty-year-old Davis, who designed delicate fan vaulting executed in plaster instead of stone, clerestory windows, and a 50-foot-tall stained-glass window overlooking the park. Alexander Jackson Davis went on to enjoy a distinguished career as one of America's leading architects, widely known for his work in the "picturesque" style, which featured bracketed woodwork and other details associated with American architecture of the Victorian era. His designs, popularized through books, were adapted for villas and cottages across the country.

Many observers remarked on the chapel's resemblance to King's College Chapel at Cambridge University in England. At the building's dedication, Chancellor Mathews claimed: "An Englishman led unexpectedly, by moonlight, through Washington Square, might, at first view of the University, imagine himself approaching King's, or Christ, or either of several other Colleges in Cambridge or Oxford." Then, he qualified: "The small growth of trees, and the light color of the building would soon correct his first impression." Toward the end of the century, the popular writer and *Punch* editor Henry Bunner expressed the opinion that the University Building looked on a dull winter day, "more than ever like some huge pasteboard toy."

Labor Troubles

With construction about to begin, the university's governing council was in turmoil. Several trustees, objecting to Mathews's interference with college curriculum and discipline, resigned over his "maladministration." Others were disturbed by the school's precarious finances, and two resigned over the expenditure of $40,000 for the land when less than that amount had been collected in stock subscription. Impending construction costs worsened the already strained situation. To finance the estimated $140,000 needed to build the neo-Gothic structure on the park, Chancellor Mathews mortgaged university property, including library books. Only $66.46 remained in the treasury at the time.

In order to reduce expenses, the council decided to contract with state prisoners at Sing Sing to cut the marble for the building's exterior. (Sing Sing, located miles upriver near Ossining, opened in 1829, replacing Newgate Prison on the Greenwich Village waterfront.) This was not unusual: Sailors' Snug Harbor had used prison-cut stone for its home on Staten Island, completed the year before. But when local marble cutters learned of the university's arrangement with Sing Sing, they, along with hundreds of stone workers petitioned the state legislature in protest. In the ensuing anti-prison-labor campaign, the workers, joined by trade unionists, passed resolutions to protect themselves from being "monopolized by the convicts," and organized parades to proclaim their cause, but the university was implacable and work continued. The contractor for the university was Elisha Bloomer, who was notorious for using prison labor to cut costs.

Late on Friday night, October 24, 1834, about 150 stonecutters quietly approached Bloomer's shop at Broadway and West Fourth Street and attacked with rocks and brickbats, smashing windows and breaking marble mantels. Bloomer assessed the damage at $2,000 and posted a reward of $250 for the apprehension of anyone involved, but no arrests were made and the riot ended. To keep the peace, the mayor called out the Twenty-seventh Regiment, a socially prestigious cadre of about 1,000 men, which camped out across from the construction site and stayed on duty for four days in the Square. Only three days before the riots, the regiment had held its annual inspection and review on the Square.

After the disturbance, the university completed its building without further incident, using the stone cut by prisoners, but it was the last time that prison labor was employed that way. Peaceful views of the medieval-looking university building give little evidence of the class and ethnic enmities rocking the city in these years. In addition to the stonecutters' riots in October, there were two other violent disturbances in 1834 that required the intervention of the Twenty-seventh Regiment: one in April arising from election disputes between Whigs and Democrats, and the other in July, when mobs attacked abolitionists and blacks.

A Gothic Revival Neighbor

At the end of 1835, the South Dutch Reformed Church located downtown near Broad Street was destroyed by fire, and the congregation were divided over where to build the new church. One branch chose to relocate to Washington Square, where their pastor, Reverend Mathews, was chancellor of the new university. Church trustees purchased property along Washington Square East for $44,000 and, early in 1839, commissioned Minard Lafever to prepare drawings and specifications for the structure. Contracted for $67,000, the final cost of building the church rose to $80,000.

Lafever, an accomplished architect, was widely known through his publications, *The Young Builder's General Instructor* (1829) and *The Modern Builders' Guide* (1833), which supplied builders around the country with designs for houses and public structures. A few years earlier, he had completed the Snug Harbor complex in Greek Revival style. But compelled by the growing enthusiasm for things medieval and the example of the University Building directly across Washington Place, he designed the new church in the Gothic style. Built of roughly cut dark granite with red stone trim, the South Dutch Reformed Church featured two tall towers twenty-four feet square, rising twenty feet above the gabled roof. Lafever's design was later praised as "one of the most imposing examples of Gothic style in the City—high roofed, with slender Gothic columns and arches, and a deep recess in which a magnificent organ carries out the design in a miniature Gothic front facing the altar and pulpit."[24] The church was dedicated on October 1, 1840. While it was under construction, the congregation rented the chapel in the University Building.

Art and Invention on the Square

From the beginning, New York University planned to derive rental income from its ambitious Gothic Revival home. In addition to hosting the South Dutch Reformed Church, the university rented space to other educational and cultural institutions, a strategy that became even more essential after the financial panic of 1837, when banks failed and businesses went bankrupt. The school's shaky financial condition exacerbated ongoing internal strife and forced Mathews's resignation a year later. Theodore Frelinghuysen, his successor as chancellor in 1838, managed to bolster the fledgling school's finances with support from the well-to-do families living nearby. Members of the Washington Square community regarded the university not only as an ornament but also as a continuing responsibility, as the urban historian Bayrd Still has documented. In addition to Tallmadge and Johnston, several neighbors on the Row, among them Robert Kelly, Thomas Suffern, John C. Green, James Boorman, and Johnston's son John Taylor Johnston, were members of the school's governing council. They and others in the community contributed generously to keep the new institution afloat. In 1853, when the university sought to meet a deficit of $532,646, eight of the ten largest donors were residents of the Square.

NYU's decision to rent rooms turned out to have far-reaching benefits beyond the university's financial solvency. The institutions housed in the University Building—the New-York Historical Society, the New York Academy of Medicine, and the American Geographical Society—along with the faculty tenants, enhanced the Square's reputation as a place of culture and intellectual distinction. Since a number of the individual tenants were artists, the area also became identified as the center of New York's art community. One of the first tenants was Samuel Finley Breese Morse, the university's new professor of the literature of the arts of design, who rented chambers in 1835 before the Gothic Revival structure was completely finished. Although he was a trained and practicing artist, Morse is best known for inventing the telegraph, a feat he accomplished in his rooms on the Square. Using electromagnetic impulses tapped in code, Morse made it possible to transmit information over distances instantaneously and ushered in a revolution in modern communications that has continued to this day.

Morse's achievements as both artist and inventor illustrate the close interrelationships that existed among artists, writers, scientists, and the city's merchant aristocracy. A New Englander by birth, the son of a prominent Connecticut minister, Morse attended Yale University and studied at London's Royal Academy of Art. He chose to settle in New York after carefully considering other American cities. More than Philadelphia or Boston or Baltimore, Morse believed, New York exuded the wealth and power necessary for art patronage to flourish. Cognizant of the potential impact of the Erie Canal then under construction, he wrote with optimism to his wife in 1823: "New York does not yet feel the influx of wealth from the Western canal but in a year or too she will feel it, and it will be advantageous to me to be previously identified among her citizens as a painter." Later he worried that the city was "wholly given to commerce. . . . Every man is driving at one object—the making of money—not the spending of it."

Articulate and better educated than some of his artistic peers, Morse participated actively in the city's social life and maintained close friendships with the literary lions of the period, particularly William Cullen Bryant and James Fenimore Cooper. With other artists of his generation, he founded the National Academy of Design in 1826 and served as president of this association run strictly by and for professional artists. Morse was also on good terms with many of the city's wealthiest citizens. In 1829, twenty-one merchants and professional men financed an extended trip made by the artist to Italy and France, paying him in advance a total of $3,000 to make copies of famous works or to execute something of his own. Philip Hone, for one, paid him $100 "to be disposed of in such way as may be most agreeable to Mr. Morse," specifying only that the picture be no larger than twenty-five by thirty inches. Upon returning from Europe, Morse became involved in politics, publishing vitriolic tracts on the dangers of immigration. He later penned pro-slavery leaflets. In 1836, he ran for mayor on the anti-Irish ticket of the Native American Democratic Association, a nativist, anti-Catholic movement that targeted the large numbers of Irish immigrants in New York. Morse's politics, later represented by the American Party, or "Know Nothings," reflected the sentiments of many respectable neighbors in the elite enclave around the Square, not then the tolerant community it would later become.

In 1835, before construction of the University Building was completed, Morse, then a widower, took six rooms there—four on one floor to use as studios for teaching and two more in the northwest tower above for his personal studio-laboratory. Continuing his professional art activities, but concerned about his financial situation, he turned to science to make money and embarked on work that led to the telegraph. His scientific interest and abilities would not have been considered unusual for an artist. In Morse's day, American artists were of necessity skilled at making or inventing what they needed for their craft, sometimes turning to science on behalf of their art. Although it seems less conceivable now, art and science then were not opposite poles but part of a continuum of knowledge accessible to any curious individual. It was not uncommon for gentlemen to engage in utilitarian scientific pursuits: Benjamin Franklin, printer and statesman, experimented with electricity using kite and key; Robert Fulton, painter and engineer, invented the first commercially successful steamboat in 1808. Only when science became more theoretically based later in the century did it became a more exclusive realm.

Morse's successful telegraph benefited from the research and ingenuity of several of his contemporaries. Yet because of the signaling system of dots and dashes he invented, known as the Morse code, the invention is forever linked to his name. The telegraph was based on electromagnetism, the fundamentals of which he had learned in lectures by a Columbia College professor, James Freeman Dana, at the New York Athenaeum in 1827. (The Athenaeum presented popular lectures to the public held in the chapel of Columbia College located near City Hall. Morse, secretary of the association, had delivered lectures on art the year before.) After settling into his university quarters, Morse drew on the expertise of his fellow tenants and faculty colleagues. Leonard Gale, professor of chemistry, and Alfred Vail, a former student, were his chief assistants. John William Draper, professor of analytical chemistry, devised the chemical battery that powered Morse's telegraph. Samuel Colt, a designer of firearms who lived in the university's north tower, supplied the necessary cable. Colt achieved fame as the inventor of the revolving-breech revolver, patented in 1835–36, which became known as the "six-shooter" and was quickly put to use by U.S. troops fighting the Seminole in 1837.

Morse held a formal demonstration, issuing printed invitations to a select group "to witness the operation of his Electro Magnetic telegraph," in Washington Square on January 24, 1838, at twelve noon. From Professor Gale's laboratory overlooking the park, he and his colleagues ran ten miles of coiled copper wire out to the Square, wrapped it around some trees, and brought it back to the laboratory, where it was connected to the tapping device. That afternoon, employing his code of dots and dashes for each letter of the alphabet, Morse successfully transmitted the first public telegraph message: "Attention! The Universe! By Kingdom's Right Wheel."[25]

Several years later, Morse persuaded Congress to underwrite a telegraph line between New York and Baltimore. To inaugurate the connection in 1844, he tapped "What hath God wrought" to Vail waiting in Baltimore, and then asked, "Have you any news?" Within a short time, the telegraph revolutionized the relay of news and information across the country. Morse offered to sell his invention to the government, but Congress refused, and so the inventor rounded up enough private backing to establish the Magnetic Telegraph Company, with service between Philadelphia and New York. In reality, the line went only as far as Jersey City; messages were rowed the last leg across the Hudson to New York. Poles strung with telegraph wires rapidly became a familiar feature of Manhattan's streets. In 1846, six New York newspapers began a telegraph-based wire service called the Associated Press to transmit news of the Mexican-American War in Texas. Lines soon stretched from Maine to Mexico, with New York at the receiving end. Thanks to Morse's telegraph, born on Washington Square, the city became the communications capital of the country.

The telegraph was not the only far-reaching advance achieved through the collaboration of colleagues in the University Building.

William Draper, inventor of the battery that contributed to the success of Morse's telegraph, was an esteemed professor at the university from 1838 to 1882. So highly regarded was Draper that his lecture notes for biology, chemistry, and physiology were sold nationally, imprinted with a picture of the University Building on the cover. Among his chief interests was light reactive chemistry, a field that overlapped with Samuel Colt's pursuits in the 1840s. In running electric current through platinum, Colt had produced an incandescent reaction that he and Draper later incorporated into temporary illumination for the University Chapel. Draper's write-up of their experiment in 1847 contributed to the development of electric lighting.

Draper was also involved in the early development of photography. In the late 1830s, Louis Daguerre collaborating with Nicéphore Niepce in France perfected the daguerreotype, a photograph produced on a silver-coated copper plate. Daguerreotypes, however, required very long exposure times. Working in his lab on Washington Square, Professor Draper found a way to cut the exposure time from forty-five minutes to about fifty seconds, thus making it more feasible for a photographer to capture the image of a human figure. In June 1839, he took a picture of his sister, Dorothy Catherine Draper, on the roof of the University Building. To ensure that her features would emerge clearly in the light, her face was caked in flour. The resulting image of her, sitting with her hands in her lap, her face framed by a large round bonnet, is one of the first photographic portraits on record.

Morse, too, became an enthusiastic photographer. In March 1839, while on a trip to England and France seeking capital for his telegraph, he met Daguerre in Paris. Deeply impressed by the Frenchman's work, he wrote to his brother that it was "one of the most beautiful discoveries of the age. . . . no painting or engraving ever approached it." After returning home and receiving Daguerre's published text with detailed instructions for creating plates and making exposures, Morse began collaborating with Draper. On the roof of the University Building, overlooking the Square, the two men set up a glass-top studio, where they experimented and taught the new photographic process. One of Morse's photography students was Matthew Brady, who later achieved fame for his compelling photographs of soldiers in the Civil War. By then, there were some two hundred photography studios in New York, accounting for $2 million in annual income.

The Art Boom

Through the end of the century, more than sixty artists took advantage of studio space in the University Building. One of the first artist tenants was Alexander Jackson Davis, the architect of the University Chapel, who leased rooms while overseeing the building's final stages of construction. The painter Eastman Johnson, a leading genre and figure painter at midcentury, worked there for a while later on, as did the landscape painter George Inness, who commuted to the Square from his home in New Jersey. They and other artists around the Square formed the core of what would become the most vital art community in the nation.

Before the 1820s, art collecting was generally limited to the patrician families of Boston, Philadelphia, Baltimore, and, to a lesser extent, New York. Although a few American artists were able to establish successful careers, mainly through portraiture, European art was generally thought to be superior. But during the 1820s, some prominent New Yorkers started to take an active interest in the careers of younger, home-grown American artists—sponsoring Morse's trip in return for paintings, for example. Just as they competed in business, these new patrons vied to enrich their art collections.

John Taylor Johnston, the eldest son of the Row's founder John Johnston, was one of this new breed of collectors. Although educated as a lawyer, John Taylor made his fortune from railroads, starting with a short line in New Jersey. After becoming president of the company in 1849, he extended the rail, acquired the Lehigh and Susquehanna and consolidated the lines into the Central Railroad of New Jersey. To ensure a direct link between the Pennsylvania coalfields and New York harbor, Johnston bought the flatlands of Jersey City across the river from the southern end of Manhattan and built rail yards there. All the while, he was befriending artists and buying pictures. After moving into the grand limestone mansion that he built on the corner of Fifth Avenue and Eighth Street, Johnston established a picture gallery in the stables behind the house. Open every Thursday to visitors admitted by card, his gallery was one of the first such exhibition spaces in the country. Johnston also helped found the Metropolitan Museum of Art and served as its first president from 1870 until his death in 1889.

The promise of such patronage, coupled with the perception of New York's energetic and less conservative atmosphere compared to that of Philadelphia or Boston, attracted more artists to the city. Intellectual life in the city was blooming. In the mid 1840s, New York literati met on Saturday evenings for tea and cookies at Anne Lynch's home on Waverly Place, a few steps west of Washington Square. Lynch, a schoolteacher and poet with a gift for fostering conversation, established what was perhaps the first salon in New York, where creative and intellectual men and women came together on equal terms. Early in 1845, Edgar Allan Poe, then living a block south of the park, gave his first reading of "The Raven" in her parlor.

The city's flourishing literary life was good for artists. It meant that there were writers to create new subjects for painters and to pen reviews of art shows. There were publishing houses that required illustrations for their books and magazines, and by the 1840s, there were a half dozen art dealers and three major art institutions exhibiting contemporary art. In addition to local collectors, there was the potential patronage of out-of-town merchants, who visited the city regularly. New York provided color and excitement, the potential for exhibiting work, finding patrons, and forging friendships—all that an artists' colony needed to thrive.

In June 1860, the twenty-four-year-old Winslow Homer from Boston took studio space in the University Building and, like many of his talented peers, found work as an illustrator at *Harper's Weekly* magazine, earning the goodly sum of $30 a week, plus train fare. At the outbreak of the Civil War, Homer was sent to the front as an artist-correspondent to record what he saw. His realistic illustrations of soldiers and camp life printed in the magazine attracted wide attention, and by 1864, visitors were seeking him out in his quarters on the Square. Preferring to work by natural light, the artist often posed figures on the rooftop of the building. A reporter for the *New York Leader* advised, "If you wish to see him work you must go out upon the roof and find him painting what he sees." One of Homer's first works to gain popular acclaim was an oil painting, *Prisoners from the Front,* based on an incident of the war and completed in his New York studio. Visitors remembered seeing elements of the painting in his room—the soldier's overcoat dangling from a wooden peg and a rusty regulation musket in one corner. The painting was purchased by J. T. Johnston and now hangs in the Metropolitan Museum of Art.

Among Homer's contemporaries at the university was Theodore Winthrop, an aspiring author who moved into a tower room of the University Building in 1860 and began writing a novel. At the start of the Civil War, Winthrop enlisted with the Seventh Regiment (formerly the Twenty-seventh) and marched off to battle, to be killed two months later. His novel *Cecil Dreeme* was published posthumously by Ticknor & Fields, one of the most important literary publishers of the day. The book attained such popularity that it was reprinted several times in the first year after its publication.

Winthrop's tale revolves around a young woman who has run away and hides out in an all-male college disguised as a man. Robert, a young artist at the school, befriends the runaway "Cecil" (nee Clara). As his feelings for Cecil/Clara deepen from affection to love, Robert confronts questions of sexual ambiguity, homosexuality (before the word was in use), and the male-female differences imposed by society. The book offers a rare discussion of gender issues before the Civil War and also provides a glimpse of Greenwich Village life at the time. Winthrop set his story in and around the Square, transparently called "Ailanthus Square," and renamed New York University "Chrysalis College." "There it stands, big, battlemented, buttressed, marble. . . . The halls and lecture rooms would stand vacant, so they let them out to lodgers. . . . It's not old enough to be romantic. But then it does not smell of new paint, as the rest of America does."

The Tenth Street Studios

In the short time that he lived on the Square, Winthrop numbered among his friends Richard Morris Hunt, a young architect just returned from Paris—the first American to have studied at the prestigious École des Beaux Arts. In 1856, Hunt moved into rooms on the second floor of the University Building, filling his studio with artwork, antique furniture, and a comprehensive collection of books about art and architecture, which he made available to all who were interested. A year later, he founded the American Institute of Architects, whose headquarters remained in the University Building until 1861. Hunt went on to gain a distinguished reputation as the architect of choice for the Vanderbilts, Astors, and Lenoxes, but few of his public or private commissions survive. He and his wife later resided at 2 Washington Square, down the block from his father-in-law, Samuel Howland, of No. 12. Hunt was also connected to the Row by one of his first projects—the Tenth Street Studio Building developed by James Boorman Johnston, the second son of John Johnston of 7 Washington Square.

James Boorman Johnston was well aware of the public's growing interest in art—his brother John was an avid collector—and he recognized the increasing demand for studio space. Although the neo-Gothic University Building buzzed with the prodigious talent of its occupants, it was dark by design and dreary with neglect, and it could not adequately accommodate the many artists clamoring at midcentury for well-lit studios. In 1857, Johnston hired Hunt, whom he had met on his European travels, to design an entirely new kind of building devoted exclusively to the making, showing, and selling of art. Located between Fifth and Sixth Avenues, the Tenth Street Studio Building included about twenty-five ample studios centered around a very large exhibition hall, lit by an ingeniously designed expansive glass roof. Nothing like it had ever existed. James Johnston, a successful businessman, regarded the project as a good investment, and he was right. Rents ran on average between $200 to $300, a bit high for the time. Yet as soon as the building was completed, it was fully rented. Hunt himself was one of the first tenants, and Winslow Homer kept a studio there from 1871 to 1880. Contributing substantially to the area's reputation as a hospitable place for artists, the Tenth Street Studio Building provided artists with studio space until 1956, when it was demolished to make way for an apartment house.

Later in the century, another popular residence for artists and writers was developed near the southeast corner of the park at 80 Washington Square East. It was called the Tuckerman Building after its developer Lucius Tuckerman, and designed by McKim, Mead & Bigelow in 1879. (Stanford White replaced Bigelow as partner in the firm about two months before the building opened in November that year.) Intended as an upscale residence for bachelors, the Tuckerman eventually came to be known as the "Benedick" after the confirmed-bachelor character in Shakespeare's *Much Ado About Nothing.* Among the early occupants was Winslow Homer, listed as "painter" at the address in the 1880 census. As had been his habit at the University Building, Homer often worked up on the roof. A visitor described finding him on the rooftop splashing models with water in preparation for making studies for *Undertow,* a beach scene he completed a few years later while living on the coast of Maine.

99

Croton Water and the Fountain in the Square

By the time the Benedick opened, the city was providing most New Yorkers with a dependable supply of water for drinking, bathing, and cooking. Among affluent households, private baths and working toilets were becoming more common. Half a century earlier, such amenities had been unheard of and clean drinking water alone would have been regarded as a precious commodity. What made the difference was one of the great engineering feats of the nineteenth century—the Croton aqueduct. The fountain at the center of Washington Square is a manifest symbol of that aqueduct and the safe, plentiful Croton water it carried to New York.

Through the eighteenth century, Fresh Water or "Collect" Pond was the city's main source of "fresh" spring water. The seventy-acre pond, located about a mile and a half south of Washington Square's site, had become so contaminated by excrement, dead animals, and industrial wastes that in 1803 the city filled it in. To this day, pumps run underneath the municipal buildings in the area to control the old pond's springs. After Fresh Water Pond was filled in, most city dwellers relied on impure well water carried by the pailful from pumps located at four-block intervals. To cover the taste of the tainted water, they often added brandy even to children's drinking water, a practice that prompted temperance advocates to join the campaign for a better water supply. Residents of private homes who could afford it arranged for water from outside the city to be delivered by hogshead—large wooden barrels holding 63 to 140 gallons. In 1799, Aaron Burr and other investors established the Manhattan Company ostensibly to dig wells, lay pipes, and deliver water. While the company's hollowed-out log pipes did supply water to a few hundred homes, the business was only a front for Burr to start a bank, the forerunner of Chase Manhattan (now J. P. Morgan Chase & Co.). New York would have to wait another forty years for a dependable water system.

Established households on Washington Square received water deliveries and kept cisterns in their yards to catch rainwater. The cistern at No. 7 was so huge that it was "large enough for a horse to swim about in," according to Emily Johnston De Forest. In the biography of her grandfather, *John Johnston, Merchant,* she relates how neighbors in the Square relied on "a pump with a long handle which afforded the boys no end of amusement."

Lack of a safe, dependable water supply posed a continuous problem for the growing city, not only endangering health but also increasing the risk of fires. Blazes had badly damaged the city in 1776 and 1828. Following the so-called "great fire" of 1835, when nearly 700 buildings were destroyed and twenty blocks leveled, authorities were compelled to address the water problem. The Croton aqueduct was begun two years later.

The aqueduct was a system of large iron pipes protected by stone and brick masonry that carried water over a distance of forty-one miles from the mouth of the Croton River in Westchester to a receiving station at Eighty-sixth Street. From there the water flowed to a reservoir at Forty-second Street, where the New York Public Library now stands. Thousands of immigrants were employed in the project, which required 150 miles of pipes to carry water to locations throughout the city. Details about construction filled the newspapers, with reporters stoking the public's excitement by tracking the daily progress of the water's flow. On July 4, 1842, thousands of proud New Yorkers assembled before daybreak to witness the culminating moment when the Croton water was introduced into the reservoir at Forty-second Street. "Nothing is talked of or thought of in New York but Croton Water," wrote the commissioner of the Croton project, the former mayor, Philip Hone, in his diary for October 12, 1842. "It is astonishing how popular the introduction of water is among all our classes of citizens, and how cheerfully they acquiesce in the enormous expense which will burden them and their posterity with taxes to the latest generation. Water! Water! is the universal note which is sounded through every part of the city, and infuses joy and exultation into the masses."

To demonstrate the distribution of Croton water—even as some poor sections remained without it—the city decided to erect fountains in public spaces. Stephen Allen, a former mayor living at 1 Washington Square, requested approval from the Common Council to raise funds for statuary to ornament Washington Square's proposed basin, "and for this purpose, it was said, a large amount of money had been subscribed by residents in the vicinity." A fountain at the center of the Square would diminish the green's usefulness as a parade ground, but it would create an atmosphere reminiscent of a European pleasure garden, which the neighbors much preferred.

But the fountain project was delayed. Finally, the city applied $2,000 of funds left over from erecting an iron fence around the Square to build the fountain, with an impressive circular basin of bluestone measuring a hundred feet in diameter, which was completed in January 1852. The ample flow of Croton water under pressure enabled the spray from the fountain's jets to rise higher than nearby trees. Tompkins Square, about a half-mile away on First Avenue and Tenth Street, also received a fountain. While the Tompkins fountain was twenty feet larger, "Washington Square's basin had a greater number of jets, and made a finer display," the *Evening Post* declared on January 31, 1852. Placed at the midpoint of the park's east-west axis, the fountain gave the Square a definitive central focus. Much to the neighbors' satisfaction, it reduced the lingering parade ground feeling and heightened the impression of the park as a pleasure garden.

Henry James and the Square: "A Riper, Richer, More Honorable Look"

Washington Square in midcentury is Henry James territory; ever since his eponymous novel appeared in 1881, James's portrayal of it has shaped perceptions of the place. James was born on April 15, 1843, in a house at 21 Washington Place (now demolished), around the corner from New York University. The plot of his novel *Washington Square,* about the strong-willed Dr. Sloper, his unmarried daughter Catherine, and her suitor Morris Townsend, was based on a family situation related to him by the English actress Fanny Kemble. But James, then living in England, set the tale on the Washington Square of forty years earlier, "so decent in its dignity, so unpretentious," drawing on memories of the home of his maternal grandmother, Elizabeth Walsh. James had known his grandmother's house at 18 Washington Square North only as a young child. After her death in 1847, the dwelling was sold, and he never again saw its interior.

The James family moved around a great deal. The author's father, Henry James Sr., had inherited enough of a fortune to be free to study, lecture, and write, to pursue his interests in theology and socialism— and to travel. James was six months old when he first went to Europe on an extended trip lasting a year and a half. Not long after their return, the Jameses moved to Albany for several years to be near the paternal grandparents. The family shuttled back and forth, finally resettling in New York on West Fourteenth Street in 1850, when Henry was seven. Over the next five years, one of the more stable periods of his young life, the boy attended school on Waverly Place and played regularly in the park, accompanied by his older brother William, later the renowned psychologist and philosopher. James seems to have delighted in the sights and even the smells of his city surroundings and to have remembered them well. Forty years later in London, he transcribed his powerful childhood memories, infusing his novel with nostalgic affection.

"In front of them was the square, containing a considerable quantity of inexpensive vegetation, enclosed by a wooden paling, which increased its rural and accessible appearance." (The wooden fence was replaced with a wrought-iron one in 1848.) "I know not whether it is owing to the tenderness of early associations, but this part of New York appears to many persons the most delectable. It has the kind of established repose which is not of frequent occurrence in other quarters of the long, shrill city; it has a riper, richer, more honorable look . . . the look of having had something of a social history. . . . it was here that your grandmother lived, in venerable solitude, and dispensed a hospitality which commended itself alike to the infant imagination and the infant palate; it was here that you took your first walks abroad, following the nursery-maid with unequal step, and sniffing up the strange odor of the ailanthus trees which at that time formed the principal umbrage of the Square, and diffused an aroma that you were not yet critical enough to dislike as it deserved."

Toward the end of the book, the ailanthus-tree motif recurs. Mrs. Penniman, Catherine's aunt, usually eager for a visit to the country in the summer, sits before a window on a hot July evening and "seemed quite content with such rural impressions as she could gather at the parlor-window from the ailanthus trees behind the wooden paling. The peculiar fragrance of this vegetation used to diffuse itself in the evening air." James recalled kicking the fallen ailanthus leaves as a child, and the olfactory sensation lingered in his mind all those years later. Nowadays only one very large ailanthus stands in the Square, near the edge of the dog run, but it might please James to know that numerous others stubbornly shoot up like weeds in courtyards and cracks of sidewalks all around the Village.[26]

Through James's words, generations of readers have imagined the Square of long ago. Since the 1940s, even more people have come to know Washington Square through stage and screen versions inspired by his book. *The Heiress*, a play written by Ruth and Augustus Goetz, opened on Broadway in 1947 and was promptly adapted for William Wyler's 1949 Oscar-winning film of the same name, starring Olivia de Haviland and Montgomery Clift, with a score by Aaron Copeland. The stage version of *The Heiress* was revived on Broadway in 1995, and a new film titled *Washington Square* was released in 1997.

James's evocation of Washington Square's "pleasanter, easier, hazier past," so compelling to modern audiences, is corroborated by D. Maitland Armstrong, who as a young boy in the 1840s spent afternoons at the parade ground playing marbles and other games. In his memoirs *Day before Yesterday, 1836–1918,* Armstrong describes militia officers dashing about on their steeds and "a quaint old Irish candy-man named Jimmy" who "carried a tray, holding it in both hands, supported by a leather strap around the back of his neck. We had recess at one o'clock and Jimmy would always be on hand at that time and had excellent custom. His tray contained squares of molasses candy, white and pink cocoanut-cakes, and 'all-day suckers' . . . very durable. All of these were one cent each."

Colliding Worlds at the "White Kid Glove Opera"

The cloudless visions of a tranquil and secure New York conjured up by Armstrong and James overlook the realities of a complex society beset by ethnic and class divisions. The metropolis of Henry James's youth was really two cities—physically close, economically unequal, and mutually distrustful. To the elite families of the city, the greatest pressure in these years was from the expanding immigrant population. Old-time New Yorkers at midcentury saw themselves as a minority culture in the city of their birth, outnumbered by thousands of Germans and Irish newcomers, just as Morse had warned would happen in his political tracts. In the 1830s, German émigrés began to settle in the northeast part of the city between the East River and the Bowery, where they recreated the culture of their homeland in an area known as Kleindeutschland. Next came the Irish, the largest single group of immigrants. By 1845, nearly 100,000 Irish had arrived, swelling the city's total population to 371,000. Through the next two decades, over a million more Irish people escaping the grip of the potato famine would find their way to New York. Most of them settled in an old section of the city, now the Lower East Side, where landlords converted single-family dwellings into "tenant houses," or tenements. Defined by nineteenth-century law as any house where three or more families cooked separately, a tenement commonly held six or more people per room, with several families sharing a kitchen and toilet and little light or fresh air.

Among the worst places was the Five Points, a slum district near City Hall where five streets intersected. Built over the filled-in Fresh Pond and inhabited mostly by immigrants, the Five Points was notorious for its wretched living conditions and violent gangs. The contrast between the filth and poverty of Five Points and the sequestered prosperity of Washington Square piqued the curiosity of some visitors. When the thirty-year-old Charles Dickens visited New York in 1842, he requested to be shown Washington Square. The popular English author, intrigued by the city's underbelly, also went to see the Five Points, "where dogs would howl to lie," he wrote.

Insulated by wealth, the world of Washington Square was presumed to be a safe distance from the Five Points. But in May 1849, what appeared to be a trivial rivalry between two actors and their admirers triggered ethnic English-Irish and class hostilities that ultimately led to a deadly confrontation on Astor Place, a few blocks away from the Square. The Astor Place Opera embodied the cultural aspirations of New York's upper class and was particularly dear to residents of the Square. Emily Johnston De Forest's maternal grandfather, James Colles, and some of his friends had built the theater to be convenient to their elegant new homes in the area. Only those in formal attire and the requisite white kid gloves were admitted to performances.

In May 1849, the British actor William C. Macready was scheduled to perform *Macbeth* at the "white kid glove opera," as some called it. During the previous months while Macready was performing on tour, he and the American actor Edwin Forrest had been trading slurs, which were well publicized in the national press. Philip Hone, expressing the anti-Irish bias shared by many of his peers, attributed the actors' rivalry to "no cause . . . except that one is a gentleman, and the other is a vulgar, arrogant loafer, with a pack of kindred rowdies at his heels." As a young man, Forrest had become a star of the Bowery Theater, and he was revered by the two major gangs of the Five Points, the Bowery Boys and the Dead Rabbits. When Forrest's loyal fans first threatened to disrupt Macready at the opera house, forty-nine merchants, lawyers, and writers—Washington Irving, Herman Melville, and Samuel Ruggles among them—petitioned Mayor Caleb Woodhull for protection. They were determined to guard their institution and their aesthetic standards from the onslaught of what they perceived as the inferior tastes of the lower classes—namely, the Irish immigrants, who were disdained for their poverty as well as their Catholic faith.

Macready was playing Macbeth on a Thursday evening, May 10, 1849, when some 15,000 supporters of Edwin Forrest gathered outside the Astor Place Opera House. Some of the crowd started throwing paving stones through the windows and began to pound on the theater doors. Three hundred unarmed policemen, stationed there to keep order, were unable to control the mob. Artillery, cavalry, and infantry companies of the Seventh Regiment—formerly the Twenty-Seventh, the same regiment that had suppressed the 1834 stonecutters' riot—had been readied ahead of time and supplied with ammunition. As was usually the case, the elite regiment was defending well-to-do property owners or employers against the working class. As rioting continued, members of the regiment, "men of means and property, the very cream of our society," were ordered to shoot into the crowd. At least twenty-two people died, and many more, including over fifty to seventy policemen, were seriously injured.[27]

Protected by police and soldiers, Mrs. John Taylor Johnston (Francis Colles) of 7 Washington Square and her family ran with opera cloaks over their heads to the safety of their homes around the Square. Macready, in disguise, escaped to a friend's house on Eighth Street, then made his way by train to Boston and immediately sailed back to

England, never to appear on the American stage again. For months, members of the Seventh Regiment, who regularly drilled on Washington Square, felt unsafe wearing their uniforms in public, the city's mood being deemed too dangerous. Following the riots, the bullet-riddled Astor Place Opera House was pejoratively called "the Massacre Place Opera House." It lingered on briefly after being repaired but was sold a year later and converted to the Mercantile Library, a lending library open to subscribers.

The Square's Decline

The Astor Place riot was a defining moment for New York at midcentury. In the wake of such an event, it was impossible to ignore the seismic changes brought about by immigration and industrialization. Washington Square had been nicknamed the "American Ward" because of its high percentage of native-born citizens. But by the 1850s, foreign-born tenants squeezed out of the Lower East Side in the 1850s were moving into dwellings recently converted to tenements on Bleecker Street, two blocks south of the Square. Manufacturing activity, previously confined to the waterfront, was rapidly pushing inland. To the east around Broadway, factories and lofts employing thousands of immigrant workers were replacing single-family residences built barely two decades earlier. The new commercial structures, forerunners of New York's metal-frame skyscrapers, were run up quickly, using prefabricated cast-iron parts manufactured at the Novelty Iron Works on the East River. Today, those cast-iron buildings along Broadway from Canal to Eighth Street have achieved landmark status, but at the time of their construction, they would have contributed to the erosion of the neighborhood's exclusive residential ambience.

Many of the moneyed set around Washington Square chose to move "uptown," defined then as between Fourteenth and Fortieth Streets. The change was dramatic: A survey published in the *Herald* reported that in 1846, 180 of the 200 richest individuals in the city lived south of

Fourteenth Street. Five years later, half had moved to homes along Fifth Avenue from Fourteenth to Twenty-third Streets. The general population was moving north as well, slowly making tangible with brick and stone the grid that once had only been lines on a map. By the 1850s, as many New Yorkers lived above Fourteenth Street as below it. Washington Square remained a place redolent of history. "It is remarkable that the streets intersecting Broadway up to Washington Square have historical names but beyond there are numbered 1 to 131, as if history had become exhausted and refused to serve the imagination," Alexander Lakier, a Russian visitor, observed in 1857.

Conditions on the old parade ground reflected the changes in the neighborhood. Henry James fondly described the park of his childhood as "rustic." But in April 1849, when the six-year-old James would have been scuffing leaves in Washington Square, the *Evening Post* complained about the park's "shabby appearance and dirty looks." A year later, on August 5, 1850, the *Post's* editor William Cullen Bryant, an indefatigable champion of green space in the city, railed that the Square was "totally neglected," which he blamed on the city's meager appropriation for public parks. The situation only worsened after 1857, when other factors hastened the park's downward slide: economic depression, the development of Central Park, and the Civil War.

On October 13, 1857, New York banks failed and all cash outlays were suspended indefinitely, precipitating a financial panic and severe economic depression. By the end of the month, 25,000 city workers had lost their jobs and 150 businesses were failing each week; 40,000 homeless and jobless people sought shelter in police stations. To relieve the suffering, Mayor Fernando Wood, otherwise something of a scoundrel, proposed a sweeping program of public works, engaging laborers to construct fire and police stations, pave streets, repair docks— and build the long-awaited Central Park. Frederick Law Olmsted and Calvert Vaux, winners of the park design competition held in 1857, began to remake the natural terrain above Fifty-ninth Street the following spring. Over the course of the first year's construction, 20,000 workers blasted out rocks, removed millions of years of soil, planted 270,000 trees, and built a new reservoir. By the winter of 1859, thousands were skating on lakes built over former swamps.

Downtown parks languished as attention was lavished on Central Park. In 1860, when the Central Park commissioners were requesting another $5 million from the state legislature for the new park uptown, the total expenditure for all other city parks was $27,389, half of which went for an iron fence around Tompkins Square. "Madison Square looks dilapidated," reported the *Tribune* on January 26, 1860; City Hall Park, the paper said, "presents a shabbiness of appearance in keeping with the seedy politicians that lounge about in it." Washington Square was equally bleak, if we trust Theodore Winthrop's depiction of the park in his antebellum novel *Cecil Dreeme:* "It was a wretched place, stiffly laid out, shabbily kept, planted with mean twiggle trees, and in the middle the basin of an extinct fountain filled with foul snow through which dead cats and dogs were beginning to sprout at the solicitation of the winter's sunshine."

The Civil War Years on the Square

After the outbreak of the Civil War, Washington Square deteriorated further from heavy use as a training ground for Union soldiers. Many New Yorkers had been reluctant to wage war on the South. The city's business interests were firmly linked by trade with the southern states, and Mayor Wood had even urged the city to secede. But following the Confederates' attack on Fort Sumter and Lincoln's call to arms on April 15, 1861, New York quickly mobilized its resources. Military companies around the city began to expand their ranks and prepare in earnest. George Templeton Strong of the New York Rifles confided in his diary on April 26, 1861, how his "squad of about 100 men or thereabouts was marched to Washington Parade Ground, where we were drilled and marched by 'Captain Levy,' a very efficient and authoritative drill officer, for an hour and a half. I confess myself tired and footsore."

The Square was also home to one of the city's most colorful recruiting centers—that of the Zouave movement, which, the *Tribune* reported April 19, 1861, "is taking exceedingly well among volunteers." The Zouaves, named for a Berber corps of the colonial French army in Algeria known for their fighting prowess, were readily identified by their exotic uniform of red pantaloons, blue embroidered jackets, and soft red hats with blue tassels. In their drill-room at Thompson Street on the south side of the Square, the Zouaves immediately attracted two hundred men, who started rigorous nightly training.

Draft Riots—"The Town Is Taken by Its Rats"

Through that spring and in the months that followed, military companies headed off to war confident that the South would soon yield. But duty in the field, expected to be a matter of weeks or months, stretched on. Two years later, the Union army was suffering from 100,000 illegal absences. With horrifying tales of carnage circulating, even the most stout-hearted hesitated to reenlist. In March 1863, when the Union cause was at a low point, the government passed a draft law to replenish its forces. All white men between twenty and thirty-five, and up to forty-five years old if unmarried, were eligible for the draft unless they could present an "acceptable substitute" or pay a fee of $300. Forty thousand potential draftees, including the future President Grover Cleveland and Teddy Roosevelt's father, Theodore Sr., paid for substitutes, netting the U.S. Treasury a windfall of nearly $12,000,000. Edith Wharton's father, George Jones, in Newport with his family, simply avoided registering and was never caught. But for thousands of wage earners, the fee for a substitute far exceeded their means and was patently unfair.

The draft began on Saturday, July 11, 1863, a few days after the battle of Gettysburg. On the following sultry Monday morning, when drafting was to continue, violent rioting brought the city to a halt. Mobs stormed the drafting places, raided armories, looted stores, and torched buildings. Protestors cut telegraph lines to sever the city's communication links and used crowbars to pull up railroad tracks. Although precipitated by the start of the draft lotteries, the fury of the riots was fueled by economic hardship, working-class resentment, and deeply entrenched racism. Toward the end of the week, the riots took on a more specific racial cast. Gangs of Irish laborers and adolescent boys aggressively sought out black men for vicious treatment, often of a sexual nature. Some of the worst racial conflict took place in Greenwich Village south and west of the Square, where blacks had lived for decades. Although reports at the time claimed up to a thousand casualties, scholars have revised the number killed to about 120. Among the dead were at least eighteen black men, deliberately mutilated and murdered.

Toward the end of the week, Union regiments were brought back from the battle of Gettysburg to restore order in the city. Members of the Seventh Regiment occupied factories uptown and guarded streets. Soldiers from the Thirty-seventh Regiment Massachusetts Volunteers set up camp on Washington Square, where they stayed through the summer. In early August, a second round of drafting began in Greenwich Village. By then, however, the war was at last turning in the Union's favor, and with better preparation and political strategy, the draft came to a peaceful conclusion.

After the riots, public life in the city became a more noticeably white domain. Many blacks were unable to reclaim their former jobs. White longshoremen kept them off the waterfront; white omnibus drivers and passengers prevented them from using public transportation. "A large number of colored families have left the city with the intention of never returning to it again," reported the *Tribune* on August 3, 1863.

In 1860, there were more than 12,400 blacks in New York; by 1865, their number had shrunk to 9,943. Of these, more than a quarter continued to live in the vicinity of Washington Square.

After the Civil War, the Square no longer served as a parade ground. It was the end of an era. "The Town is taken by its rats. . . . All civil charms . . . these like a dream dissolve, / And man rebounds whole aeons back in nature," Herman Melville had written in his poem "The House-Top: A Night Piece," referring to the draft riots. Many of Melville's friends around the Square would have agreed. A quarter century earlier, the green had been a magnet for New York's mercantile aristocracy, who dominated the city's economic, cultural, and political life. But as the 1849 riots at the Astor Place Opera suggested and the draft riots made clear, that group was no longer unequivocally in charge. Washington Square and the buildings around it would soon feel the impact of a different power base in the city.

(a) Plan of Washington Parade Ground, 1827; (b) plan of Washington Square Park, 1871. Drawn by Christopher M. Crowley, New York City Parks & Recreation

14

A comparison of these two plans of Washington Square reveals the changes to the space that occurred in the nineteenth century and reflects the influence of Olmsted and Vaux's picturesque landscaping of Central Park. The early layout of the parade ground, appropriate for military reviews, was rigidly symmetrical. Diagonal paths and broad east-west and north-south walkways converged at the geographic center, where in 1852 the fountain was added. The north-south walk angled almost imperceptibly in order to connect Fifth Avenue on the north with Thompson Street on the south.

Thompson Street was already established when the parade ground was converted from the potter's field in the 1820s, but Fifth Avenue was a dirt road, opened only in 1824 in compliance with the 1811 grid plan. A half-century later, Fifth Avenue had become a distinguished address and an important element in the Parks Department redesign. The 1871 plan indicates broad roadways carrying traffic between Fifth Avenue and streets south of the park. In place of the parade ground's ruler-straight walks, gently curving pathways now wind around grassy areas lined with trees. The fountain, enlarged to one hundred feet in diameter, sits midway on the east-west axis of the park and dominates its center. Despite later changes, the legacy of the 1871 design lingers on in today's Washington Square.

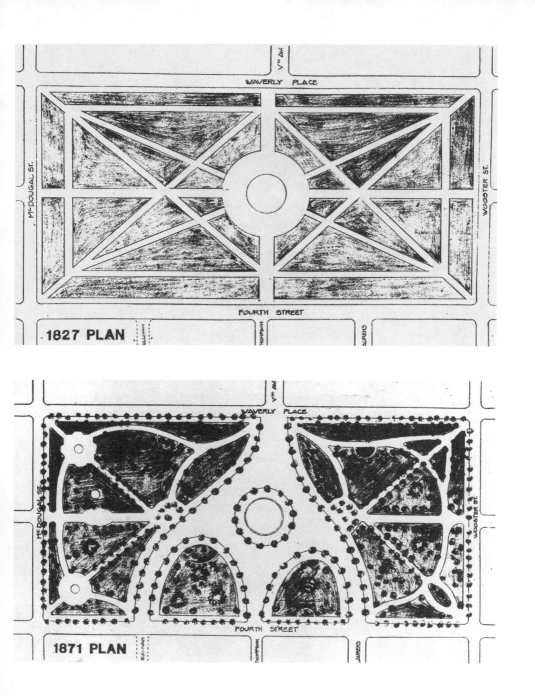

Washington Square, N.Y. From *50 Views of New York and Environs,* Charles Magnus, Publishers, ca. 1870s. Eno Collection, Miriam and Ira D. Wallach Division of Art, Prints and Photographs, The New York Public Library, Astor, Lenox and Tilden Foundations

Looking north across the park towards Fifth Avenue, this bird's-eye view of exaggerated scale dramatically conveys the results of the 1870s redesign. The central north-south road, barely visible as a crosswalk in earlier prints (cf. page 41), is now a major element on the left side of the picture, leading to Fifth Avenue, visible on the horizon as a narrow opening between rows of townhouses on Washington Square North. There is no fence around the park, but benches and occasional gas lamps have been set at various places along the curving walkways. For the first time, we see horse-drawn carriages and civilians riding in the grounds. Mariana Van Rensselaer noted that a good deal of traffic was passing through the Square at the end of the century, "But it can hardly be called one of traffic's highroads, except at dawn, when farmers' carts rumble plentifully through on their way to Jefferson Market." The market, located on Sixth Avenue at Tenth Street, was replaced years later by the Jefferson Market Courthouse, now a landmarked building housing a branch of the New York Public Library.

Garibaldi statue. Photograph, ca. 1890. New York University Archives

Standing in the Square since 1888, the commanding bronze of Giuseppe Garibaldi by Giovanni Turini testifies to the great Italian presence in the city. The wave of immigration in the late 1800s brought so many of Garibaldi's countrymen to these shores that by the early 1900s, more Italians were living in New York than in Rome. Set upon a granite pedestal about eleven feet high, the hero of the Italian struggle for unification assumes a Michelangelesque pose, his upper body twisting back as his right hand reaches across to grasp the sword hanging at his left side. With head raised and eyes gazing into the distance, the mature, bearded Garibaldi dressed in the full-sleeved shirt and cape of a romantic hero appears ready to act, confident yet contemplative. The front of the pedestal is inscribed "Garibaldi 1807–1882." On the base below, the stonecutters carved their names—Azzaro & Barton, Woodlawn. The back of the pedestal carries the dedication: IL II GIUGNO / MDCCCLXXXVIII. GLI ITALIANI / DEGLI STATI UNITI / D'AMERICA. / ERESSERO. (JUNE 2, 1888. ERECTED BY THE ITALIANS OF THE UNITED STATES OF AMERICA).

Alexander Lyman Holley bust. Photograph, ca.1905. Collection of the New-York Historical Society (#20932)

Alexander Lyman Holley is considered the father of the modern steel industry because he successfully adapted the Bessemer method he had seen in England for commercial steel production in the United States. Holley was a man of many talents. Trained as an engineer at Brown University, he contributed hundreds of articles on science topics to the *New York Times,* organized the first professional associations in his field, and was known as an accomplished amateur artist. This memorial bust, commissioned in 1886 for $2,000, was to be completed in one year, but it took the sculptor John Quincy Adams Ward three years to finish the work to his satisfaction. The architect Thomas Hastings, whose firm of Carrere & Hastings built the New York Public Library in 1911, designed the stately winged pedestal of white marble. Above the rolled collar of his coat, Holley's head is turned slightly to the left, his hair blown by a light breeze. His mouth turns up and eyes crinkle in a barely suppressed smile, suggesting the ebullient personality, described by his contemporaries, of a man who took a warm and lively interest in everything around him.

Inscribed on the statue's pedestal are the following words, now almost totally worn away: "Holley / born Lakeville Conn. July 20th, 1832 / died Brooklyn N.Y. January 29, 1882 / In honor of Alexander Lyman Holley foremost among those whose genius and energy established in America and improved throughout the world the manufacture of Bessemer steel this memorial is erected by engineers of two hemispheres." The Holley memorial was cleaned and restored in 1999.

121

Francis Luis Mora, *Robert Louis Stevenson and Mark Twain in Washington Square Park*. Watercolor, 1907. National Arts Club Permanent Collection, New York

In 1887, Mark Twain took a train from his home in Hartford, Connecticut, to meet Robert Louis Stevenson, who was visiting New York City before heading to a sanitarium in Saranac, New York, where he hoped to improve his health. The two authors were then among the most popular of their time—Twain for *The Adventures of Tom Sawyer* and *Huckleberry Finn;* Stevenson for *Treasure Island, Kidnapped,* and *The Strange Case of Dr. Jekyll and Mr. Hyde.* The Scottish-born Stevenson was staying near the Square at a hotel on Tenth Street and University Place. Since his doc-tor recommended that he take the sun, he and Twain walked down to the park and settled on a sunny bench for their visit. Stevenson died seven years later in 1894, at age forty-four. Twain moved to New York in 1900, resided at 21 Fifth Avenue north of Washington Square from 1904 to 1908, and died in 1910 at the age of seventy-five. In his trademark white flannel suit, Twain was a familiar sight in the park. Many a time he would have sat on benches, which he may not have realized had been provided by Boss Tweed, a figure he had satirized in *The Gilded Age: A Tale of Today* (1874). In the book, Tweed is thinly disguised as William W. Weed, a politician whose friends sell nails for $3,000 a keg. Mark Twain's title became the descriptive term for that epoch of American history.

The Tuckerman Building (the "Benedick"). Photograph, ca. 1920s. New York University Archives

The Tuckerman on Washington Square East opened in 1879 as an upscale residence for bachelors—"that fortunate or unfortunate class" who, the *Tribune* of August 8, 1879, noted, were often refused tenancy in the better class of flats. Filling this niche, the Tuckerman eventually came to be known as the "Benedick" after the confirmed-bachelor character in Shakespeare's *Much Ado About Nothing*. The Benedick's thirty-three rooms were quickly filled by tenants including the artists Winslow Homer, J. Alden Weir, and Albert Ryder. Another artist tenant, John LaFarge, had just been hired to decorate Cornelius Vanderbilt's mansion on Fifth Avenue and 52nd Street. Several years later, LaFarge's friend Stanford White rented rooms in the Benedick for a group calling themselves the "Sewer Club." White was no bachelor, but his wife Bessie didn't like the city and preferred to stay at their Long Island home. His biographers speculate that the architect and his friends used the rooms for private parties and illicit encounters. Acquired by New York University in 1925, the Benedick is now the Pauline Goddard Hall and functions as a dormitory.

The Temporary Arch with Buggy and Vendor. Photograph, 1889. Collection of the New-York Historical Society (# 43389)

The temporary arch for the 1889 Centennial honoring George Washington's inauguration in 1789 stood a half-block north of Washington Square on Fifth Avenue between the Rhinelander mansion on the left, and Edward Cooper's house on the right. Designed by Stanford White, the classically styled arch, constructed of pine and painted an ivory white, was embellished with laurel wreaths and a frieze of garlands rendered in papier-mâché. In order to allow sufficient room for two-way traffic to pass under the arch and pedestrians to pass on the sidewalks, White of necessity made the arch's span very wide in proportion to the narrow supporting piers, giving the monument a slightly top-heavy appearance.

Poised at the top of the arch is a painted statue of Washington dressed in a blue dress coat, buff riding breeches, and riding boots. Legend has it that the folk-art figure of the president stood at the Battery in 1792, but most likely it was carved for a celebration in the 1820s or 1830s. Senator T. Coleman DuPont, U.S. Senator from Delaware, discovered the statue in front of a cigar store in New York in 1912 and rescued it for his home state. The sculpture is in the collection of Delaware Historical Society.

The Washington Arch at Fifth Avenue and Washington Square—Drawn by Charles Graham from the Architect's Drawing. Harper's Weekly, May 4, 1889

In his proposed design of the temporary arch, Stanford White specified that the decoration would "have a somewhat formal basis in the use of bunches of flags arranged as trophies in rather an architectural manner, with streamers running off in different directions." After dark, the arch was to be lit with electricity, "picked out with small incandescent lamps which will sparkle all over the arch like fireflies." His instructions, accompanied by sketches, were carried out by Theodore Gunsel of the Metropolitan Decoration Establishment, at 2 Fourth Avenue, opposite the Cooper Institute, for $200.

Harper's Weekly, one of the most popular journals in the nation, featured extensive coverage of the Centennial, copiously illustrated. Until the beginning of the twentieth century, it cost too much to reproduce photographs for mass publication, and so to obtain pictures quickly, *Harper's* and the other firms employed artist-reporters like Charles Graham to make drawings on the spot. Winslow Homer had worked as an artist-reporter for *Harper's* during the Civil War. Specially trained engravers would transfer the artists' finished drawings to wood blocks, which could then be printed along with the text.

The Washington Arch—North Elevation. McKim, Mead & White, 1892. Collection of the New-York Historical Society (# 58654)

Stanford White planned an elaborate program of decoration to embellish the classic form of the Arch and turned to his friend and frequent collaborator Augustus Saint-Gaudens to execute the work. The most highly regarded sculptor in America at the time, Saint-Gaudens was too busy to do the work, but recommended two of his former apprentices who were already accomplished sculptors. The first was Frederick MacMonnies, whom White chose to do all the relief decoration, including the spandrels and the frieze. The second was the Alsatian-born Philippe Martiny, who designed the eagle perched on the keystone of both the north and south faces of the Arch. Martiny's model for the spirited bird met with such success that Tiffany & Co. and the silver manufacturing firm of Gorham Manufacturing Co. replicated the eagle, with the artist's permission, for an exhibit at the 1893 Columbian Exposition in Chicago.

TO COMMEMORATE THE ONE HUNDREDTH ANNIVERSARY
OF THE INAUGURATION OF GEORGE WASHINGTON
AS FIRST PRESIDENT OF THE UNITED STATES

ERECTED BY THE PEOPLE OF THE CITY OF NEW YORK

Letter to Stanford White from William Stewart on the Washington Arch, February 23, 1892. Collection of the New-York Historical Society, Department of Prints, Photographs, and Architecture, McKim, Mead & White Papers: Washington Arch correspondence file

Handwritten letters like this one from William Stewart to Stanford White were an efficient form of communication, since mail delivery was quick in those days. Stewart kept a record of what he wrote by penning his letters in correspondence volumes that provided carbon paper and a blank page behind each sheet of stationery. The image of the Arch at the top of the letter was an engraving of one of White's preliminary designs, which had featured a sculptural group on top of the monument.

As is still customary in fundraising, the names on the masthead are meant to impress readers and add credibility to the cause. Members of the Arch Committee, drawn originally from the larger Centennial Art and Exhibition Committees, were actively involved in a range of civic enterprises and generous benefactors of universities, hospitals, and other charities. Several were founders and trustees of the Metropolitan Museum of Art; Robert W. De Forest served as the museum's president. Political leaders are listed as well: Grover Cleveland, president of the United States, 1885–89; Levi Morton, vice president under Benjamin Harrison in 1889 and governor of New York, 1895–97; and William L. Strong, New York's reform mayor, 1895–97.

Office of *Wm. R. Stewart, Treasurer,* 54 William St.

Stanford White Esq,
   1 West 20th Street.

New-York, 23rd February, 1892.

My dear White.

    I was on top of the Arch this morning. They are erecting a circular iron frame about 9 feet high in which will be the door to the roof. It seems to me this is much too high, and even when the last two courses of marble are set I fear it will be seen at a distance of a block or two from the Arch. This would be a great pity. A trap door would be better, but I think you can have two feet taken off the height of this structure, and still allow access by it to the roof.

    On this subject may I suggest a glass roof to this little iron structure as this will light the stairs. The workmen said the roof was to be fire brick.

    The inscriptions proposed for the attic of the Arch are the following viz: For the North front

Men on Scaffolding Inspecting the Arch. Photograph, 1892. Collection of the New-York Historical Society (#51942)

Before the internal stairs of the Arch were completed, a climb up the scaffolding was the only way to inspect the monument. Here, checking on the Arch is William Rhinelander Stewart at the center of the group, distinguished by his tall top hat, with Stanford White on his right. Above them are Martiny's eagle and sections of the frieze by MacMonnies. White specified that the frieze was to include thirteen wreath-encircled stars, one for each of the original states, alternating with W's for Washington. Above the gentlemen's heads is the coffered ceiling of the arch, decorated with carved rosettes in the center of each square. Still to be completed are the reliefs for the spandrels, the slightly curving triangular panels on either side of the archway.

Stewart kept a tight rein on all phases of the Arch and never hesitated to voice his impatience. In a letter dated November 19, 1891, he had complained to White that the pace of building was so slow "as to make me wonder if I shall live to see the structure finished" (New-York Historical Society, New York City Misc. MSS, Washington Arch Papers, box 2, folder 6). As the Arch neared completion, he became concerned about the pedestal figures, writing to White on December 27, 1893: "I think the designs for these should really be pushed or we will be old men or dead before the groups are finished" (ibid., box 3, folder 1).

135

(a) Herman A. MacNeil, *Washington in War* (east pier of the Arch) (b) A. Stirling Calder, *Washington in Peace* (west pier of the Arch). Photographs by Adam F. Kies, 2001. Collection of the author

The sculptor MacNeil intended the figure of *Washington in War* on the Arch's east pedestal to appear alert and intent, as if watching the maneuvers of his army. Behind Washington are two allegorical figures carved in high relief: Fame holds a flaming torch, and Valor supports a shield encircled by a wreath, which forms a kind of halo around Washington's head. The figural group was completed in 1916.

For the west pedestal, A. Stirling Calder depicted *Washington in Peace* as standing "bareheaded in Colonial civil dress, as of some sixty years of age, firmly planted on his feet with

head erect, regarding the vision of the future," he wrote in his official description. Behind the president are two figures in high relief symbolizing Wisdom and Justice—Wisdom as the modern Athena in a helmet; Justice, draped and crowned, holding a balanced set of scales with one hand and an open book in the other. The pages of the book are inscribed with the words "Exitus acta probat"—"The end justifies the deed."

Unfortunately, the west group has suffered badly with the passing of time. Washington's right hand had to be replaced in 1949 and is out of scale with the rest of the figure. The new hand, carved of Vermont marble, did not match the original stone and was later painted over to minimize the difference. Finally, sandblasting of the 1960s ate away at the stone of Washington's face.

Main Building, New York University. Photograph, ca. 1920s. New York University Archives

For about thirty years, the American Book Company shared the Main Building with NYU's Schools of Law, Commerce, and Pedagogy, until increased enrollment enabled the university to take over the entire building in 1927. After World War I, a Collegiate Division on the Square, established for the benefit of those who could not attend the Washington Heights campus, attracted thousands of students, many of them immigrants who commuted to school by subway. Thomas Wolfe sustained himself as an English teacher at NYU in the late 1920s while writing what became his best-known work, *Look Homeward, Angel* (1929). Wolfe found many of his lower-class, immigrant students terrifyingly inquisitive. Although he befriended some students, he later characterized them cruelly in *Of Time and the River* (1935). Several years later, he acknowledged the value of his experiences at NYU: "I can think of no other way in which a young man coming to this terrific city as I came to it could have had a more comprehensive and stimulating introduction to its swarming life, than through the corridors and classrooms of Washington Square."

F. C. Martin, *A City Tramp at Work. Century Magazine,* March 1894

This image of a ragged fellow begging from a well-dressed woman in Washington Square, an illustration for Josiah Flynt's article on "The City Tramp," testifies to Washington Square's split personality at the end of the nineteenth century. The Square had many tramps, wrote Mariana Van Rensselaer in the *Century Magazine,* December 1892—one section of the park was even known as "Tramp's Retreat"—but it also had "a sprinkling of baby wagons and white-capped nurses; for this is the boundary-line between very poor and crowded and very

140

well-to-do and roomy streets of homes—South Fifth Avenue, with its teeming French, German, Irish and Negro population, ending against one of its sides, and the true Fifth Avenue starting from another."

The editor of the *Century* was Richard Watson Gilder, who lived on Eighth Street around the corner from the Arch. Gilder was deeply concerned about the hardship and deprivation he witnessed in the city around him and frequently published articles that addressed these issues. In the 1890s, he also served as chairman of a state commission on tenements and wrote recommendations for health and safety standards that were signed into law in 1895.

Fernand Lungren, *A Winter Wedding—Washington Square, 1897.* Oil on canvas. Private collection, courtesy of Berry-Hill Galleries

Despite the poverty lapping the south side of the Square and tramps frequenting the park, Washington Square North retained its aura of social status into the 1890s. This picture shows New York's upper crust arriving at the Square on the afternoon of December 17, 1896, to attend the wedding reception for Fannie Tailer and Sydney Smith held by the bride's parents in their home at 11 Washington Square North. (Bruce Weber ties the painting to the Tailer-Smith wedding in his book *Homage to the Square.*) Fannie's mother, Agnes Suffern Tailer, was the daughter of Thomas Suffern, the merchant who had built No. 11 in the 1830s. The father of the bride was Edward Neufville Tailer, a cloth merchant, importer, and bank director active in the city's social life. The wedding, one of the largest and most fashionable of the season, brought out New York society—Astors, Belmonts, Havemeyers, Cooper-Hewitts, and others. Lungren seems to have observed the scene from the doorstep of his lodgings at 3 Washington Square, a Row house converted into artists' studios in 1879.

The contrasts between deprivation and wealth so evident at Washington Square were well catalogued in this era. In 1890, the year Jacob Riis published *How the Other Half Lives*, Ward McAllister wrote *Society As I Have Found It*, a recounting of his experiences with the elite group known as "the 400," named for the number of guests who could be accommodated in Mrs. William Astor's ballroom. Pasted into Edward Tailer's diary (preserved in The New-York Historical Society collection) is a clipping from the *World* of December 18, 1896, headlined "A Wedding in the 400."

Childe Hassam, *Washington Arch, Spring*. Oil on canvas, 1890. Phillips Collection, Washington, D.C.

An engraving of this painting appeared in the *Century Magazine*, November 1893, to illustrate Mariana Van Rensselaer's article on Fifth Avenue. Childe Hassam, a good friend of the *Century*'s editor, Richard Gilder, was a popular American Impressionist who adopted the soft colors, flickering brush strokes, and candid "snapshot" approach of French Impressionism. Hassam's luminous urban views, like this one looking from Fifth Avenue at Eighth Street toward Washington Square, exemplify the ideals of the City Beautiful movement.

Although signed and dated 1890, this painting could not have been completed until about 1893, by which time the actual Arch would have corresponded to the one in the picture. Another pictorial element keys the painting to a later date: the white-clad municipal street cleaner shown sweeping at the curb was part of a citywide system, initiated in 1891, in which individual workers, known as "White Wings" because of their uniforms, were assigned to sweep up specific blocks. The trash they collected in their small carts was carried away by horse-drawn wagons that circulated through the streets and brought the refuse to specified collection places along the river.

Waiting for the parade of the 71st Regiment returning from Cuba. Photograph, 1899. New York University Archives

Eager crowds packed the sidewalks and available stoops waiting to greet victorious soldiers who were returning home from Cuba at the end of the Spanish-American War. This photograph, taken from the roof or top floor of a house just north of Eighth Street, offers a view of the many loft building already in existence south and east of the Square. In the left foreground, on the west side of the Fifth Avenue, we see the four old houses that had been converted to Miss Lucy Green's Academy for Young Girls. The school had opened in 1835 under the leadership of Mrs. Esther Boorman Smith. One of Mrs. Smith's pupils was Lucy Green, who with her sister Mary ran the school until 1869. Still in existence just before World War I, Lucy Green's was one of the most fashionable and select schools of its kind. The financier Leonard Jerome's daughter Jenny, who was later to be the mother of Winston Churchill, was a student there in the mid nineteenth century. The school buildings were replaced in 1927 by One Fifth Avenue, first a hotel and now a cooperative apartment building.

Funeral Procession after the Triangle Fire, April 5, 1911. Tamiment Institute Library, New York University

"The skies wept," reported the *World* in describing the funeral procession for the seven unnamed victims of the Triangle fire. "Rain, ever and again, descending in a drenching downpour." Following the empty hearse, marchers wound under the Washington Arch and headed up Fifth Avenue. Dressed in black and carrying labor slogans, they marched through the city in complete silence as heavy rain continued to fall and street mud oozed through their shoes.

New Yorkers were generous in the wake of the disaster. Robert De Forest and Jacob Schiff, both members of the Arch Committee, immediately organized a Red Cross Emergency Relief Committee of the Charity Organization Society to raise money for the victims' families. The coal and steel magnate Andrew Carnegie sent $5,000. There were benefits with George M. Cohan at the Metropolitan Opera and Al Jolson at the Winter Garden, and movie theaters turned over days' worth of receipts for the cause.

TWO

A New City Park Takes Shape

"The park was quiet and shadowy after the war," recalled Mariana Griswold Van Rensselaer, architectural critic and historian, and granddaughter of the Griswolds on the Row. "It had then a high wooden paling . . . and only children and very peaceful decorous loiterers filled its paths and benches. Here, too, were the pop-corn and cake-vendors, and old Irishmen who sold ballads. . . . printed on little sheets of very bad paper, strung with clothespins on lines against the palings, and sold for a cent a piece. And as the middle of February drew near, their place was taken by comic valentines which, despite their gaily tinted pictures, were disposed of at the same temperate price."[1]

This tranquil interlude ended a few years after the Civil War when the forces of politics and philanthropy—the public and private interests that defined New York in the Gilded Age—redefined the Square. Under the reign of one of Gotham's most brazen politicians, the newly formed Department of Parks remodeled the parade ground into a green in the pastoral style of Central Park. Private citizens embellished the park with statuary and built the iconic Washington Arch, soon the centerpiece of civic demonstrations and a favorite subject of artists and photographers. But by the early 1900s, good intentions and a marble Arch were not enough to stem the accelerating decline of the park and surrounding neighborhood. While prosperity and promise were still evident in the houses along Washington Square North, tenements and manufacturing lofts were proliferating on streets to the south and east. Poised midway between the poor immigrant sections downtown and the uptown world of wealth, the park encapsulated the extreme social and economic inequities of the metropolis.

Boss Tweed's Legacy

Washington Square began to acquire its current appearance when it was refashioned from parade ground to park by the newly formed Department of Public Parks in 1870. Renovations of the Square and the other small parks downtown were engineered by Tammany "Boss" William Magear Tweed, an immense figure with beady eyes, a jovial swagger, and a large diamond in his shirtfront. Tweed had attained power by way of New York's volunteer fire companies, historically an entrée into municipal politics for ambitious young men without money or connections. Inducted into the Democratic stronghold of Tammany Hall, he built up a loyal constituency by courting Catholics and helping to feed, clothe, and shelter the poor, who were neglected by most politicians then. At the time of the draft riots, Tweed had secured the allegiance of working-class New Yorkers by arranging a low-interest loan fund enabling them to pay for substitutes just as the rich did. Many of his supporters were not eligible to vote because they were non-naturalized Irish immigrants. But Tweed's Tammany-appointed magistrates granted them citizenship at the breathtaking rate of 2,000 a day—three new voters a minute. Tweed was elected state senator in 1867; a year later as "grand sachem" of Tammany, he proudly hosted the 1868 Democratic National Convention at the new Tammany Hall on Fourteenth Street and Third Avenue.

Tweed was born downtown on Cherry Street, a fourth-generation Scots Protestant and chair maker by trade. He became a very wealthy man from various business schemes, kickbacks, and real estate investments, and was for a time one of New York's largest property owners. His power and patronage were so extensive, his charm so beguiling, and his bookkeeping so creative that a committee of irreproachable businessmen led by John Jacob Astor III was unable to uncover any wrongdoing after having reviewed his books. Later investigations conservatively estimated that Tweed and his associates had stolen between $45 and $75 million from the city, and some put the figure as high as $200 million. "The fact is that New York politics were always dishonest," Tweed testified. "There never was a time when you couldn't buy the Board of Alderman."

In April 1870, Senator Tweed, chairman of the senate committee on cities, led the state legislature to pass a new charter restoring home rule to New York City. Among other changes, the charter established ten municipal departments, which allowed Tweed to appoint himself and his cronies, known as "the Ring," to positions of unchecked power in the city. Tweed appointed himself head of the Department of Public Works and installed Peter B. Sweeny, said to be the "brains" of the Ring, as commissioner of the Department of Public Parks. Sweeny brought two of the state-appointed Central Park commissioners onto his new Parks Board and added two loyal Tammany men.

With Central Park completed, the new Parks Board intended to improve the city's smaller green spaces. They declared their intentions in the *First Annual Report of the Board of Commissioners of the Department of Public Parks for the Year Ending May 1, 1871*: "The present Board, having long been residents of the City of New York . . . all felt a sensitive regard for the eminent public demand that these parks should be converted from the neglected, repelling, and unpleasant places they had been for many years, into breathing-spots that should afford pleasure to the people frequenting or passing through them, and to the masses who have not the means of frequent access to Central Park." Curiously, they felt it necessary to state their credentials as longtime city dwellers. And they practically guaranteed themselves a measure of success by labeling these parks "neglected, repelling and unpleasant." In referring to them as "breathing-spots," they expressed the belief, widely held before germ theory was understood, that exposure to fresh air would increase robustness and prevent the sicknesses thought to be brought on by the dense, urban-industrialized atmosphere. Improving the few open spaces in lower Manhattan would benefit Tweed's downtown constituents unable to afford the ten-cent train fare to Central Park. And new projects would also offer ample opportunities for Tammany patronage.

The Park's Redesign

Washington Square was one of the Parks Department's first redesign projects. The job was entrusted to Ignaz Anton Pilat, assisted by Montgomery A. Kellogg, both of whom had been closely involved with the construction of Central Park. Kellogg, chief engineer of the new Parks Department, had as young man supervised job assignments at Central Park. Pilat, an Austrian-born landscape designer, had studied at the University of Vienna and served as assistant director of a Viennese botanical garden before emigrating to the United States in 1848. As Frederick Law Olmsted's chief gardener after 1861, he was responsible for shaping slopes, arranging boulders, planting lawns, and selecting and planting all trees and shrubs. Central Park's pastoral appearance—and Washington Square's adaptation of that style—is very much due to Pilat's efforts.

Pilat applied the soft, undulating layout of Central Park to the small, flat plot of the former Washington Parade Ground. A comparison of the park's old and new plans reveals the striking changes. The strict symmetry of the old Square gave way to a web of curving pathways outlined by plantings and interrupted by small round gathering places. In place of the parade ground's two equally wide crosswalks, Pilat's plan provided a broad road that led from Fifth Avenue to the fountain, then widened like a pitchfork into three parts to connect with the three streets on the park's south side.

Today's Washington Square still retains aspects of Pilat's design in its shaped lawns and curving paths. Yet the contemporary park must contend as well with the less attractive legacy of the 1870s redesign—the wide swath of paving intended to serve as a main traffic artery through the heart of the park. The reason for the road—an indication of Parks Department obvious priorities—is openly stated in the 1871 *Annual Report:* "The construction of these roadways across the grounds converging into Fifth Avenue affords direct access for travel between the upper and lower portions of the city, at least as far down as Canal Street, by three separate streets . . . all of which parallel Broadway, and if properly paved cannot fail to relieve materially that crowded thoroughfare from Canal Street to 23rd." By conspicuous co-incidence, Boss Tweed, self-appointed commissioner of Public Works, also controlled city streets and paving. Indeed, he was having a grand time paving and repaving streets, sometimes the same ones over, until local residents protested the continual disruption. In tandem with the park's redesign, Tweed arranged for traffic to funnel through Washington Square via three access roads—Thompson, Laurens (West Broadway), and Sullivan. Although Sullivan only reached Third Street then, it was to be extended one block to connect with Fourth Street at the park. The extension was not cut through until 1903.

Given the extensive real estate holdings of Tweed and his associates, it is likely that the road through the park was expected to enhance property values to the south, a conjecture reinforced by Tweed's re-naming of Laurens Street as "South Fifth Avenue." The nomenclature did little to change the street's poor reputation. George Templeton Strong recorded in his diary for October 31, 1870, that he walked up-town to inspect "the improvement of Laurens Street (whilom Rotten Row) which carries that fragrant thoroughfare across Washington pa-

155

rade Ground." Some twenty years later, Mariana Griswold Van Rensselaer called it "the ill-reputed street . . . irreverently rebaptized as
South Fifth Avenue," and Arthur Barnes in *Harper's Weekly* con-
temptuously noted that "South Fifth Avenue resembles its namesake
about as much as Mulberry Bend resembles Murray Hill."[2] Mulberry
Bend was near Five Points; Murray Hill was J. P. Morgan's neighborhood. During the reform administration of Mayor William L. Strong,
the street was renamed West Broadway. In 1947, following the death
of Mayor Fiorello La Guardia, the three blocks of West Broadway immediately south of the park were named La Guardia Place. Despite
efforts in the 1950s to rename the thoroughfare, the appellations West
Broadway and La Guardia Place have stuck.

Between October 1870 and May 1871, in the course of redesign-
ing Washington Square the city graded and prepared nearly 12,000
square yards of roads, laid 4,350 square yards of pavement, set in place
3,025 feet of curb, and installed over 2,000 feet of drainpipe. The 1871
Parks Department *Annual Report* specified that the roadways were to
be covered with "S. H. Ingersoll improved wood pavement," recommended for its durability, easy repair, and relatively noiseless surface.
Road flooring and wood blocks were treated by the "Robbins process
for preserved Wood." Subsequent flooring and blocks were to be "Bur-
netized," while sidewalks were paved with "Day's Vulcanized concrete." To implement these improvements for Washington Square, the
Parks Department spent $39,961 in 1870 and $181,026 in the first half
of 1871. The smaller expenditure of $23,702 listed in the Parks De-
partment's 1872–73 *Annual Report* suggests that by then the overhaul
was nearly complete, bringing the total cost of redoing Washington
Square to $244,689.

While the Square was under construction, the Parks Department
was busily improving public spaces throughout the city, thriftily shift-
ing discarded materials from one place to another as needed. There
was so much topsoil or "muck" leftover after Washington Square's re-

design that the excess was transported a few blocks east to Tompkins Square, where it was spread over all the lawn areas of that park. Washington Square's old curbing was supplemented by dressed, two-inch curb from other parks to edge the walks, while new six-inch, bluestone curb was set around all roadways and the park exterior. Work was advancing so well, the 1871 *Annual Report* boasted, that roads, walks, curbs, and the final shaping and seeding of grounds were expected to be finished that summer.

At the center of the park, where the roadways came together, excavation for a new fountain was under way. Although the fountain's design was not yet determined, the 1871 *Report* specified that the basin was "to be surrounded with a walk twenty-five feet in diameter and well shaded. This fountain will properly be the commencement of the Fifth avenue." Recycling of materials continued. The iron railing around the old fountain came down and was transported uptown to enclose Reservoir Square, now Bryant Park at 42nd Street. And instead of a new model, the Square received a hand-me-down from uptown—a fountain from one of the southern entrances to Central Park at 59th Street. The classically designed basin of graywackie, a stone similar in appearance to bluestone, was probably designed by Jacob Wrey Mould, an architect who assisted Calvert Vaux with the stonework and structures in Central Park. Modified into a wading pool in 1934, and badly in need of restoration in the early twenty-first century, the fountain installed in 1870 remains the gravitational center of Washington Square.

Taxpayers Complain

Despite the flurry of activity in the park, people living nearby were not impressed by the Parks Department's progress. Their frustration surfaced in letters to the *New York Times*. On August 1, 1871, for example, "H. T. P." wrote:

I have watched daily, for the past four years, the very important operations on Washington Parade Ground (formerly one of our most beautiful parks) of the minions of the Ring, and would like very much to know the sum charged for the immense amount of labor bestowed on it. . . . It seems to me that the Ring kept it as a nursery for idle men to the number of hundred, whose instructions must have been to do as little real work per day as possible, so that they might not accomplish too quickly the alterations then proposed, as it might have been troublesome to the Ring to contrive alterations that led to undoing all that had been previously done so as to keep the minions on the City pay-roll.

On August 7 an even more cynical letter appeared, signed "A Taxpayer":

> Washington-square is a park no more. It is a thoroughfare short-cut for funerals, hackmen going to the boats. . . . The cost to the City Treasury for improving (!) Washington Park (!) when finished—which will be when another dollar cannot be swindled out of the City funds—will amount to about $1,600,000, more than the value of the whole square if cut into lots and sold at ten thousand dollars each lot. Since September last, so many men have been engaged . . . in such large numbers that if they had been eager to work, or had been engaged to work, their crowded numbers prevented them from doing so. These men . . . [were] patiently waiting for election day, when each laborer received a new red flannel shirt, a day's pay and a day's freedom, to go to the polls to vote early and often.

This referred to Tweed's practice, long endorsed by Tammany, of fixing elections by offering gifts to voters, inducing them to vote more than once. In May 1871, the number of votes for Tweed far exceeded

158

the total number of registered voters in the city.[3] The author of the letter described the construction process in scathing detail:

The daily surveying progressed, and the poor laborers were daily toiling their wearied footsteps, pushing before them, with fearful three inch strides an empty barrow filled with a handful of dirt, and requiring two assistants to support the sides of the barrows, and an overseer to be careful that they did not die of *ennui*. In this manner the earth was carried from the north to the south, and heaped in huge mounds; and from the south to the north, and from the east to the west . . . and after a hundred or so more surveys this earth was all carried back and distributed over the places from whence it was taken.

During the months that Washington Square was under construction, the press had been closing in on Tweed. Thomas Nast's stinging cartoons in *Harper's Weekly* focused public attention on the Ring and made Tweed's face and figure familiar to a wide audience. The *New York Times,* which had assailed Tweed for over a year, dealt the final blows in July 1871 by publishing information covertly supplied by an insider. In a series of incriminating articles listing payments, names, and dates, the *Times* fully documented the Tweed Ring's corruption. Boss Tweed was served with a warrant for arrest that October but nonetheless won reelection as state senator a month later, although his criminal indictment and arrest in December effectively ended his political career. Tweed later managed to escape from jail and flee to Spain, where the authorities recognized him from Nast's well-known cartoons and sent him back to the States—and to prison. Tweed died of pneumonia in 1878 while in jail.

Depression, Class Antagonism, and an Armory on the Square

Just as the new park was nearing completion, economic disaster struck. In September 1873, the financial house of Jay Cooke & Company collapsed after failing to market millions of railroad bonds. Following the unchecked economic expansion of the postwar years, financial panic engulfed the country. Banks failed, the stock market suspended operation, and factories across the country began laying off workers. The Panic of 1873 ushered in an economic downturn that lasted sixty-five months—the longest period of uninterrupted economic contraction, including the Depression of the 1930s, that the United States has ever known. Immigration slowed to a trickle. A quarter of New York's labor force could not find jobs that winter and hoped that the city government would undertake public projects, as it had in 1857 when Central Park was built. On January 13, 1874, thousands of working men and women and their families gathered in Tompkins Square to demand employment or relief, "Work or Bread." The demonstration turned into an ugly riot as mounted police bore down on the crowd, attacking and beating hundreds of demonstrators and arresting others. This time there would be no municipal projects and little relief. As conditions worsened, unions became more militant and violent outbreaks became more frequent, deepening the rift between classes. Throughout the country, in urban as well as rural areas, the figure of the "tramp" became a familiar sight.

The depression of the 1870s affected Washington Square in several ways. Despite the attractive new park, the neighborhood's appearance declined as many of the single-family dwellings fell into disrepair or were converted into boarding houses. Wealthy families remained, but several experienced severe financial reverses. John T. Johnston, for example, sold off the valuable art collection he had exhibited in the stables of his mansion at Fifth Avenue and Eight Street. The most profound, if less tangible, effect of the Panic of 1873 was the increased antagonism between rich and poor. As destitution pressed in on all sides and violence often accompanied increasingly bitter labor disputes, the bourgeoisie of Washington Square and their counterparts uptown became fearful and rigidly conservative.

Upper-class anxieties about the unruly lower classes fed the demand to build more armories and professionalize the military in order to ensure stability in times of trouble. Over the next quarter century, the city erected twenty-nine armories at a cost of more than $2.5 million. Much of the money came from private benefactors. One of the first places selected as an armory site was the newly renovated Washington Square Park. The armory proposed for the Square was to serve as headquarters for the First Division and its brigades, with at least four cavalry and artillery organizations and two regiments of infantry.

By law, public parks and squares were not to be used for armory purposes. Nonetheless, in February 1878, officers of the National Guard presented a bill at City Hall to amend that law by making an exception of Washington Square. The Guard promised that its structure, to be located in the eastern half of the Square, would not exceed a size of 200 feet by 400 feet, equivalent to one-seventh of the park space. City Hall had not expected that any objections would be raised, but the project was halted by the efforts of Thomas Egleston, who lived on the Square, and the elderly real estate developer Samuel Ruggles, who had created Gramercy park in 1831. Ruggles's missive, "On the Importance of Saving Small Parks," was his last piece of writing before he died. Egleston, founder of the Columbia School of Mines, organized the Public Parks Protective Association and pressured authorities to prevent the armory from usurping park land. In response, the state legislature passed a law on June 1, 1878, stating that the "public park known as Washington square or Washington parade ground shall . . . be used in perpetuity for the public as a public park, and for no other use or purpose whatsoever." The armory designated for the park was never built. At the end of 1879, the Seventh Regiment, historically associated with Washington Square, moved into a huge, well-appointed fortress uptown on Park Avenue and Sixty-sixth Street, the first and most lavish of several such structures in New York.

Leisure Time in the New Park

Through the fluctuating conditions of the 1870s and 1880s, more people sought out the open spaces of Washington Square. Gas lights and later electric fixtures enhanced and extended the hours of park use. Benches lining the walks beckoned neighbors to sit and rest or watch children at play. Shop clerks and factory workers passed to and from their jobs; professors and students at the university ambled by. The park was a natural gathering place for artists and writers. In 1887, Robert Louis Stevenson, then in poor health, was passing through New York on his way to "take the cure" upstate at Saranac. Mark Twain came in from Connecticut to meet the Scottish author of *Treasure Island* at his hotel near the Square. The two famous writers strolled down to the park and, following Stevenson's doctor's orders to take the sun every day, settled down on a sunny bench to enjoy a good talk.

Roadways of wood pavement, providing a smoother, quieter surface than stone paving, attracted bicycles, the latest sports fad. Two-wheelers became so popular that their use had to be limited. "The biped and bicycles have regularly appeared on the wooden roadway pavement of the north side of the square," chided the *New York Times* on July 25, 1871, reminding its readers that "Velocipedestrianism is prohibited in Washington Square by order of the Commissioners." More than a century later, despite activity to the contrary, bicycle riding is forbidden within the park.

One legal pleasure from those days has persisted. For several summers beginning in 1871, the Parks Department organized free outdoor "promenade" concerts at various city parks. On designated Tuesday evenings, musicians gathered at the gazebo structure located in the northwest quadrant of the park to play a mix of classical and popular selections. The tradition of outdoor concerts in the park was renewed in the twentieth century under the sponsorship of the Washington Square Music Festival. For nearly half a century, this community-supported organization has presented free summer concerts in the Square, held serendipitously on Tuesday evenings in the summer.

Literary Views:
American Respectability and International Shabbiness

One name often linked with the Square of this era is Edith Wharton, born Edith Newbold Jones. Her descriptions of "old New York"—its stylized rituals of paying calls, attending the opera, or hosting dinner parties—frequently mention Washington Square and have indelibly colored our understanding of late-nineteenth-century life. To Wharton, "Washington Square" did not allude to the green park space but to the row of townhouses on the north side inhabited by the "old money" set. It was a realm of social distinction and stifling existence that she found intolerable. As a young woman, she had observed the calcified attitudes of New York's elite in the 1870s. Years later, she still chafed at the "hoard of petty maxims which its elders preached" and wondered, "What had become of the spirit of the pioneers and the revolutionaries?"

Born in 1862 into a long-established, well-connected New York clan, Wharton knew her subject intimately. Her family members and friends provided the material for her sharply etched characterizations. Wharton's mother Lucretia was one of the "poor Rhinelander girls." In spite of her family pedigree, she suffered snubs in her youth that she never forgot nor forgave. Edith's father, George Frederic Jones, was a "gentleman of leisure" impeccably connected by blood and marriage to the most prestigious families: his cousin Caroline Schermerhorn married William Backhouse Astor and became *the* Mrs. Astor, acknowledged leader of New York society, whose party invitations determined social standing among the city's upper crust.

Wharton's maternal great-grandparents, Mary Rogers and William C. Rhinelander, lived in the Greek Revival mansion at 14 Washington Square North, on the west corner of Fifth Avenue, where she would have visited them. Edith herself resided briefly on Washington Square following her father's death in 1882. To improve the family's straitened circumstances at the time, her mother rented out both the family's townhouse on Twenty-third Street and their summer home in Newport and took rooms on the north side of the Square. Not long after, Lucretia Rhinelander Jones received her share of William Rhinelander's estate, valued at $50 to $75 million, distributed among nineteen heirs, and bought a house at 28 West Twenty-fifth Street, where Edith lived until her marriage to Teddy (Edward) Wharton in 1885.

The Wharton family, like many of the well-to-do in those days, traveled extensively. They left for Europe when Edith was four years old and stayed abroad for six years. As a young girl, she became fluent in several languages, and she remained a passionate traveler throughout her life, eventually settling in France after 1900, when she was nearly forty. *The Age of Innocence,* for which Wharton won the Pulitzer Prize in 1920—she was the first woman to be so honored—was written while she was living in Paris. Just as her revered friend and fellow expatriate Henry James had written about an earlier era in *Washington Square* while in London, so Wharton wrote about New York in the 1870s from an equally distant time and place. But there are obvious differences. James's characters in *Washington Square* inhabit a city fondly recalled from his childhood. Wharton's story, set in the decade of her own adolescence, is coolly anthropological in its study of a culture she found impossibly confining, yet compelling.

Wharton's focus on New York's upper strata of society is far different from William Dean Howells's approach. A newcomer to New York in 1888, Howells, a writer, editor, and champion of realist literature, was considered a radical in his day. His novel of 1890, *A Hazard of New Fortunes*, often described as panoramic, takes on a range of diverse characters, timely social and political issues, and the contemporary urban landscape. The plot revolves around Basil and Isabel March who leave Boston when Mr. March is offered a position as editor of a new literary magazine in New York. March's situation parallels Howells's personal experience as editor of the *Atlantic Monthly* in Boston, a post he was forced to give up after publishing his political views on a controversial subject.

Howells's fictional couple settle near Washington Square, where the author and his wife lived for a while. Unlike Wharton, Howells took notice of the Square's variegated texture and relished its split personality: "the old-fashioned American respectability which keeps the north side of the square in vast mansions of red brick, and the international shabbiness which has invaded the southern border, and broken it up into lodging houses, shops, beer gardens, and studios." The Marches, he wrote in *A Hazard of New Fortunes,* "went and sat a good deal in the softening evenings among the infants and dotards of Latin extraction in Washington Square . . . and enjoyed the advancing season, which thickened the foliage of the trees and flattened out the church warden's gothic of the University Building. The small Italian children raced up and down the asphalt paths, playing American games of tag and hide-and-whoop; larger boys passed ball in training for potential championships." On some nights, the couple stayed in the park "till the electric lights began to show distinctly among the leaves . . . and the benches filled with lovers." They "met Italian faces, French faces, Spanish faces as they strolled over the asphalt walks under the thinning shadows of the autumn-stricken sycamores. They met the familiar picturesque raggedness of southern Europe. . . . In fact, foreign faces and foreign tongues prevailed in Greenwich Village, but no longer German or even Irish tongues or faces. The eyes and earrings of Italians twinkled in and out of alleyways and basements."

A NEW CITY PARK TAKES SHAPE

The ethnic composition of the city changed dramatically during the 1880s, when over 300,000 Italians, mostly poor farm laborers from the south, swarmed to a Manhattan of 1.2 million people. Willing to work long hours for less pay, Italians displaced Irish laborers in the building trades and on the waterfront. A New York official testifying before Congress in 1890 reported that southern Italians constituted 90 percent of those involved in Gotham's public works. Some Italians moved onto streets immediately south of the park, where they gradually pushed out the small black community there. Most settled a few blocks below Houston Street, where they grouped themselves according to their old villages and provinces—Neapolitans on Mulberry Street, Sicilians on Baxter, Calabresi on Mott. Since these newcomers spoke no English, they were often dependent on *padroni*, fellow Italians who arranged jobs for them, extracted a good portion of their wages in return, and cruelly exploited children.

Although the greatest number of Italian immigrants arrived late in the century, there had been a community living south of the Square in the 1820s. Numbering 12,000 before the Civil War, this earlier Italian-born generation had established themselves as craftsmen, stonecutters, and musicians. Some had managed to obtain modest success by opening small groceries, restaurants, and coffeehouses. Their simple entrepreneurial efforts were appreciated by other city dwellers who like Howells's fictional couple delighted in encountering European-style pleasures on American streets.

Public Sculpture for the Park

The historic Italian presence around the Square accounts for the great bronze statue standing east of the fountain—the figure of Giuseppe Garibaldi, commander of the insurrectionary forces in Italy's struggle for unification. Garibaldi was one of the greatest guerrilla generals in history and the most popular Italian patriot of his time. After fighting for Giuseppe Mazzini's short-lived Roman Republic, he sought asylum in the United States where he lived for two years on Staten Island. Returning to his homeland in 1851, he led his red-shirted volunteer army on campaigns that helped bring about a unified Italy twenty years later. Garibaldi's military prowess was so renowned that at the start of the Civil War, Abraham Lincoln offered him command of a Union army corps. In writing to accept, the Italian leader demanded not just a corps but supreme command and firm reassurance that slavery would be abolished. He was turned down. Italian Americans, too, opposed slavery, associating the Union cause with the struggle for Italy's unification and its dream of freedom. They readily joined up as volunteers in the Thirty-ninth New York Infantry, the all-Italian "Garibaldi Guard," and even though Garibaldi himself did not lead them, they carried into battle a flag that had waved at the head of his columns in Europe.

At Garibaldi's death in 1882, the *Italo-Americano* newspaper opened a subscription list to raise funds for a monument honoring the general. Public sculpture was one of the most popular art forms of the nineteenth century, and it was customary then for communities to decorate parks and plazas with commemorative statues of political, military, and cultural heroes. Garibaldi's appeal was such that contributions ranging from five cents to thousands of dollars rapidly poured in from around the country. The commission for the statue went to Giovanni Turini, an Italian-born sculptor who had been a volunteer with Garibaldi's Fourth Regiment in 1866, when Italy wrested Venice from Austria. Turin had previously sculpted a bust of the Risorgimento leader Mazzini for Central Park. His statue of the freedom fighter for Washington Square turned out to be a bronze nearly ten feet tall.

On June 4, 1888, the sixth anniversary of Garibaldi's death, the monument was unveiled in the park. Thousands of spectators gathered for the celebration, waving Italian flags and cheering for members of the Garibaldi Guard, who could be identified by their red shirts, black scarves, and gray trousers. Scores of bands entertained the crowds during the long wait for the ceremony to begin. Professor Vincenzo Botta delivered a lengthy address on Garibaldi's life and accomplishments. Mayor Abram Hewitt, accepting the statue as a gift to the city, described the immigrants' bond to their birthplace "as one would recall the love of a fond mother from whom we are parted forever." Drawing a parallel between the Italian struggle for unification and the American war between the states, the mayor cited the figure of Garibaldi "as a warning against domestic strife and as a perpetual monitor of that love of union for which Italy and the United States have each in the crises of their destiny made such heroic sacrifices."[4] The imposing bronze figure of Garibaldi continues to dominate the small plaza on the east side of the park, a memorial to the man and the strength of New York's Italian community.

Two years after the Garibaldi statue was set in place, a smaller sculpture was installed on the west side of the park—the bronze bust of Alexander Lyman Holley, an engineer regarded as the father of modern American steel manufacturing. The monument is a reminder of the technological advances of the mid nineteenth century, which formed the basis for America's later industrial supremacy. While touring England in the early 1860s, Holley observed the Bessemer method of manufacturing steel and acquired the American rights to the process. At his factory in Troy, New York, Holley adapted the Bessemer process to American conditions and in 1865, he established the first steel plant of commercial significance in the United States. His innovations laid the foundation for the modern steel industry in America. A few years after Holley's untimely death at age fifty in 1882, a committee of the Institute of Mining Engineers asked John Quincy Adams Ward to create a memorial bust of the engineer. Ward was one of the most respected and prolific artists of his time, well known for his statue of Washington on the steps of Federal Hall. His memorial to Holley is on a more intimate scale and one of his finest portraits—a natural, spontaneous likeness.

The monument's unveiling was timed to occur while an international congress of representatives from the iron and steel industries was meeting in New York. On the afternoon of October 2, 1890, a lengthy tribute to Holley was held at Chickering Hall at Fifth Avenue and Eighteenth Street, after which the "iron and steel men" trooped down to Washington Square to join a big crowd gathered there for the ceremony. At the appropriate moment, Holley's little grandson pulled a cord that bound the flag around it, and the bust was revealed. The monument was set close to the center of the park beneath the shade of two giant elms, facing west away from the fountain on a little triangular grass plot, now paved over.

In surrendering the Holley memorial to the Parks Department, the spokesman for the engineering societies urged that New York's parks be decorated with monuments to those "whose work has contributed to the material progress of the Nation. If the soldier and statesman are worthy to be thus held in lasting remembrance, not less so in a republic are those who have made its industrial history and led the progress of the arts and sciences." Why the Parks Department placed Holley in Washington Square is unknown, but the memorial to the engineer-industrialist complements the statue of the Italian soldier, just as Holley's subscribers had wished.

The Centennial Celebration of 1889

At the time of the Holley dedication, work was already under way for what would become the best-known structure in the park—the Arch built to honor the first president of the United States, George Washington. This signature monument of Washington Square began as a temporary wooden structure put up for the Centennial of 1889, an event commemorating the one-hundredth anniversary of Washington's taking the oath of office, on April 30, 1789, on the steps of Federal Hall at Wall and Nassau Streets. (New York City was the new nation's first capital, but its tenure as such was brief. As a result of a deal between

Alexander Hamilton and Thomas Jefferson, the federal government moved to Philadelphia, where it functioned for ten years before finally settling in Washington, D.C., in 1800.)

Official plans for the Centennial made no provisions for any commemorative structure or ceremony at Washington Square, but one individual thought differently. William Rhinelander Stewart, whose family had lived on the park for generations, wanted to be certain that Washington Square's historic neighborhood would be included in the proceedings. He single-handedly arranged for a temporary arch to be built for the Centennial celebration and organized the funding and construction of the permanent arch as well. Conceived ostensibly to honor Washington, the two arches and their surrounding ceremonies commemorate as well a generation of New Yorkers and their social and cultural milieu.

In anticipation of the Centennial, the New-York Historical Society had begun in the mid 1880s to plan for a major celebration that would underscore New York's prominent role in the nation's early history. Philadelphia had marked the centenary of America's independence in 1876 with a major exposition of international architecture, design, and industry, which had attracted ten million people. New York's event was intended to be of a different nature and scope, more like an extended Fourth of July festival. The appointed Centennial committees, composed of civic leaders and representatives of the city's Knickerbocker families, arranged for a three-day extravaganza with a dual goal: first, to recreate as nearly as possible the historic events of Washington's time, and second, to flaunt the achievements of modern New York.

Stewart's Dream

In March 1889, while the parade route was still under discussion, Stewart began a subscription to raise money for a triumphal arch to be placed on Fifth Avenue immediately north of Washington Square

Park. In short order, he collected $2,765 from neighbors on Waverly Place, Washington Square, and Fifth Avenue. According to an interview printed in the *Commercial Advertiser* of May 4, 1889, Stewart had for some time been worrying over an appropriate way to observe the Centennial. "One night, he says, he dreamed it all. In his dream he stood at the corner of Clinton Place (Eighth Street), and looking toward Washington Square beheld this white arch looming up and beneath it a stream of troops and horsemen passing along." The next day, he called upon Stanford White, partner in the architectural firm of McKim, Mead & White, and "made him acquainted with his plan for building a triumphant arch, at the same time explaining to him the design he had seen in his dream." Stewart knew White because the architect had been working on a Rhinelander family memorial at the nearby Church of the Ascension on Fifth Avenue. The architect graciously offered to provide plans and superintend the building of the arch at no charge.

Stewart was the scion of distinguished old New York families. On his paternal side, he was a descendant of Robert Stewart, who had arrived in New York before the Revolution. On his mother's side, he was descended from Philip Jacob Rhinelander, a Huguenot seeking refuge in 1686 from Louis XIV's persecution of French Protestants. Subsequent generations of the Rhinelander family gained wealth from sugarrefining, a business that depended on the importing of raw sugar produced by West Indian slave labor. The Rhinelander Sugar House, constructed in 1732, was one of the largest structures in prerevolutionary New York. Stewart's maternal grandmother, Mary Rogers Rhinelander, was Edith Wharton's great-grandmother, thus making William a cousin of Edith's. His unmarried aunts, Serena and Julia, inhabited the house built for his grandmother at 14 Washington Square North, while Stewart lived a few doors away at No. 17. Born in 1852, he was educated at Columbia University, joined a company of the Seventh Regiment, and practiced law for seven years. In 1880, he retired to attend to his duties as executor and trustee of the family estates and to devote himself to philanthropic causes.

Stanford White, the designated designer of the arch, was an astute choice for the project. The architect delighted in the interplay of architecture, sculpture, and landscape and was adept at defining spaces and creating focal points with his designs. Born on East Tenth Street in 1853 to a family with serious literary and artistic interests, "Stanny" wanted to be a painter. But his father, a writer and music critic, feared that this would be a financially risky choice and through friends, arranged an apprenticeship for his son in Boston with Henry Hobson Richardson, one of the most influential American architects of the time. After a few years under Richardson, White went off to study in Paris for several months, returning to New York in 1879 when invited to join in partnership with Charles Follen McKim and William Rutherford Mead. Theirs soon became the busiest and most highly reputed architectural firm in New York. In the year preceding the Centennial, White, the youngest partner, was working on extensive embellishments for Prospect Park, built by Olmsted and Vaux after Central Park. He was also about to begin designing Judson Memorial Church on the south side of the Square.

The Temporary Arch

Correspondence between Stewart and White and a contract, signed in March 1889, stipulate that the arch would be executed by Joseph Cabus, a cabinet and architectural woodworker, for a cost of $1,743.[5] White based the design of his arch on ancient Roman models, but mindful of the historical context and setting, also incorporated details from the nearby Greek Revival residences. The completed arch stood 50 feet wide, corresponding to the width of Fifth Avenue, and 71 feet high, with a ten-foot painted wood statue of Washington on top.[6]

While it may seem surprising that a well-known architect would agree to work on an ephemeral structure for a parade, the idea relates back to a tradition of the late seventeenth and early eighteenth centuries, when accomplished court artists regularly devised temporary decorative structures called *apparati* to celebrate victories, royal birthdays, or state occasions for their royal patrons. The practice revived in the 1800s for the more bourgeois purpose of expositions and world fairs that were taking place around the globe. In the spring of 1889, while New York was preparing for the Centennial, an engineer named Gustave Eiffel completed an unusual iron tower for the Universal Exposition in Paris celebrating the hundredth anniversary of the French Revolution, which was due to open on May 6, just a week after New York's Centennial. As the Eiffel Tower became an enduring symbol of its city, so did the permanent arch Stanford White ultimately designed for Washington Square.

Because of the arch, the Centennial Committee diverted the parade from Broadway at Union Square back again to Fifth Avenue. "The only apparent object to be gained by this diversion is to gratify a few families on Washington-square and lower Fifth-avenue by having the parade pass by their residences," groused a critic in the *New York Times*. No doubt there was some truth to this, but the gentry around the Square claimed that they were motivated simply by public spirit and local pride. All along the parade route, the city erected public bleachers, which were supplemented by numerous stands erected on private property. In addition to the public stands at Washington Square, enterprising property owners whose homes afforded good views constructed platforms over their front yards and stoops, devised makeshift balconies, and rented out rooms for good sums, which they advertised in the newspapers. "Balcony seats, Waverly place—only a few left," reads an ad in the *Sun* on the Saturday preceding the Centennial. Another promised "large double windows from $100 to $250; two days, private parties only."

A NEW CITY PARK TAKES SHAPE

Ceremony and High Spirits

In the week before the Centennial, eager patriots in all quarters of the city hung masses of bunting and tricolor banners from every possible surface. Extremely heavy rains, not unusual for that time of year, marred some of the decorations, but opening day on Monday, April 29, dawned brightly. "Magnificent stood New York yesterday morning—grand, splendid beyond even her usual magnificence. Radiant she was, and glorious with color," crowed the New York *Sun*. The Centennial began with a solemn re-creation of Washington's inauguration, with President Benjamin Harrison playing the part of Washington. Deviating from history in the name of progress, the seven-day stagecoach journey from Washington's home at Mount Vernon to New York was reduced to a nine-hour train ride from Washington to Elizabeth, New Jersey. From there, the president was rowed across to Manhattan. (A hundred years earlier, the coxswain of Washington's boat had been Thomas Randall, the successful privateer whose land was bequeathed by his son to Sailors' Snug Harbor and leased for the Row.) When President Harrison, dressed in period costume, stepped ashore at the same spot where Washington had landed, cannons boomed and the crowds roared. Washington's first inauguration had been followed by a naval parade, which now was "to be outdone a hundredfold in the extent and elaboration of its pageantry," claimed the *New York Times*. A huge flotilla of a thousand ships and 70,000 sailors formed a city afloat in the harbor. At the formal ball held that evening at the Metropolitan Opera House at Thirty-ninth Street, ten thousand people squeezed onto the dance floor at one time.

Tuesday, April 30, was devoted to the military parade, eleven miles of marching men, "a glittering stream of waving plumes and polished steel" heading from Fifty-seventh Street south to Washington Square. By seven o'clock that morning, several hundred spectators had already claimed the hard wooden seats of the grandstands in the park facing north, directly across from the arch. Throngs of people at the park, disgorged by Fifth Avenue coaches, jostled one another as they vied for viewing space. "Half a dozen men were clubbed and fights occurred every few minutes. . . . The police were not sparing of their clubs," observed the *Sun*. Later in the morning, crowds at the northeastern corner of the park on Waverly Place near the University Building had become so dense that they completely blocked the parade route. When police on horseback attempted to gain control, reported the *Tribune*, "a thousand people rushed down toward Fifth-ave. to escape the hoofs of the mounted patrol." Policemen were faulted for engaging in unnecessary violence, but they were credited for keeping order and for having had the foresight to lock up all the thieves, burglars, and bad characters they could find before the celebration began.[7]

Later that night, several thousand people gathered in the Square to witness a magnificent display of fireworks. Five hundred rockets shot skyward from a roped-off plaza in the park, followed by "Bengal lights," "cataracts of fire," "cascades of diamond showers," and other spectacular pyrotechnic effects. Given its reputation as a metropolis driven by commerce, New York's wholehearted pride and patriotism throughout the Centennial seems to have surprised everyone. "This city, always called so mercenary, so selfish, and so lacking in public spirit, gave up three days to this festival," *Harper's Weekly* conceded grudgingly. "Four days were lost from business, for Sunday preceded the holiday."[8]

Creating a Landmark

Three arches in all were constructed for the Centennial, yet only the one at the foot of Fifth Avenue was deemed praiseworthy. As for the others, a critic wrote dismissively in the *Sun*, "a Western boom town might have been expected to do better . . . small, cheap, and either inartistic or hideous. The one at the foot of Wall street, a shell of canvas dotted with shields and hung with mere ropes of bunting does not become a great city. The one at Twenty-sixth street, distinguished by drunken soldiers cut out of pasteboard, would be refused by the manager of a Bowery variety theatre if a sign painter offered it there." Illustrations in the *Sun* show the Wall Street monument as a straightforward, if uninspired effort at ephemeral street decoration. The second arch, located near the presidential reviewing stand at Fifth Avenue and Twenty-third Street, seems an odd choice for the occasion, since it closely resembled the façade of a turreted medieval castle, with soldiers standing guard in niches on each side. Above the center of its crenellated arch towered a figure of Washington on horseback, a modern-day St. George about to slay the dragon. No wonder that White's thoughtful, more restrained design captivated the public. "The one noble, imposing, beautiful arch is that at the foot of Fifth avenue. It was designed by Mr. Stanford White, and even he may well be proud of it."[9]

Before the Centennial had concluded, the temporary arch at Washington Square had so imprinted itself in the public mind that a movement was already under way to perpetuate the arch in stone. On the last day of the official celebration, the *Sun* had described "the gorgeous spectacle" of the arch, brilliantly lit with three hundred incandescent globes, embellished with white streamers and bunches of flags. "And by the way why should not that arch become permanent in marble?" demanded the paper. "And where it is now is the place for it to stand— at the beginning of the only great thoroughfare left in this city without railroad tracks, opposite Washington Square." Before the Centennial was over, the *Commercial Advertiser* rushed in to claim credit for first proposing a permanent arch and opened a subscription list for the project, starting it off with a contribution of $100. Within the next few days, papers up and down the East Coast—Springfield, Boston, Philadelphia, Baltimore—heartily voiced support for the arch.[10] If credit for proposing a permanent arch were to be awarded, it would most fairly go to the *Critic,* a literary magazine, which had introduced the idea weeks earlier in its April 1889 issue. The *Critic* was edited by Jeannette L. and Joseph B. Gilder. Joseph was the brother of Richard Watson Gilder, editor of the *Century Magazine* and secretary of the Centennial Art and Exhibition Committee, who lived at 55 Clinton Place (East Eighth Street), around the corner from the temporary arch.

Raising Money, Breaking Ground

At a meeting of the Centennial Art and Exhibition Committee on Thursday, May 2, members approved the suggestion of making the arch a permanent memorial and appointed a special committee chaired by Henry Marquand, with Louis Fitzgerald as vice-chairman, Richard Gilder as secretary, and William Rhinelander Stewart as treasurer, to oversee the project. White once again generously offered to provide plans free of charge, and the group estimated that $75,000 would cover the cost of materials and labor. Two days later, the newly organized "Committee on Erection of the Memorial Arch at Washington Square"—hereafter referred to as the Arch Committee—resolved to build a permanent "Washington Memorial Arch" of marble, designed by Stanford White and placed in or near Washington Square. (The word "Memorial" was soon dropped from its name.) After some reconsideration, the committee decided to raise $100,000 for the arch, plus another $50,000 for its sculptural decoration. Skeptics citing the city's delay in building Grant's memorial doubted whether the sum could be collected. The tomb for President Ulysses S. Grant and his wife Julia at Riverside Drive and 122nd Street, begun in 1885, was still short of funds and not completed until 1897. "The public spirit expressed in such works does not seem to be abundant in New York," snapped the *Chicago Herald* on May 7. (New York had, in fact, spent very little on public monuments. Its rival Brooklyn, for example, was just then building a Soldiers' and Sailors' Memorial Arch at Prospect Park for $250,000.) Defending the honor of the home turf, the *Mail and Express* observed: "New Yorkers are famous the world over for 'doing things with a rush.' What we do at all we are apt to do quickly and heartily. Let us come up to the full measure of our reputation in this respect by rolling up the needed funds for the erection of the Centennial Memorial Arch with a characteristic New York 'rush.' "[11]

New Yorkers came through, thanks in good measure to Treasurer William Stewart's intuitive talent for fund-raising and publicity. His meticulous accounts indicate that $40,000 had been solicited by the end of May. Funding for the Arch slowed over the summer when charitable contributions went to relieve the effects of calamitous flooding in Johnstown, Pennsylvania, where more than 2,200 people had died. But by October 1, the Washington Arch Fund stood at $53,000, one-third from donations of $1,000, and the rest from contributions of $100 to $500. Stewart reassured White that he would be able to lay the cornerstone for the Arch on April 30, 1890, the first anniversary of the Centennial, and was hoping to see the permanent structure completed by the second anniversary.

White meanwhile was engaged in a search for the perfect stone for his project. Committee member Robert De Forest had suggested to the architect that granite would give the same visual effect as marble and be better suited to New York's climate, but White held fast. Seeking a pure white marble without flaw or discoloration of any kind, the architect wrote to sources around the country. Several firms sent samples, all of which were tested by Columbia College's Department of Engineering School of Mines. White eventually selected Tuckahoe marble from a quarry about twenty miles north of the city in Westchester County. White must not have been aware that the Tuckahoe stone, appealing to him for its crystalline quality and excellent for ashlar masonry, was problematic for decorative carving, because, when exposed, it was prone to shear off or crumble like a sugar cube over time.[12]

The marble monument was to be larger than the temporary arch, nearly 78 feet high and 57 feet wide, decorated with sculpture and inscriptions, and flanked by four columns of Victory, which were later eliminated. White envisioned the Arch as a punctuation point for lower Fifth Avenue and positioned it to straddle the roadway passing through the park. To accommodate the passage of traffic, he designed the Arch with a broad central span, thirty feet wide and forty-seven feet high, dimensions that, the architect proudly noted, outdid any single-span arch of antiquity. He reduced the bulk of the piers proportionally, with the result that the Washington Arch appears lighter and less muscular than its Roman ancestors. The impression of lightness, a trait often associated with the architect's work, is enhanced even more because White limited the decorative carving to certain areas and kept the pier surfaces unadorned. While integrating elements from Greek and Roman models—allegorical figures, wreaths, bands of decorative motifs, and the coffered ceiling (patterned squares) on the curved underside of the span—White bestowed a distinctly modern clarity and simplicity to a classic form. As Stewart remarked to White when the Arch was nearing completion, "Where-ever you have departed from strictly classic ideas about this Arch I think you have made it more original and better. . . . you and the Arch are both 19th century products, and 19th century ideas ought to have full play."[13]

White's decorative scheme for the Arch revolves around the theme of Washington as leader in war and peace. Carved panels on the north side contain shields bearing the coat of arms, crests, and mottoes of General Washington and the United States; those on the south display the arms of the state and the city of New York. Around the shields, space is filled with images alluding to war and peace—a wreath of oak around a sword hilt, for example, and wreaths of laurel for victory. In the spandrels—the triangular sections curved to fit around the arch— allegorical winged figures in flowing tunics hold banners, horns, and laurel wreaths to reinforce the war and peace theme. At the highest point of the Arch's opening, a very large eagle with outspread wings perches on the keystone. Measuring nearly eleven feet across, the regal bird forms the central motif of the decorative frieze that stretches around all sides of the Arch.

On the attic story above the frieze are inscriptions selected by William Stewart and his Committee. The north façade reads, "To commemorate the One Hundredth Anniversary of the Inauguration of George Washington as first President of the United States." On the south is a quotation from Washington: "Let us raise a standard to which the wise and honest can repair—the event is in the hands of God." White initially planned for statuary representing Washington in war and peace to be placed on the pedestals of the piers facing Fifth Avenue. Too costly to include in the initial fund-raising budget, the pedestal sculptures were not completed until 1916 and 1918.

On April 30, 1890, precisely one year after the Centennial, ground was ceremoniously broken for the Arch. Among the prayers, patriotic songs, and speeches, one talk stands out, because it hints at the ambivalent feelings about the monument and the Square itself. Addressing those who may have questioned the wisdom of erecting a costly monument in Washington Square, Henry Marquand, the chairman of the Arch Committee, declared:

> It is true someone has remarked that the neighborhood in a few years will be all tenement houses. Even should this prove true, no stronger reason could be given for the Arch being placed there. Have the occupants of tenement houses no sense of beauty? Have they no patriotism? Have they no right to good architecture? Happily there is no monopoly of the appreciation of things that are excellent any more than there is of fresh air, and in our mind's eye we can see many a family who cannot afford to spend ten cents to go to the park, taking pleasure under the shadow of the Arch. This is the Arch of peace and goodwill to men. It will bring the rich and poor together in one common bond of patriotic feeling.

Marquand's noble sentiments are characteristic of Gilded Age philanthropists, but his words also suggest that longtime residents on the park's north side feared that their neighborhood was slipping irretrievably. Struggling to recapture the grace and harmony of that "pleasanter, easier and hazier past," in the words of Henry James, these neighbors privately hoped that the Arch would stave off any further deterioration.

In April 1891, the Arch Fund at last reached its goal of $100,000, but by then the committee estimated that an additional $28,000 would be needed to complete the project and fundraising continued. The contract for building the Arch, exclusive of the sculptural carving, was awarded to David H. King, who had just finished building the pedestal for the Statue of Liberty. King, like White, agreed to do the work on the Arch at cost and waived the contractor's usual 10 percent commission. King appointed James Sinclair & Co. to prepare all the marble, except for the low-relief carving, and Sinclair, too, accepted no fee. By offering their services free of charge, these men and White in fact made the largest contributions to the Arch. The builders were fortunate in finding great talent, notably the Piccirilli brothers—six of them recently arrived from Tuscany and all trained as sculptors. Working in their studio at 142nd Street in the Mott Haven section of the Bronx, they carved all the decorative reliefs and statues on the Arch following the sculptors' designs. The Piccirillis went on to chisel many of New York's monuments, including the beloved lions of the New York Public Library. An invoice shows that another new family business— the Guastavino Fire Proof Construction Co., established in 1889—was hired to do the brick leaders, roofing, interior staircase, and the room over the arch. The Rafael Guastavinos, a father and son from Spain, brought with them an old Catalan building technique in which flat bricks are used to create curved surfaces on walls and ceilings. Like the Piccirillis, the Guastavinos' work may be seen all over New York—

in train stations, under bridges, in churches, and most dramatically in the soaring vaults of St. John the Divine. Since their work on the Arch was interior, however, it is not visible to the public.

Stewart and White Correspond

Correspondence between Stewart and White at the end of 1891 conveys the growing relationship between the two men and the good humor with which they dealt with their frustrations and conflicts. It was "a complete surprise," wrote Stewart to White on December 7, upon learning that the cost of the Arch was $10,658.50 higher than first estimated. Extra costs were due to changes made by the committee, replied the architect the next day, and neither the figural sculpture nor the iron staircase were included in the original contract. "Now, the last man to whom I should wish to write an angry letter would be yourself," wrote White in response to what he called a "haircurling official letter" from Stewart. If he could not clearly demonstrate that all the extra costs were due to changes asked for by Stewart, his committee or Washington Square residents, then, said White, "I will agree to curl my hair permanently."[14] Most often, their communications demonstrate Stewart's unwavering devotion to the project and his vigilant supervision of all its aspects.

After two years of working together, Stewart finally took a step that says much about upper-class etiquette at the turn of the century: "We have so much in common on the Arch that I feel you will not think I take too much liberty in dropping the 'Mr.'"[15] Henceforth he addressed the architect simply as "White." February 23, 1892: "My Dear White, I was on top of the Arch this morning. They are erecting a circular iron frame about 9 feet high in which will be the door to the roof. It seems to me this is much too high, and even when the last two courses of marble are set I fear it will be seen at a distance of a block or two from the Arch. This would be a great pity. A trap door would be better, but I think you can have two feet taken off the height of this structure, and still allow access by it to the roof." Two days later, White replied that the stairway was only five feet above the roof line, would be painted white, and could only be glimpsed by someone standing 210 feet off. "If you wish it lower, amen! It will be very uncomfortable getting up the staircase."[16] The lower door did create an awkward opening for anyone climbing to the top, but it preserved the Arch's silhouette unimpaired.

In March 1892, the Washington Memorial Arch Fund received a boost from an unlikely source. The renowned Polish pianist Ignace Jan Paderewski who had debuted at the new Carnegie Hall the previous fall, volunteered to give a farewell benefit concert for the Arch with the Boston Symphony Orchestra at the Metropolitan Opera House. Colonel Henry Higginson, founding director and patron of the Boston Symphony, paid for the musicians, and New York piano maker William Steinway covered the cost of advertising and the rent on the Opera House. The March 27 concert featured selections by Wagner, Berlioz, Schumann, Saint-Saëns, and Liszt, as well as a performance of Paderewski's own piano concerto, to which the audience responded enthusiastically. Proceeds from the event enriched the Arch Fund by $4,500.

At the end of April, the scaffolding came down, and the Arch was revealed without obstruction for the first time. At a ceremony to mark the completion of this phase of work, Stanford White, Richard Gilder, and William Stewart set the last three block of marble, each chiseled with their respective initials, into place at the top of the Arch. That June, the Arch Fund reached its goal of $128,000.

The Arch's Debut:
"Few Such Nights in the History of the World"

The Arch made its grand debut during the Columbian Celebration of 1892, the four-hundredth anniversary of Christopher Columbus sighting the new world from his ship on October 12, 1492. Chicago claimed the place of honor, with ambitious plans for a World's Columbian Exposition, to be held in a specially created "White City "on Lake Michigan. The dazzling aggregation of Roman-style buildings designed by America's leading architects, including White's partner McKim and the New York architect Richard Morris Hunt, did not officially open until 1893.

The city on the Hudson was not about to be outdone by its rival on Lake Michigan. New York arranged for a towering statue of Columbus to be unveiled on the site subsequently known as Columbus Circle at Fifty-ninth Street and Eighth Avenue and organized yet another round of naval, military, and civic parades. This time, the Arch at Washington Square was on the program from the start. Stewart had alerted White that the Columbus Day parades would be passing under the Arch and pressed him to finish as much as possible before then. By September, most of the carved panels were in place.

"One of the most attractive spots along the route of the parade was the beginning of Fifth Avenue just above the new Washington Arch," remarked the *New York Times*. Neighbors on the east side of Fifth Avenue had collaborated in erecting a viewing platform 250 feet long draped entirely in red. Students and faculty from Cooper Union packed the stands around the Coopers' home on the east corner. Across the way, the Rhinelanders filled a stand in their courtyard with students from many of the charity schools in the city. Stewart provided all the boys and girls with bags filled with buns and cakes. The city had erected two sets of platforms along the north and east sides of the Square, each accommodating 2,800 ticket holders, who had paid $1.50 apiece. One reporter noted that women sightseers, in the majority at Washington Square, were packing the stands "as close as gowns in a boarding house clothes closet. The future historian in his introduction to the great Columbus celebration . . . will doubtless note that by a special providence hoops had disappeared from the feminine form divine some years before."[17]

IT HAPPENED ON WASHINGTON SQUARE

For the October 11 opening parade, 25,000 schoolchildren and college men marched under the Arch and past the mayor and thousands of viewers assembled on lower Fifth Avenue. The next day every rooftop was filled with spectators as 3,000 bicyclists led off a spectacular succession of floats. For the evening pageant the city was in "an elfin mood transformed into a city of lights. . . . There have been few such nights as this was in all the history of the world," exulted the *Sun* the next day. The Edison Electric Illuminating Company had installed a permanent double row of electric lights all along Fifth Avenue. To illuminate the Arch, the company fastened 348 lights to one-inch iron pipes that had been attached to the monument in advance and enameled to match the stonework. In the evening, Chinese lanterns illuminated the Coopers' mansion on one corner, while across the way colored lights gleamed at the Rhinelanders. Between them, the Arch appeared "in a bath of colored light from a calcium apparatus on Fifth avenue, about twenty-five feet from the square. The effect was highly pleasing. . . . The east side reflected red, the west side blue, and the crown white." Stewart expressed his great pleasure in a note to White dated October 13: "The last three days have been simply grand. . . . lighting of the Arch was immense and one of the great features of the night parade."[18]

While appearing to be structurally complete at the time of the Columbian festivities, the Arch was still lacking whole sections of sculptural decoration. Over the next year, the trophy panels on the north were completed and the inscriptions set in place, but the spandrels—the carved victory panels of War and Peace on either side of the opening—were delayed. In June 1893, Stewart informed White that he was "especially anxious to have Mrs. Stewart's profile and Mrs. White's for the figures of the West and East spandrels on the North front. To see them there will be additional reward to us for all the trouble we have taken to make the Arch. . . . I count upon you to see that the models are satisfactory in this particular."[19] Viewed from Fifth

A NEW CITY PARK TAKES SHAPE

Avenue, Mrs. White was to be on the left or east side, and Mrs. Stewart was to be on the right, or west, facing her home across the street.

White passed along the request to the sculptor Frederick MacMonnies, a former Saint-Gaudens apprentice whom he had commissioned to design the all the sculptural relief on the Arch. Working from his studio in Paris, MacMonnies, one of White's favorite collaborators, had already completed most of the work. But when the architect received the sculptor's studies for the spandrels, he was evidently dissatisfied. In a letter to MacMonnies in Paris dated November 8, 1893, White wrote that the spandrel drawings "bother me in certain ways a good deal. . . . I dislike the leg up in the air very much, and the figures seem to me meagre." White softens his criticism with a coy disclaimer: "Of course, you must take everything I say 'Cum grano salis,' because I am an Architect, and it may be bad taste in me but, I would really like here a thoroughly quiet, severe and architectural treatment of the sculpture."[20]

When Stewart viewed the models some time later, he thought them "very artistic, but I do not think that the profiles resemble in the least either Mrs. Stewart or Mrs. White . . . cannot this be improved." After many months, White's friend Saint-Gaudens took a turn at the spandrel reliefs, and one year later, in January 1895, they were installed on the Arch. In the end, the profiles of the winged figures resembled neither Mrs. Stewart nor Mrs. White, but there were no further words on the subject. Stewart's press release announcing the completion of the spandrels credited only MacMonnies and referred to the triangular panels as "masterpieces of relief sculpture." MacMonnies, "high in the front rank of American sculptors," Stewart announced, was now preparing studies for the pedestal statuary.[21]

On May 4, 1895, six years after the Centennial, the Washington Arch was formally dedicated. Again crowds gathered to witness an imposing ceremony; bands played and regiments paraded. People filled the big turkey-red stands put up for the event, while three hundred policemen struggled to control the crowds on the streets. Grover Cleveland, in his second term as president (1893–97), came up from Washington for the dedication. Cleveland had attended the ground-breaking shortly after his first term ended in 1889, and must have considered the Arch and its benefactors important enough to warrant his personal appearance once again.

Among the many speeches was a short address by Henry Marquand, who had spoken so movingly at the cornerstone ceremony in 1890. This time Marquand emphasized the democratic support for the Arch: "The money was not raised among a few wealthy subscribers, but has come from widely different sources, and the interest has been general. . . . It has shown, also, the popular desire for good architecture." The Arch was formally transferred to the city in a brief ceremony, and since that day in 1895, the Washington Arch has been in the care of the Parks Department.

The City Beautiful

It is evident that the Arch held profound meaning for the generation that erected it. Over a period of six years, every stage of its construction was marked by a well-attended ceremony. A year after its dedication, the Arch Committee produced *The History of the Arch in Washington Square,* written by William Stewart and published in a limited deluxe edition in 1896. The fully illustrated and detailed volume chronicles every phase of building, records all the speeches from every ceremony, and lists each donor and dollar contributed. The hundreds of large and small donations, many from beyond the city, are an impressive indication of the monument's appeal.

Created as a patriotic gesture to call attention to the historic Square, the glistening marble Arch epitomized what private wealth and focused energy could accomplish. Committee members and other donors believed the monument would be an asset to the city as a whole. Having harvested or inherited their wealth in an era of excessive greed and materialism, these benefactors belonged to a circle of philanthropists who acknowledged their obligation to society. Prompted by duty and a sense of righteousness, they founded and magnanimously supported the hospitals, cultural institutions, schools, and welfare associations that continue to benefit New Yorkers of today. Their generosity and that of their counterparts across the country occurred at a time when there was no tax on income, and hence no advantageous deductions for charitable giving.

At the cornerstone ceremony in 1890, Marquand had alluded to the socially redeeming power of architecture to effect change—"the Arch of peace and goodwill to men" that would "bring rich and poor together in one common bond of patriotic feeling." His sentiments reflect the dual influences of Social Darwinism and the City Beautiful movement, which were sweeping the country in the 1890s. The City Beautiful idea was supported by generally conservative civic leaders like those of the Arch Committee. It offered an approach to city planning that was inspired by Baron Georges-Eugène Haussmann's redesign of Paris in the 1850s and most fully realized at the 1893 Columbian Exposition in Chicago. Proponents believed that classically inspired architecture would not only beautify the urban environment but also benefit the physical and moral well-being of city dwellers' lives. Such beliefs intersected with the application of Darwinian ideology to human behavior—namely, that humans, like other species, adapt to their environment. Advocates of the City Beautiful movement found allies among the social workers and reformers who were then crusading for better housing, cleaner streets, and more parks and playgrounds. Together these groups worked to solve the pressing social problems of their time and enlarged the scope of what a metropolis should provide for its citizens.

Those involved with building the Arch understood that it would take more than a classically styled monument to improve the lot of New York's poorest inhabitants. Richard Gilder, secretary of the Arch

Committee, had just completed his duties as chairman of a state-appointed commission on tenements. Forty years earlier, Gilder had been taken by his father to see Five Points, and the experience had left its imprint. Too prim to print Walt Whitman's verse in his magazine, Gilder nonetheless marched tirelessly through the worst slums to observe conditions personally. His specific recommendations for health and safety standards were adapted by the legislature and signed into law by Governor Morton on May 9, five days after the dedication of the Arch.[22]

For his exhaustive investigation, Gilder enlisted the help of the well-known reformer Jacob Riis, a Danish-born immigrant who knew the slums firsthand through his work as police reporter for the *New York Tribune*. Riis's stories and compelling photographs formed the basis for his groundbreaking study of tenement life, *How the Other Half Lives*, published in 1890. The "other half" then numbered close to a million people, in reality accounting for closer to two-thirds of the city's total population of 1.6 million.

Washington Square was not insulated from the problems Gilder and Riis were confronting in their tenement study. Those down on their luck had been frequenting the Square for many years. In *How the Other Half Lives*, Riis tells of a well-known charitable stove manufacturer who opened a sort of breakfast shop at the southwest corner of the Square, offering a free cup of coffee and a roll to all who had no money. The first morning, he had a dozen customers, and the next day, about two hundred. Two weeks later, when he found by actual count 2,014 shivering creatures waiting in line, he had to close shop, ruined by too much business.

Across the Square on the north side of the park, however, conditions seemed to take a turn for the better, or at least to have stabilized around the time the Arch was built. Mariana Griswold Van Rensselaer, then living on Ninth Street, wrote optimistically in *Century Magazine* in 1893: "They are not the fashionable streets they were in my childhood; but 'good people' still live in them, and the number is now increasing again year by year, desecrated dwellings being restored within and without, and a belief steadily gaining ground that . . . this quarter mile will remain a 'good residence neighborhood.'"

Second Growth around the Square

"The principal business in our goodly city seems to be to unmake what has cost years of labor and heaps of money in the erection." So wrote the New York correspondent for the *Baltimore Transcript* in 1839.[23] His words would hold equally true a half-century later.

When Henry James was visiting New York in 1904 after an absence of twenty years, he was unsettled by the changes at Washington Square. Readily acknowledging that lower Fifth Avenue still possessed "a value, had even a charm for the revisiting spirit," the expatriate author saw little to praise about "the little lamentable Arch of triumph . . . lamentable because of its poor and lonely and unsupported and unaffiliated state." The "melancholy monument," as he called it in *The American Scene,* was too assertive for his taste next to the low-scaled dignity of the Greek Revival houses around it. Most disturbing for James was the loss of his birthplace on Washington Place, torn down ten years before to make way for NYU's Main Building. The effect, he wrote, "was of having been amputated of half my history." Gone, too, were the familiar neo-Gothic spires of the old University Building and the Dutch Reformed Church, displaced by second-growth commercial-style lofts. In the course of a few years, two sides of the old Square had been significantly altered. The only tower punctuating the skyline of 1904 belonged to the new Judson Memorial Church, a structure unfamiliar to James.

A Mission Church

Construction of Judson Memorial Church began a few months after ground was broken for the Washington Arch. Like the Arch, it was designed by Stanford White. Edward Judson, pastor of the Berean Baptist Church in the south Village, wanted to erect a church to commemorate the one hundredth anniversary of his father's birth. His father, Adironam Judson, the first American missionary to be sent abroad, had served in Burma and had translated the scriptures into the language of his converts. To honor his father's memory, the son sought to create a splendid church that would reach out to the needy people of downtown New York.

Transposing his parents' missionary zeal to an urban setting, the younger Judson left a wealthy Baptist Congregation in New Jersey for service in lower Manhattan and moved with his wife to 35 Washington Square West. He believed that the Protestant neglect of immigrant masses posed a serious threat to the American way of life and he had "come to regard foreigners not as a menace but an opportunity."[24] From his experience at the Berean church, Judson decided to expand his work among the immigrants from southern Italy, who were baptized Roman Catholics but remained unaffiliated and beyond the reach of clergy. He deliberately selected the south side of Washington Square for his church because the spot was surrounded by struggling Italian newcomers, yet "within reach of a most respectable and aristocratic neighborhood, from which it is hoped many will come to engage personally in Mission work."

To support his work at the Berean church, Judson had depended on wealthy Baptists and had come to know John D. Rockefeller, a fellow Baptist and generous contributor to Protestant causes. Rockefeller, then the nation's richest individual, had accumulated millions of dollars after seizing control of the oil industry in the aftermath of the 1873 crash. Based on mutual needs and respect, the friendship that developed between the pastor and the head of Standard Oil continued for over three decades. Judson often accompanied Rockefeller on his travels and was a frequent dinner guest at his house. Along with other Baptist clergymen benefiting from Rockefeller's largesse, Judson was able to overlook some of Standard Oil's harsh business practices and find righteousness in his patron's benevolent use of wealth. In 1887, when Judson began fund-raising efforts for the Memorial Church, his patron offered him a challenge grant: for every $50,000 raised, Rockefeller would contribute $15,000, with a cap of $40,000. Judson traveled tirelessly for two years, ultimately collecting $256,331. Exhausted and overwhelmed by his fund-raising responsibilities, he wrote to Rockefeller that it was "far more to my taste to build a *spiritual* house than one of brick and stone."

Between May and December of 1888, Judson and his wife acquired three and a half contiguous lots with houses on the south side of Washington Square. Once the tenants' leases expired, the houses on the property were leveled and ground was broken in 1890. The main part of the church was finished in April 1891. The building's design combines elements reminiscent of Roman basilicas and Italian Romanesque and Renaissance churches. Its richly articulated exterior, enhanced by a multistoried campanile, or bell tower, is composed of tawny-colored brick and pale terra-cotta trim. For the sanctuary interior, White enlisted Saint-Gaudens and John LaFarge, both of whom had collaborated with him in remodeling the Church of the Ascension on lower Fifth Avenue. Saint-Gaudens designed the Judson's marble panels and reliefs, as well as the gilded organ screen with freestanding angels guarding the pipes, considered to be one of the most magnificent of its kind in the country. LaFarge was responsible for the altar mural and the Renaissance-style stained glass windows portraying the full figures of saints and martyrs. The glowing, jewel-like colors of the fifteen-foot windows were fully restored in 1998.

Some may have wondered at Edward Judson's motives for adorning a missionary church with such costly art, but he was determined that his future congregation should receive the best in preaching, music, and architecture. "If I had my way, I would put the most beautiful churches among the homes of the poor, so that it would be only a step from the squalor of the tenement houses into a new and contrasted world," wrote the pastor. "The rich have beautiful objects in their homes. They should be content with plainness in church. But when we bring together the poor and the sad, let their eyes . . . find repose and inspiration in the exquisite arch, and the opalescent window, through which shimmer the suggestive figures of the saints and martyrs."

The new church welcomed all denominations and promptly assumed an activist stance, hosting community meetings on controversial subjects and offering a wide range of social welfare programs. One generous donor, Hiram Deats, contributed $40,000, of which $25,000 was earmarked for establishing a children's home on the lower floors of the bell tower. The church also offered classes, vocational training, a health center, and an employment bureau. Edward Judson initially counted on support for these activities to come from the prosperous neighbors north of the park, but their help never materialized. Rockefeller, however, continued to contribute about $3,000 a year. In addition, Judson expected to generate revenue, as other Baptist churches did then with some success, by running a hotel, a kind of lodging house adjacent to the church and integrated into its design.

When the church complex was complete, Judson leased the upper floors of the bell tower and the house immediately west of it to James Knott, "to be occupied only as an apartment and boarding house of the first class, principally for young men. . . . no liquor or intoxicating beverages allowed." According to the very specific terms of the lease, Knott was to furnish the premises "in a tasteful manner" for not less than $8,000; cover all the operating costs, and pay the church 75 percent of his profit after expenses.[25] Knott, accompanied by his wife and two young sons, moved into the Judson Hotel in 1894. He proved to be an adept manager. Within a few years he built the Holley Hotel, named after the nearby bust in the park and later remodeled into NYU's Hayden Hall on Washington Square West, and took over the Earle, now the Washington Square Hotel on Waverly Place, diagonally across from the northwest corner of the park. After Knott died in 1907, his sons William and David expanded the hotel chain to include thirty-four hostelries nationwide. Stock certificates for the Knott Hotel Corporation bore an engraving of Judson Memorial Church.[26]

Designated a city landmark in 1966, Judson Memorial was listed on the National Register of Historic Places in 1974. Its interior was restored a year later and the exterior was completely refurbished at the time of the church's centennial in 1990. The Judson Hotel in the tower was purchased by NYU in 1925 and converted eight years later into a dormitory called Judson Hall. In the 1990s, the Judson was reconfigured by the architect James Stewart Polshek into New York University's Juan Carlos I Center for Spanish Studies. Although its interior is entirely new, the exterior has been restored in accordance with Stanford White's original design.

The needs of the neighborhood must have been great in the late nineteenth century. Directly west of the Judson at 49–50 Washington Square South stood the Wetmore Home for Fallen and Friendless Women, founded by Apollo Wetmore in 1865 and relocated on the Square in 1881. The home sought to "protect young girls against temptation and to rescue them when they have been led astray." Over 3,000 young women and girls received shelter there before the Wetmore was torn down when Sullivan Street was cut through to the park in 1903. The Young Women's Christian Association had a similar mission. Founded as the "Ladies Christian Association of New York" in 1858 by well-born women living around the Square, the organization purchased 27 and 28 Washington Square North in 1868 to look after "the temporal, moral, and religious welfare of women, particularly young women dependent upon their own exertions for support." And in 1902, Greenwich House, dedicated to improving the health and welfare of immigrant families in the area, was established by Mary Kingsbury Simkhovitch according to her concepts of neighborhood settlement work.

NYU's Expansion

During the 1890s, the ubiquitous White was engaged in work for a third client on the Square. NYU was looking to move its undergraduate program to a more residential area, where there would be space for libraries, laboratories, residence halls, and playing fields. Graduate programs would stay at the Square. The university invited McKim, Mead & White to submit a proposal for their campus situated on the grounds of an estate in the Bronx, high above the Hudson. White's first suggestion was to move the University Building on the Square stone by stone to the new location, a process calculated to cost many times more than erecting a new structure. The architect then designed a symmetrical layout of dormitories, classrooms, and a colonnaded pavilion, which had as its centerpiece a library in the form of a classic basilica. Construction of the University Heights campus was completed in 1899.

While work on the Bronx campus was progressing, the school expected to renovate the University Building, which had been suffering from leaks and other structural problems for many years. Drawings by McKim, Mead & White, dated March 1893 and rediscovered in 1996, indicate detailed plans for redoing the old neo-Gothic edifice. But the cost, estimated at $250,000 or more, was judged excessive.[27] Believing that the money would be better spent constructing four or five new buildings uptown, the trustees ordered the sixty-year old university building, previously compared to Oxford and Cambridge and so proudly displayed to the visiting Prince Albert, to be torn down. As demolition began on May 21, 1894, students, former students and onlookers carried off souvenir chunks of masonry, keys, and pipes from the chapel's organ. Today, the one vestige of the original Gothic Revival structure is Founders' Memorial, a towering composite sculpture standing in the plaza immediately east of Bobst Library on Washington Square South. Fashioned from pieces of the old University Building's Gothic Revival façade, the memorial was dedicated at University Heights in 1894 and rededicated at Washington Square in 1973 after the uptown campus was closed.

NYU replaced the University Building with a new ten-story structure designed to house a commercial business on several of the floors. University trustees accepted the American Book Co. as a long-term tenant and, in March 1894, approved a design by Alfred Zucker, a German-born architect who had built a number of nearby industrial lofts. The American Book Co. was to occupy the lower seven floors of the new building, and the university's graduate and professional schools would reside in the upper three. While the building was under construction, classes continued in a small wooden shack tucked amid the pillars and girders of the new structure. During the bitter winter of 1894–95, law students complained about the unbearable classroom temperatures.

Zucker's design for the Main Building, faced in light-colored stone, brick, and terra-cotta trim, was intended to correspond to the McKim, Mead & White architecture of the University Heights campus. The architect also strove to incorporate elements that would harmonize with the classicism of the Arch and the Greek Revival Row on the Square. Following the tripartite division common to façades of commercial buildings of the time, Zucker established a sturdy base on the first two stories using thick, fluted Doric columns. The five stories of the central section are plainer in design, featuring paired windows with little decoration. On the upper level, a deep recession with four pairs of freestanding Ionic columns interrupts the flat façade to distinguish the three floors reserved for the university. Two pediments rise above the roof line. The university's motto: "Perstando et Praestando Utilitati" (Striving and Excellence in Useful Pursuits) was originally displayed below the cornice.

The second Gothic Revival landmark torn down in the 1890s was the South Dutch Reformed Church on Washington Square East, built by Minard Lafever in 1839–40. After many of its congregants had moved away, swept along in the uptown migration of wealth, the congregation disbanded, and in 1876 the building and land were sold to the Asbury Methodist Church, formerly of Greene Street. In 1893, the Asbury congregation merged with the Washington Square United Methodist Church across the park on West Fourth Street. Two years later, Lafever's gem on the Square, cited in the *New York Times* in 1881 as "one of the most perfect Gothic structures in the United States," was demolished. In its place arose a warehouse, acquired by NYU in 1925 and named Pless Hall.

The six-story Benedick, built in 1879 and home to White's coterie, remains standing on Washington Square East. Next to it is another commercial loft—the Celluloid Building, now NYU's Paulette Goddard Hall, at the south end of the block. By the end of the 1890s, the once-tranquil residential streets around Henry James's birthplace east of the Square had yielded almost entirely to warehouses or factories bulging with immigrant workers in sweatshops. These commercial lofts, many of which were designed by Alfred Zucker, exhibited elements similar to those employed on the university's Main Building. As NYU gradually acquired these second-growth loft buildings and adapted them for academic use in the early twentieth century, the downtown campus achieved a distinctly urban harmony.

Of Gold Bugs and Butterflies: More Parades through the Park

The changes along the park's perimeter contributed to Washington Square's shift from a predominantly residential enclave to a place of mixed use. With the added focus of the Arch, it gained appeal as a gathering place and became a frequent rallying point for parades and demonstrations. One of the most unusual events to pass by was the "sound money" parade on October 31, 1896. Known officially as the Business Men's March, it was organized to protest the free-silver platform of the Democratic presidential candidate, William Jennings Bryan. The free-silver movement, supported by Populists, Democrats, Nevada silver-mining interests, and indebted farmers of the South and West, proposed unlimited coinage of silver. This would allow borrowers to pay back debts with inflated silver dollars worth intrinsically less than gold dollars. Firmly opposed to such policy, New York's conservative business interests backed Republican William McKinley, whose advocacy of the gold standard and a protective tariff won him the election that year.

Hamilton Fish Armstrong, then a young boy living on Tenth Street off Fifth, described the event as a dull occasion in his memoirs, *Those Days:* "Businessmen, merchants, stockbrokers, clerks and college students have been gathering downtown since noon and are now moving north from Washington Square, line after line, hour after hour, uninterested-looking citizens in ordinary clothes with only a very occasional band for diversion." But daily papers reported the event with customary hyperbole. "Never before in the world's history have so many citizens in time of peace in any country rallied to march under their country's flag," trumpeted the *New York Times.* More than a hundred thousand marchers filled the streets on the three-mile route between the Battery and Fortieth Street as three-quarters of a million spectators looked on. Wealthy merchants and heads of financial institutions marched side by side with clerks and assistants and representatives of every trade and profession—scholars and journalists, publishers and advertisers, hatters, cloak makers, saddlery and hardware dealers. Many of the paraders and onlookers carried yellow chrysanthemums, a symbol of the cause, and sported a variety of gold badges, the most popular of which were in the shape of an insect called the "gold bug."

Perhaps the most spectacular feature of the day was a kite show over Washington Square arranged by Gilbert T. Woglom, a member of the Jewelers' Sound Money Club. From a vantage point in the Judson tower, Woglom floated three pilot kites in red, white, and blue, followed by a string of bright gold ones. After the kites reached a height of about 3,000 feet, he attached a twelve-foot golden silk flag to the line and let it out until it was suspended almost directly over the Arch. Hidden within the gold silk were hundreds of tiny flags. As the jewelers' division approached the Arch, the gold banner unfurled and the flags fluttered toward earth. The display glittering in the sun was visible far up Fifth Avenue.[28]

Three years later on September 29, 1899, a bright day when the air over Fifth Avenue was unexpectedly filled with butterflies, a full-scale military parade marched down Fifth Avenue in honor of Admiral George Dewey, hero of the Spanish-American War. Following Spain's declaration of war on the United States in the spring of 1898, Dewey led the American navy to a spectacular victory over the Spanish fleet in the Philippines. The conflict then spread to Cuba, where the young Theodore Roosevelt and his Rough Riders charged up San Juan Hill, helping free the island from Spanish dominion and adding to the future president's mythology. Intense nationalism, stirred to a feverish pitch by the sensationalist "yellow journalism" of American newspapers, furthered the cause of the war and made heroes of Dewey and Roosevelt, who was elected New York's governor in the fall of 1898. As a result of the short-lived war, the Spanish empire dissolved and the United States emerged as an international power, with overseas protectorates including Guam, the Philippines, Puerto Rico, and Cuba.

The centerpiece of the three-day Dewey celebration was an enormous arch, a temporary wood and plaster confection erected for the occasion near Madison Square at Fifth Avenue and Twenty-third Street. Troops paraded through the Dewey arch and past its four pairs of victory columns, continuing down Fifth Avenue to Washington Square, where thousands of viewers filled the roadways and formed a thick circle on the stone rim of the fountain. Younger spectators claimed places in the trees. From a position near the Arch, Governor

Roosevelt on horseback reviewed the New York troops. At the end of the day, he rode off with his old squadron.[29]

Following the example of the successful Washington Memorial Arch, the committee that had organized the Dewey event sought to make their temporary monument a permanent one and opened a subscription list for donations. But the admiral's hold on the public imagination could not compare to George Washington's or Teddy Roosevelt's. Dewey's popularity waned, and after he failed to win the Democratic nomination, subscriptions ceased. Plans to build a permanent arch for Dewey were abandoned, and in December 1900, the plaster model for the arch at Madison Square was carried off to the city dump.

Final Statuary for the Arch

The example of Dewey's failed arch must have nagged at the Arch Committee. Although officially the Washington Arch belonged to the Parks Department, the committee had pledged to complete the monument and felt responsible for the pedestal statues that were still lacking. As far back as 1893, Stewart had asked White to see about groups for the pedestals. The design should be pushed, he wrote prophetically, "or we will be old men or dead before the groups are finished."[30] White requested that MacMonnies be commissioned to do the pedestal figures. After viewing photos of his plaster models for the statuary in 1896, the committee approved the designs and recommended raising an additional $35,000 to pay for the sculpture.

It would take another twenty years until the statuary was complete. William Stewart tried to obtain half the sum for one group, but the country was experiencing an economic downturn in the mid 1890s, and donations were meager. Furthermore, MacMonnies was involved with the sculptural groups for the Soldiers' and Sailors' Monument in Brooklyn. Not until 1913 was enough money accumulated to undertake the pedestal sculpture. By then Stanford White was dead, and William Kendall of McKim, Mead & White was overseeing work on the Arch. MacMonnies, far away in France and lacking White to plead his case, lost favor and his commission was cancelled. At Kendall's recommendation, contracts were extended instead to two other well-known sculptors: Herman Atkins MacNeil, famous for statues of American Indians (and for designing the Liberty quarter for the U.S. Mint), and Alexander Stirling Calder.

MacNeil's contract for the east pedestal, signed on June 25, 1913, specified a group of figures in high relief around a central statue of Washington in War. Carved from a block of Dover marble quarried south of Poughkeepsie, New York, the figure of Washington as general in chief of the Continental Army stands twelve feet eight inches high and reportedly weighs sixteen tons. For reasons that are not clear—perhaps a large enough block of marble was not available—the relief figures behind Washington were carved from a slab of Georgian marble slightly different in color from the Dover stone used for the general. Installation of the enormous statuary proceeded slowly and ran behind schedule, forcing a delay in the unveiling until sunset on Monday evening, May 30, 1916, when Stewart pulled away the red, white, and blue cloth covering the sculpture.[31]

Standing among the group gathered for the unveiling of MacNeil's work was A. Stirling Calder, who had just signed a contract to do the statuary for the west pedestal. His sculpture of Washington in Peace accompanied by relief figures of Wisdom and Justice was completed two years later. Calder was a member of a distinguished family of sculptors. His father, Alexander Milne Calder, created the statues on Philadelphia's City Hall, including the building's crowning thirty-seven-foot landmark figure of William Penn. His son, a sculptor of the same name, is best known as the inventor of the mobile. Work on Calder's marble group was progressing when the United States entered the war in Europe. As might be expected, the installation of the statuary was a more subdued event than previous ceremonies related to the Arch.

While preparing for the installation of Calder's sculpture that winter, those involved with the Arch were discouraged to see how the relatively young monument, just over twenty years old, was visibly deteriorating as a result of water damage. When the Arch was first cleaned in 1892 to remove the stains left by the wooden scaffolding, the ever-vigilant Stewart had informed White that the top was not draining properly and water was falling from a pipe in the keystone. The water problem was never adequately resolved. Two decades later, in May 1914, Parks Commissioner Cabot Ward wrote to McKim, Mead & White seeking recommendations on how to alleviate the leakage problem found throughout the Arch.

When MacNeil's pedestal group was installed in 1916, Stewart and others noticed that the roof was still leaking and all the exterior marble work required repointing. It was also evident that the stone chosen for the pedestal figures differed in color from the Arch's masonry, an unfortunate disparity aggravated by the monument's water-stained surface. Days before the first pedestal statues were unveiled, McKim, Mead & White complained to the Parks Department that what was "originally erected as a marble arch . . . has lost all resemblance to any such thing. You are probably aware that a group of figures are about to be set on the northeast pedestal and they will simply serve now to emphasize the dirty condition of this arch." Efforts to obtain a small appropriation from the city failed.

Two years later, when Calder's sculpture was about to be installed, the Arch Committee, advised by McKim, Mead & White, again pleaded with city officials to attend to the monument. Conditions were alarming. Several inches of water had leaked through the roof and collected in the large interior room over the Arch's span. Low winter temperatures had caused the water to freeze, but when that interior ice melted in the spring, warned the Committee, it would leak through and damage the Arch even more. Stewart and his group recommended that the monument be cleaned to unify its color with the marble of the new pedestal figures and filed a request to the Board of Estimates, asking that about $3,500 be allocated for preserving the Washington Arch.[32] During the exceptionally cold winter of 1917–18, snow and ice did accumulate on the roof and leaked as predicted, hanging in great icicles from the stonework. The city made only minimal repairs. Instead of taking up the tiles and relaying them, as should have been done, workers applied a coat of cement to prevent leakage.

Water damage continued to plague the Arch. In 1997–98, with federal funding, the city ordered a thorough study and attempted to stabilize conditions to prevent further damage. The Arch received a new roof and was entirely repointed, but only the lower sections of the piers were cleaned. While doing the work, conservators discovered that the individually carved rosette panels on the arch ceiling (directly under the room flooded eighty years before) were crumbling away. Other areas of decorative carving were also endangered. Both statues of Washington had suffered over the years, and remedies such as the sandblasting of the 1960s had unintentionally caused more harm by removing the outer layer of the sculpted marble. President Washington's pockmarked face on the west pedestal was one of the sad results.[33] Nearly $3 million in funding from public and private sources has finally enabled the Arch to be restored beginning in 2002. In addition to stabilizing the interior structure, the fragile exterior marble and decorative panels will be conserved and the statues of Washington restored.

Stanford White did not live to witness the monument's deterioration, nor did he even see the Washington Arch complete with all its statuary. By the turn of the century, his health was failing—he had been diagnosed with renal disease in the 1890s—and his lavish lifestyle had sent him deep into debt. In 1905, when he was fifty-two, he was

203

forced to relinquish his partnership in McKim, Mead & White, and William Kendall took over supervision of the Arch. A year later, on June 25, 1906, at Madison Square Garden, White was shot and killed in a jealous rage by Harry Thaw, who suspected him of having had an affair with a young chorus girl, Evelyn Nesbit, before she married Thaw. After a sensational trial, Thaw was sent to a mental institution, but he was later freed. Eclipsed by his reputation as a notorious playboy, Stanford White's standing as an architect and designer suffered for decades.

A Courthouse for the Square

At the turn of the century, the Square with its new Arch was a favored subject of artists and photographers, but it did not seem to garner much respect from other quarters. In January 1909, the city's Courthouse Board recommended Washington Square as the site for a new courthouse, claiming that the City Hall area was too crowded for any more construction. District Supreme Court Justice Samuel Greenberg gave his full support. Washington Square was "peculiarly well-adapted" for such a purpose, he wrote. "With space added to the existing park as law requires, the building could be erected within the park, affording a maximum of light, air and quiet."[34] He made no mention of how a court might affect the park, its users, or the surrounding neighborhood. Members of the New York County Lawyers Association opposed the proposed location, not out of concern for Washington Square's well-being, however, but on grounds of convenience. They preferred that a new courthouse be close to the existing courts and municipal buildings around City Hall, where they frequently had to conduct business.

Other parties chimed in with their objections. On behalf of the community, the Washington Square Association—the earliest neighborhood civic organization in the city, founded in 1906—vigorously protested what its members considered an "invasion of Washington

Square by the City."[35] Devoted to maintaining the desirable character of the neighborhood, the Association included affluent local residents, members of the original Arch Committee, and offspring of the Rhinelander, Delano, Schermerhorn, and other "old money" families living between the Square and Fourteenth Street.

The *New York Times* objected to the courthouse as well. "Washington Square, which is now a very useful playground and place of recreation, would be totally changed," it editorialized on January 21, 1909. "The Washington Arch, in which the people of New York take a good deal of pride, would be dwarfed and robbed of its dignity and effect." The newspaper recommended Union Square as an alternative, but the courthouse was eventually constructed near City Hall, where the lawyers had wanted it to be all along. While only a blip in the annals of the Square, the courthouse incident, reminiscent of the armory proposal of the 1870s, gains significance in light of later assaults on the park's integrity. Like other "improvements" proposed for the park by "outsiders" and defeated by the community, the courthouse, if successful, could have obliterated historic Washington Square.

Those who advocated building a courthouse in the Square believing its atmosphere would "encourage the calm, quiet, deliberate administration of justice," as one judge wrote, could not have seen the park on a normal day. Densely populated by a cross-section of the city's population, the Square exhibited the extremes of urban vitality and variety. Walter Prichard Eaton, writing in the *Atlantic Monthly* of July 1909, described the shrill cries of ragged children playing at the fountain and the sounds of a hurdy-gurdy floating up to his room on Washington Square East. From his perch on the sixth floor of the Benedick, he observed the ring of yellow tulips at the fountain, and the curve of asphalt around it roped off into a skating rink. Neatly attired nursemaids sat on benches next to "sad wrecks of the under-world" waiting for the Bread Line, while nearby, he wrote, "a young man richly dressed sat scribbling on his knee with a gold pencil. . . . And everywhere, on walks and asphalt, the children swarmed, skating, playing strange, half-remembered games with chalk-marks, shouting, falling down." At certain hours, a corner of the Square would fill with "a mighty river of sweat-shop workers . . . both men and girls pathetically under-sized, foreign, babbling in a dozen tongues." And at night, while men and women slept "behind those red-brick aristocratic fronts that line the Square, on the benches, under the lamps and the vivid-green leaves, like stage foliage, more men are sleeping."

The jarring inequalities of city life were in stark evidence at the end of September 1909, two months after Eaton's piece appeared in the *Atlantic.* Barely a half-block from the Square, a major labor battle was brewing. Yet there in the park, if any of the homeless seeking refuge at night cared to look up, was the Washington Arch, dramatically lit for the Hudson-Fulton celebration. Once again New York was observing an anniversary, this time a double one to commemorate two men whose achievements were fundamental to the city's development. New York's Dutch foundation was due to Henry Hudson's exploration of the harbor and eponymous river, and the city was indebted for its economic prosperity to Robert Fulton's invention of the steamboat. In 1609, Hudson, an English explorer searching for the fabled North West Passage on behalf of the Dutch East India Company, had entered the harbor on his ship the *Halve Maen* ("Half Moon"). In 1807, two hundred years after Hudson's voyage, Fulton successfully launched his steamboat the *Clermont* on the river named for the explorer. Throughout the last week of September 1909, there were naval processions, parades, fireworks, and trial airplane flights by the pioneer aviators Orville Wright and Glenn Curtiss. Streets and monuments were illuminated as never before. The entire length of Fifth Avenue was strung with lights, and closing the vista at the avenue's southern end stood the Washington Arch, silhouetted as if by magic with thousands of Thomas Edison's new light bulbs.

The Triangle Fire:
"If the Union Had Won, We Would Have Been Safe"

On September 28, 1909, while the Hudson-Fulton revelry was in full swing, two hundred young immigrant women, mostly Jewish and Italian, went out on strike. They were protesting the working conditions at the Triangle Shirtwaist Co. located in the Asch building on Washington Place, just behind NYU's new Main Building. The strikers would have been among the "mighty river of sweat-shop workers" whom Eaton observed passing through the park, "pathetically undersized, babbling in a dozen tongues." Emboldened by a speech by the American Federation of Labor leader Samuel Gompers at nearby Cooper Union, Triangle workers had voted to strike, and their action soon spread to all the shirtwaist shops in the city, involving 15,000 female workers—the largest strike by women up to that time. With amazement, followed by newfound respect, news reporters relayed the impressive courage of the women strikers, who donned their best clothes and withstood the threats of hecklers to march on the picket lines. When police arrested the strikers and brought them before the magistrate in the Jefferson Market Court on Sixth Avenue and Ninth Street, wealthy society women who supported labor and women's suffrage were there to provide bail, led by the indomitable Mrs. August Belmont. After thirteen weeks, the International Ladies' Garment Workers' Union Local 25 signed contracts with 354 firms for a shorter work week of fifty-two hours, a 12–15 percent wage increase, and improved physical conditions. At the beginning of February, the women finally returned to work. But even then Triangle refused to recognize the union or meet the workers' demands.

A little more than a year later, on Saturday, March 25, 1911, a fire broke out at the Triangle Shirtwaist Factory shortly before closing time. As was customary in this shop, the owners, Max Blanck and Isaac

Harris, had locked their six hundred workers in the densely packed workrooms to prevent latecomers from slipping in or anyone from leaving early. Although the building was technically fireproof, the fire rapidly spread through the highly flammable cotton shirts hanging in rows over the workers' heads. Within minutes, the top floors of the building were engulfed in flames. Young women and men started jumping from the ninth floor windows. William Gunn Shepherd, a young reporter for the United Press, happened to be crossing the Square at the time. The only newsman on the scene, he found a telephone and dictated his story to his city editor in the *World* building downtown. Shepherd counted the thuds of sixty-two falling bodies before the first fire engine came around the turn. Fire company ladders reached only to the sixth floor and were useless in evacuating those stranded on the higher floors. Some workers on the top floors came down in the elevator, but its rails quickly melted from the heat. Others used the one exterior fire escape, which soon crumpled from the excessive weight.

Frank Sommer lecturing to fifty law students on the tenth floor of NYU's Main Building next to the factory heard the alarms and saw the fire. He and his students found ladders left by painters on the roof and quickly arranged them to reach the roof of the Triangle building ten feet below. Forming a line along the ladders, NYU students assisted the frantic workers to safety. The fire was brought under control in eighteen minutes and all over in a half hour. By then, 146 young men and women, mostly between sixteen and twenty-three years old, were dead; more died the next day.

As word of the fire spread, thousands of friends and relatives poured into Washington Square hoping to find their loved ones alive. By seven o'clock on Saturday evening, there were twenty thousand people in the area. Family members broke through the police lines on the east side of the Square to search among the charred bodies piled in mounds, recognizing daughters by a burned fragment of skirt or a familiar bit of jewelry. It had been payday. Some of the dead were identified only by the pay envelopes found in their pockets or clutched hands.

On Sunday morning, the crowds of people descending on the Asch building were pushed back by the police and settled in for the day on Washington Square. If he had not known better, observed a reporter in the *New York Tribune* on Monday, March 27, "the general atmosphere was that of a country circus or Vanity Fair." Every place of vantage from which any angle of the burned building could be seen was occupied. Gaily dressed people, men in top hats, stepped off the Fifth Avenue double-decker buses. At an intersection of footpaths, a vendor of ice cream tinkled a small bell and extolled the virtues of his stock. Hawkers who overnight had assembled and packaged a stock of penny rings, glass jewelry, and other trinkets, plied their wares: "Souvenirs of the big fire! Get a dead girl's earrings!"[36]

Throughout the following week, families buried their dead. On Wednesday, April 5, the city buried the seven unidentified victims of the fire. Union groups organized a citywide parade, specifying no bands, no banners, no propaganda signs, only union banners draped in black. Two divisions of the procession were to convene at Washington Square, one starting from Twenty-second Street and the other from the lower East Side. Rain was falling heavily, thoroughly drenching the mourners. Silently, the somber march continued until the two masses of city's workers entered the park. When they came within sight of the Asch building, there was "a long-drawn-out, heart piercing cry, the mingling of thousands of voices, a sort of human thunder in the elemental storm—a cry that was perhaps the most impressive expression of human grief ever heard in this city." From three o'clock in the afternoon until six in the evening, rain fell relentlessly while a steady stream of mourners marching eight abreast passed under the Arch. The nameless victims of the Triangle Fire were buried at Evergreen cemetery in Queens.

"If union had won, we would have been safe," Rose Safran, a Triangle factory worker, said. "Two of our demands were for adequate fire escapes and for open doors from the factories to the street. But the bosses defeated us and we didn't get the open doors or the better fire escapes. So our friends are dead."[37]

In the wake of the fire, the city established a Bureau of Fire Investigation to inspect safety standards, and the New York State legislature created a Factory Investigating Commission chaired by two Tammany men, State Senator Robert Wagner Sr., assisted by Alfred E. Smith. Both men would go on to have distinguished political careers: Wagner would become a U.S. senator and leading spokesman for the New Deal, and Al Smith would be elected New York's governor in 1918, the first Catholic in the country to achieve a gubernatorial position. Samuel Gompers and Mary Dreier, president of the Women's Trade Union League, also served on the Factory Commission. As a result of the commission's work, between 1912 and 1914 New York State passed thirty-three new labor laws, which formed the basis for the state's progressive Industrial Code. With meager funding for investigators, however, the laws were not well enforced, and sweatshop conditions persist in many places to this day.

The fire made a profound impression on Frances Perkins, a young woman who happened to be visiting friends on the other side of the park that Saturday. She had rushed out at the sound of fire engines and seen the employees jumping. "I shall never forget the frozen horror which came over us . . . watching that horrible sight, knowing that there was no help."[38] Perkins, a consumer advocate, later volunteered as executive secretary of the Factory Investigating Commission. In 1932, President Franklin Delano Roosevelt appointed her secretary of labor, the first woman to hold a cabinet position. Perkins believed that the stirring up of public conscience after the Triangle Fire was a formative experience that contributed to the realization of Roosevelt's New Deal.

Blanck and Harris, owners of the Triangle Shirtwaist Company, were accused of ignoring their employees' safety and indicted for manslaughter. After a three-week trial, they were acquitted. Fiorello La Guardia, then a lawyer in private practice and later a congressman and mayor of New York, represented the Triangle victims' families in a suit against the factory owners. In 1914, a judge ordered Blanck and Harris to pay the families who had sued—only twenty-three in all—a mere $75 for each employee who died.[39] The exterior of the Asch building showed hardly any signs of the disaster because of its fireproof construction. It continued to function as a factory until 1929, at which time NYU purchased the building and renamed it after their donor, Frederick Brown, a realtor. The Brown Building, now used for science classrooms, laboratories, and offices, bears two plaques on its façade. One, dated 1991, cites the facts of the fire and designates the building a National Historic Landmark. The other, presented by the International Ladies' Garment Workers Union, is a memorial to the workers who lost their lives: "Out of their martyrdom came new concepts of social responsibility and labor legislation that have helped make American working conditions the finest in the world."

The Triangle Fire marks a nadir in Washington Square's history when all the pressures intensifying through the nineteenth century— immigration, economic and ethnic inequities, exploitation of labor— resulted in a tragic outcome. Yet just then the Square undergoes another kind of upheaval and pulls out of its seemingly irretrievable decline to make a comeback. Revitalized not by any physical change this time but by one of spirit, Washington Square shortly assumes new life as the heart of a creative and progressive community known around the world.

A NEW CITY PARK TAKES SHAPE

Labor Day Parade, 1912. Brown Brothers, Sterling, Pennsylvania

With memories of the 1911 Triangle Fire still fresh, 20,000 workers—a quarter of them women—marched briskly down Fifth Avenue to Washington Square in the Labor Day Parade of September 2, 1912. Many of the women marchers wore fitted, tucked-front blouses like those manufactured by the Triangle Shirtwaist Company. Copied from a style worn by wealthier women, the white shirtwaists and simple long skirts had become the working woman's uniform and a symbol of female independence, reflecting the alliance of the labor and suffrage movements. Both causes were taken up by a coalition encompassing downtown radicals as well as uptown society women. Their efforts through the 1910s culminated in the passage of the Nineteenth Amendment to the U.S. Constitution guaranteeing women the right to vote in 1920.

William Glackens, *A Spring Morning in Washington Square, New York*. Charcoal and gouache, ca. 1910. Collection of Mr. and Mrs. Arthur G. Altschul

Omnibuses, motorcars, carriages, horses, policemen, and mischievous children vie for the viewer's attention in Glacken's lively portrayal of the Square. The picture, full of narrative detail, was reproduced on the cover of *Collier's* on April 16, 1910, where it would have reached a wide audience and contributed to Washington Square's growing reputation around the country.

Glackens made many drawings and paintings of the park viewed from his studio on Washington Square South. His interest in depicting contemporary city life was shared by a small circle of his colleagues known as The Eight—George Bellows, Arthur B. Davies, Ernest Lawson, George Luks, Maurice Prendergast, Everett Shinn, and John Sloan, most of whom lived on or close to Washington Square. After some of their work had been rejected by the National Academy, the group came together and organized an exhibition of their own. Davies, Glackens, Sloan, and their cohorts also helped arrange the Armory Show of 1913, the international art exhibition that first introduced the work of Picasso, Matisse, and other European modernists to a stunned American public.

FARE TEN CENTS

John Sloan, *Arch Conspirators.* Etching, 1917. Private collection

Sloan's etching commemorates an evening escapade when this small band climbed the internal stair of the Arch to stage a "revolution." After calling on President Wilson to recognize the "Free and Independent Republic of Washington Square," the group pledged themselves to serve the State of Greenwich and drank to her prosperity. Sloan depicts himself at the right, and the French artist Marcel Duchamp is shown standing at the left, eating a sandwich. Both Duchamp and the seated figure next to him are leaning against the low, domed structure that covered the stairway. Beyond the parapet are the rooftops and houses of lower Fifth Avenue.

The 1917 declaration of the Republic of Washington Square was, in fact, preceded by a similar effort years earlier, organized by Ellis O. Jones, an editor of *The Masses.* In 1913, Jones and some friends intended to proclaim Washington Square a free republic. Believing that the park would be too small for the large turnout anticipated, they announced that their revolution would take place uptown on the Mall in Central Park. On the designated day, there were heavy rainstorms, and only Ellis and a few friends showed up, to be met by vanloads of police.

Jesse Tarbox Beals, *Grace Godwin's Garret and the Oasis of Washington Square*. Photograph, ca. 1917–18. Collection of the New-York Historical Society (# 58128)

218

The corner house, now demolished, was at one time the grave digger's residence at the potter's field. In the early 1900s, it was occupied by a popular ice-cream and soda shop on the ground floor and, for a while, by Bruno's Garret on the second floor. By the time this photograph was taken, Bruno was gone, and Grace Godwin, visible in the second-story window, had taken over the upstairs. Godwin added window boxes and served breakfast, afternoon tea, and after-dinner coffee. Several similarly independent women ran establishments along Washington Square South. At 60 Washington Square, Marian Powys presided over the Devonshire Lace Shop, where she demonstrated techniques and offered lace of all kinds, from simple collars and caps to the most exquisite museum pieces. Further along the street, Alice Palmer ran the Village Store, a basement-level craft shop where visitors could browse, take refreshments and warm themselves by the fireplace. Similar shops, teahouses, and restaurants, many operated solely by women, dotted the streets of the Village.

The photographer Jessie Tarbox Beals managed to earn a living from her art by reprinting images like this one on postcards, which she sold as tourist souvenirs. After moving to California in the late 1920s, Beals expressed her lingering affection for the city and the Village in a poem that concluded: "I'd give all California's damn flowers / For the sight of Washington Square."

Evolution of a Speakeasy: Speako de Luxe. Barney Gallant's, 19 Washington Square North, 1933. Lithograph by Joseph Webster Golinken. Museum of the City of New York

During Prohibition, speakeasies, cabarets, and clubs in Greenwich Village provided alcoholic beverages to an eager clientele from all over the city and beyond. Barney Gallant, one of the colorful figures of this era, first opened a speakeasy on the south side of the park at 40 Washington Square. He then started a place around the corner at 85 West Third Street, where Edgar Allan Poe had briefly resided, and finally established Speako de Luxe at 19 Washington Square North, next door to the venerable dwelling built by Henry James's grandmother. Gallant's posh speakeasy attracted well-heeled clients who could afford his steep prices—$16 for a bottle of Scotch, $25 for champagne.

Only a few years before becoming a speakeasy, 19 Washington Square had been the scene of a bold crime. In 1922, the family of the house were locked in their wine cellar while a burglar escaped with loot worth $80,000.

Washington Square West. Photograph, September 8, 1905. Collection of the New-York Historical Society (# 20962)

On the west side of the park at the corner of Washington Place stood the Hicks-Lord house, built for James W. Alsop in 1851 and named after a later occupant, the aspiring hostess Annette Hicks-Lord, who made the house a center of city social life. The widowed Mrs. Hicks caused a sensation in New York society when she married Thomas Lord on the last day of 1877. Her groom, aged eighty-three, was one of the wealthiest retired merchants in the city, heir to $6 or $8 million. She gave her age at the time of her marriage as forty-eight. Before World War 1, the Hicks-Lord house was headquarters for Teddy Roosevelt's short-lived Bull Moose party. In 1925, the Hicks-Lord house was replaced by a fifteen-story apartment house, the first tall building to be erected on the Square's perimeter.

Washington Square West. Photograph, 1962. New York University Archives

The west side of the park has been lined with tall residential apartment houses since the 1920s. The relatively low building on the left was originally the Holley Hotel, built by the Knott family, who ran the hotel associated with Judson Church. The Holley, named for the nearby memorial statue in the park, with the taller Holley Chambers to the right, was purchased by New York University, remodeled as a residence for law students and later converted to a dormitory for undergraduates. To the right, on the north, stands 29 Washington Square West, where Eleanor Roosevelt lived for several years. Both it and No. 37 on the southernmost corner belong to the university and house senior members of the faculty and administration.

Fountain with Children Swimming. Photograph, 1930s. New York University Archives

When the fountain was repaired in 1934, the Parks Department added four concrete steps around the inside of the stone rim. The steps strengthened the fountain's structure and allowed access to the shallow pool of water that collected to a depth of sixteen inches. Photos from the mid 1930s show children happily splashing in it. Nowadays, people may splash their feet in the shallow water of the basin when the fountain is on. After NYU's graduation ceremonies in the park, students sometimes jump in, but officially there is no swimming allowed.

Thomas Hart Benton, *The Artists' Show, Washington Square Park*. Oil and tempera on canvas, 1946. Gift of Jerome K. Ohrbach. Courtesy of the Herbert F. Johnson Museum of Art, Cornell University

Begun during the Depression as a way to help artists sell their work, the semi-annual outdoor art show continues to draw crowds to Washington Square every May and September. During the first Washington Square Outdoor Art Exhibit, held May 28 to June 5, 1932, participating artists sold 1,698 pictures and received orders for more. Following on that success, a second exhibition with three hundred artists was held the following November. Sales totaled nearly $10,000 that first year. Over time, the show extended be-

yond the perimeter of the park to streets north and south of the Square, from Bleecker up to Twelfth Street. Artists are now selected by jury and pay a fee to exhibit.

Thomas Hart Benton, who painted this scene, is usually identified as a Regionalist artist for his images of rural or small-town America, but from 1912 to 1935, he spent most of his time painting and teaching in New York City and lived near the Square for a while. (This painting was, however, completed in Kansas City.) Benton's most famous pupil was Jackson Pollock, who worked from 1938 to 1941 for the Federal Art Project, a New Deal initiative to keep artists employed. For many years, Pollock lived on East Eighth Street, about two blocks from the park.

Passengers Waiting for Buses in Washington Square. Photograph, ca. 1930s. Collection of the New-York Historical Society (# 58649)

Before traffic was eliminated from the park, passengers would line up west of the fountain for the double-decker buses of the Fifth Avenue Coach Company. Washington Square, the last stop on the line, was the turnaround for buses heading back up Fifth Avenue to 110th Street. Fifth Avenue traffic ran two ways until 1966. After other vehicular traffic was prohibited from driving through the Square in 1958, buses continued to use the park as a terminal until they were completely banned in 1963. Since then, Fifth Avenue buses have turned east on Eighth Street before heading uptown.

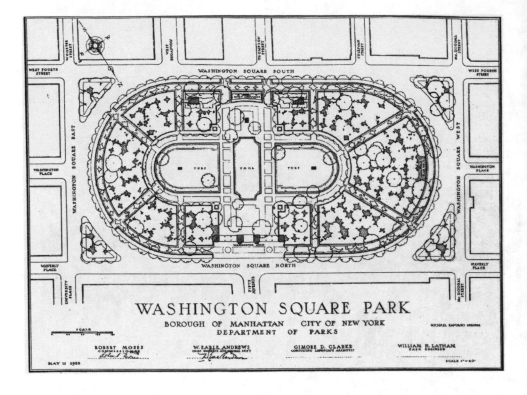

WASHINGTON SQUARE PARK

BOROUGH OF MANHATTAN   CITY OF NEW YORK
DEPARTMENT OF PARKS

(a) Plan for Washington Square Park by Gilmore Clarke and Michael Rapuano, 1935; (b) plan with Two Depressed Roadways and Bridge, 1958. New York City Parks & Recreation Map File

Robert Moses' first proposal for redoing Washington Square completely eradicated all traces of the 1870 design and imposed a formal symmetry on the landscape. The fountain was to be replaced by an ornamental pool, and triangular islands at the corners, lopped off from the rest of the grounds, were to be used for boarding and exiting from buses. Successive proposals eliminated the fountain, straightened the roads, and added space for bus turnarounds in the park. Finally, in 1958, the city recommended that two depressed roads, each twenty-four feet wide and separated by a narrow mall, be cut through the Square with a pedestrian overpass linking the two sides of the park. Decades of resistance by Villagers eventually

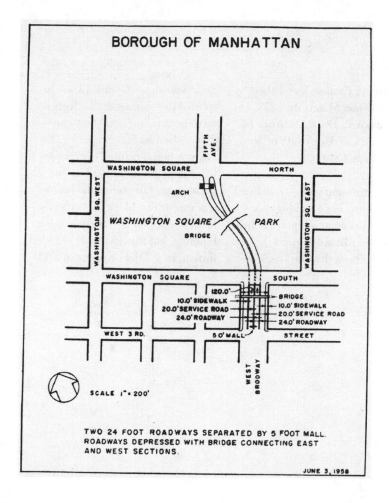

BOROUGH OF MANHATTAN

WASHINGTON SQUARE NORTH

FIFTH AVE.

ARCH

WASHINGTON SQUARE PARK

BRIDGE

WASHINGTON SQ. WEST

WASHINGTON SQ. EAST

WASHINGTON SQUARE SOUTH

120.0'
10.0' SIDEWALK
20.0' SERVICE ROAD
24.0' ROADWAY

BRIDGE
10.0' SIDEWALK
20.0' SERVICE ROAD
24.0' ROADWAY

WEST 3 RD.

50' MALL

STREET

WEST BRODWAY

SCALE 1" = 200'

TWO 24 FOOT ROADWAYS SEPARATED BY 5 FOOT MALL.
ROADWAYS DEPRESSED WITH BRIDGE CONNECTING EAST
AND WEST SECTIONS.

JUNE 3, 1958

wore down Moses and other city officials. The park design was left unchanged until the community-planned renovation of 1970. "Nowhere was opposition to change so vociferous as in the rehabilitation and reconstruction of the older Squares . . . notably at Washington Square," Moses wrote in his 1956 book *Working for the People: Promise and Performance in Public Service.* "We simply struck the improvements off our list and left the field to local residents to battle over for the time being."

The House of Genius demolished. *Herald Tribune,* March 18, 1948. The Seymour B. Durst Old York Library at The City University of New York Graduate Center

So many artists and writers had lived in the boarding houses along this section of Washington Square South between West Broadway and Thompson Street that the block became known as "Genius Row." In spite of the community's efforts to save the dwellings, the first one was demolished on Saint Patrick's Day, 1948. A mural painted over a fireplace appears on the wall in this photograph taken after the house was razed. The block was to have been developed into an apartment building, but the developer decided instead to sell the property to NYU.

Washington Square South. Photograph by Joseph Roberto, 1947. New York University Archives

The lodging houses where Jack Reed, Lincoln Steffens, and Eugene O'Neill had lived were old single-family homes that by 1900 had been converted into four- and five-story walk-ups with large studio windows on the top floors. In 1923, Columbia University leased the property on the westernmost block between Sullivan and MacDougal Streets to "Papa" Albert Strunsky and his brother. Strunsky modernized the interiors, refaced the exteriors of the houses with new brick or stucco, and rented rooms to the creative people he favored. A legendary Village character, "Papa" Strunsky was an extraordinarily kind-hearted landlord who instead of kicking out a delinquent tenant would carry the struggling writer or artist for years. His daughter Lenore said of her father that he had "a pathological compulsion for charity." Strunsky and his wife Mascha lived at 47 Washington Square. Lenore married Ira Gershwin in 1926.

New York University purchased the entire block from Columbia University in 1948 and a year later demolished all the houses in preparation for building a new law school. When excavation of the Law Center began in 1950, construction workers disturbed the long-buried Minetta Brook. Pumps had to be installed to control the gushing water.

Looking north over the park: One and Two Fifth Avenue. Photograph by Mitchell Koch, ca. 1950s. New York University Archives

This photograph from the 1950s illustrates the dramatic changes to Washington Square North and lower Fifth Avenue by the middle of the twentieth century. To the right, on the east side of Fifth Avenue, behind the remodeled Row, rise the soaring towers of One Fifth Avenue. Built to be a stylish residential hotel by Helmle, Corbett & Harrison in 1927, it augured change on lower Fifth Avenue. One Fifth was acquired by NYU in 1966, but several years later, the university sold its interest in it. The building is now a cooperative apartment.

To the left, on the west side of Fifth Avenue, stands another large apartment house, Two Fifth Avenue, completed in 1951. In response to the community's strenuous objections to its first plans for Two Fifth Avenue, Emery Roth & Sons compromised, lowering the section of the building that ran directly along Washington Square North to approximate the cornice height of the Greek Revival homes across the way, facing that part of the new building with red brick, and adapting some architectural details to match the Row.

Musicians in Washington Square
Park. Photograph by Nat Norman,
late 1950s, early 1960s. Museum of
the City of New York

Around the time Washington Square
was closed to traffic, growing numbers of folksingers were gathering
around the fountain basin to sing
and play together. Despite the
complaints of some neighbors and
the city's short-lived ban on their
music-making, folksingers—including the young Bob Dylan and Joan
Baez—remained a steady fixture of
park life.

Avant-garde artists, too, found
Washington Square a congenial
place. Mark Rothko had first met
Willem de Kooning on a park bench
here in the 1930s. The two painters,
along with Pollock, Adolph Gottlieb,
Franz Kline, Robert Motherwell,
and other Abstract Expressionists

came together regularly at their fabled hangout, Cedar Street Tavern,
an undistinguished bar (now demolished) two blocks north of the park
on University Place. In 1949, led by
de Kooning, they rented space at 39
East Eighth Street and organized
what soon became known as "the
Club," whose programs attracted a
younger generation of painters and
sculptors, among them Robert
Rauschenberg, Helen Franken-
thaler, Larry Rivers, Joan Mitchell,
Red Grooms, and Claes Oldenburg.
Through the 1950s, blocks north
and east of the Square between
Eighth and Twelfth Streets were
filled with artists' studios and galleries. With the addition of performances and exhibitions at the Judson
Memorial Church after 1960, the
Washington Square area was a dy-
namic center for the most advanced
and experimental work of the time.

Judson Memorial Church. Photograph, ca. 1970s. New York University Archives

When Howard Moody became the pastor of Judson Memorial Church in 1956, he expanded on Edward Judson's founding mission and during his forty-year tenure adapted a "bar-sitting evangelism," as he called it. If congregants were reluctant to fill the church pews, the Texas-born cleric and graduate of the Yale School of Divinity reached them by going out on the streets of his parish. A committed social activist, Moody founded the Village Aid and Service Center, where drug addicts could receive help, offered abortion counseling, provided shelter for runaways and battered women, and reached out to AIDS victims before such help was readily available elsewhere. Through the 1960s and 1970s, the minister was involved with civil rights demonstrations and anti-war protests, many of which took place in the park. During the Vietnam War, he posted daily body counts on the signboard at the church's front door.

Acting on his conviction that all parts of the community should be reached by the church, Moody became involved with young artists living downtown who were having a hard time getting their work shown. Claiming to know nothing about art, he enlisted the help of Associate Minister Al Carmines. Around 1960, they began arranging art exhibitions at the church featuring the work of abstract painters and many of the later well-known Pop artists, including Jim Dine, Red Grooms, Claes Oldenburg, and Tom Wesselman. Through the 1960s, the church sponsored avant-garde performances by Meredith Monk and Yoko Ono, "happenings" by Alan Kaprow, and experimental dance. Robert Rauschenberg, a participant in the Judson's Dance Theater program, designed sets for performances at the church with Andy Warhol.

André Kertész, *Washington Square Park*. Photograph, 1971. Courtesy of the Estate of André Kertész

Washington Square continued to be a rich subject for artists and photographers throughout the twentieth century. In 1952, the Hungarian-born Kertész moved into an apartment on the twelfth floor of Two Fifth Avenue overlooking the Square. For nearly a quarter century, he took pictures of the park, many of them shot from his terrace. The photographs were published in 1975 in a small book entitled *Washington Square,* with an appreciation by Brendan Gill. Among the photographs in Kertész's book is this aerial view of the park showing the renovations made after the Square was closed to traffic.

At the time the photograph was taken, the World Trade Center was still under construction. Thirty years later, after the attack on September 11, 2001, crowds fleeing the downtown financial district took refuge in the Square and watched as the World Trade towers, in clear view to the south, collapsed. In the aftermath, daily vigils took place around the fountain, and the chain-link fence around the Arch became a memorial plastered with pictures of the missing. Flowers, flags, candles, pictures by schoolchildren, and written messages by neighbors and visitors from around the world expressed the nation's profound grief.

THREE

Radicals and Real Estate

*I*n the years before World War I, Washington Square was shedding its old skin to emerge as the center of a young bohemian community. Artists, writers, and radicals from all over the country were making their way to Greenwich Village and the Square to pursue their art and lend support to the causes of labor, pacifism, and women's rights. After the war, the enlivened neighborhood around the Square, still characteristically split between north and south—"satin and motorcars on this side, squalor and pushcarts on that"—became a magnet for fun-loving visitors from uptown and out-of-town. But around the same time, it also became prey to developers. From the 1920s to the 1950s, residents struggled to maintain the historic character of the area against the formidable threats of real estate development, New York University expansion, and the wiles of Robert Moses.

Ambitions to Get to New York

Painters, poets, aspiring actors, journalists, and musicians had been living in Greenwich Village for decades, integrated into the society around them. Some, like William Dean Howells, Walt Whitman, and Horace Greeley, were regulars at Pfaff's, a beer cellar opened in 1856 on Broadway near Bleecker Street, known as a meeting place for bohemians and the intelligentsia. Later in the century, the term "bohemian," derived from a French word for the gypsy population of Central Europe, was used to describe impoverished young *artistes* living as they pleased while in pursuit of their muse—like the characters in Puccini's 1896 opera *La Bohème*. In the United States, thousands of readers were captivated by George Du Maurier's novel *Trilby*, the tale of a young artist's model in Paris who falls under the influence of a mesmerizing Hungarian *bohémien* named Svengali. First run as a serial in *Harper's Monthly* in 1894, the popular story of Trilby, retold in song and stage versions around the country, encouraged countless young Americans to seek a bohemia of their own.

Those who were yearning to live in a garret or work in a studio perceived Greenwich Village as the New World equivalent of the Left Bank of Paris. Magazines such as *Bohemian*— published first in Boston, then in Deposit, New York, and Philadelphia—and stories by William Dean Howells ("Coast of Bohemia") and O. Henry ("A Philistine in Bohemia") popularized the idea. Around 1900, as New York became the acknowledged center of American publishing, Washington Square became the literary center of the Village. Hopeful authors from all across the country made their way to the rooming houses on the south side of the Square where they found cheap accommodations of appealing, if somewhat decaying, charm. European-style restaurants in the neighborhood provided inexpensive meals, the local population was tolerant, publishing houses were within walking distance, and exhilarating company awaited just outside the door.

"Of all the ambitions of the Great Unpublished, the one that is strongest, the most abiding, is the ambition to get to New York," wrote Frank Norris, one of the country's first "naturalist" writers. Shortly before the turn of the century, Norris came to New York from California to work for *McClure's Magazine.* The young man rented a small front bedroom in a three-and-a-half-story red brick house at 61 Washington Square South run by Katherine Branchard. A legendary Village landlord, the Paris-born Branchard had leased the old building in 1886 and took in tenants until her death at age eighty in 1938. Her boarding house was later labeled the "House of Genius" because creative people such as the writers Stephen Crane and Theodore Dreiser had reputedly lived there at one time or another. There is no documentation that those two authors were ever boarders, but they did live nearby and visited the premises. Dreiser mentions some of Madame Branchard's renowned dinners in his novel *The Genius*. The poet Alan Seeger, a documented lodger, was living in the house when he penned "I Have a Rendezvous with Death" shortly before going off to war and his death in France. And on at least one occasion, the famed soprano Adelina Patti rehearsed her entire opera troupe in the parlor for a production of *Cavalleria Rusticana* while Madame Branchard looked on from the fire escape.

Gelett Burgess, one of Norris's friends from San Francisco also lodged with Branchard. He is most often remembered as a poet of nonsense verse: "I never saw a purple cow. . . ." Years later, reminiscing about his experiences while living at 61 Washington Square, Burgess described an encounter with Mark Twain in Washington Square. Twain, attired in his customary white flannels, was sitting on a bench feeding pigeons in the park. When Burgess sat down next to him, the older author offered him a cigar and asked what he did. Burgess confessed he was trying to be a serious writer but was handicapped by his reputation as a humorist and couldn't get rid of his "damned Purple Cow." Twain laughed, slapped him on the knee and told him there were "lots of mighty poor humorists nowadays, and most of 'em are so damned poor they can't even keep a cow."[1]

Most of Burgess's peers around the Square rejected Twain's humorous style as a model for their writing and chose instead to work in the naturalism favored by Norris. Before his premature death in 1902, Norris completed *The Octopus*, a fictionalized account of the California wheat industry and the railroad interests he believed were strangling the wheat farmers. Stephen Crane, author of the Civil War epic *The Red Badge of Courage* (1895), wrote *Maggie: A Girl of the Streets,* a novel about the tragic fate of a working-class woman in the New York slums, in 1892. Dreiser's first novel, *Sister Carrie,* the frank story of a kept woman who becomes a star of the New York stage but nonetheless fails to find happiness, was published in 1900 with Norris's help. Norris, then working as a reader at Doubleday, arranged the contract while F. N. Doubleday was away in Europe. The concern of these writers for the social and economic injustices of modern urban-industrial America—including the plight of women and the evils of capitalism—reflected the ideas of the Progressive movement at the turn of the century and later informed the radical agenda of political activists in the Village.

Norris had come to New York to work for Samuel Sydney McClure, whose relatively young publication called *McClure's Magazine* was well regarded for its fine fiction and uncompromising journalism. Colleagues at *McClure's*—who included Ida Tarbell, Upton Sinclair, and Lincoln Steffens—were writing and receiving national attention for their studies of business and labor, racial discrimination, and municipal corruption. Later on President Theodore Roosevelt dubbed the *McClure's* writers "muckrakers," a term borrowed from an image in Paul Bunyan's *Pilgrim's Progress:* a man with a muckrake in hand would rather rake filth than look upward to nobler things. *McClure's* soon folded, but the muckrakers' righteous anger and socialist outlook were formative influences on American journalism and the generation arriving in Washington Square.

Another star in McClure's constellation of writers was Willa Cather, who had been working as a schoolteacher in Pittsburgh when her first published stories caught the publisher's attention. Invited to join the magazine, Cather came to New York in 1906. Although her interest was fiction not reform, within a short time she became managing editor. Cather, described by Alfred Kazin as being about as rakish as

Calvin Coolidge, took a studio at 60 Washington Square with Edith Lewis, the woman who was to be her lifelong companion. In Lewis's biography of Cather, *Willa Cather Living,* the Square of those years is described as "then one of the most charming places in New York. On the north side the long row of houses of rose-red brick, residences of aristocratic old New York families, gave it an aura of gentility and dignity. On the south side, writers and artists lived. But it was a very sedate Bohemia: most of the artists were poor and hardworking." Two years later, Cather moved to Washington Place just off the Square, and then to a second floor apartment at 5 Bank Street, where she wrote her acclaimed novel *My Antonia* (1918), set in the Nebraska Plains, and *Death Comes to the Archbishop* (1927), a story of the Southwest. Cather relied on the city for cultural and intellectual stimulation but almost always drew her subject matter from other regions of the country.

One of her rare stories set in the city was "Coming Aphrodite." Published in 1920, it reflects her experience of Washington Square in the first years of the new century, "when young people coming to New York to 'write' or 'paint' . . . desired artistic surroundings." The story recounts the relationship between Don Hedger, a "modern" painter, and Eden Bower—born Edna in Illinois and later a famous singer— and their different measures of success. It is set in an old house on the south side of the Square, very much like the one Cather had inhabited, where the two occupy studios on the top floor and share the one bathroom in the hall. They often meet in the Square.

"It was almost the very last summer of the old horse stages on Fifth Avenue. The fountain had but lately begun operations for the season and was throwing up a mist of rainbow water which now and then blew south and sprayed a bunch of Italian babies that were being supported on the outer rim by older, very little older, brothers and sisters. Plump robins were hopping about on the soil; the grass was newly cut and blindingly green. Looking up the Avenue through the Arch, one could see the young poplars with their bright sticky leaves, and the Brevoort glistening in its spring coat of paint, and shining horses and car-riages,—occasionally an automobile." (The Hotel Brevoort on Fifth Avenue at Ninth Street was a favored meeting-place for those with money in their pockets. It featured a Parisian-style restaurant and one of the first outdoor cafes in the city.)

While Cather was living on the Square, one of her neighbors a few doors away was the Philadelphia-born artist-illustrator William Glack-ens, who arrived in New York in 1896 after a year's study in Paris. Glackens rapidly developed a successful career as an artist-reporter for several New York papers and magazines, including *McClure's,* which sent him to Cuba during the Spanish-American War. Married in 1904, he moved with his wife to 3 Washington Square North and took a stu-dio across the park at 50 Washington Square South near the Judson Memorial Church. He remained in the immediate neighborhood until his death in 1938. Looking out from his studio window, Glackens had a clear view of the park and sketched it frequently from different an-gles and in all seasons. His drawings and illustrations, rich in anecdotal detail, provide a glimpse of the bustling park life in the early 1900s.

Glackens, more conservative later on, was one of the group of in-surgent artists whose earthy urban subjects, painted with vigorous re-alism, offended the staid American art establishment. After the Na-tional Academy of Design—the institution founded by Samuel Morse in 1826—refused their work for its annual exhibition, the young artists held an independent show at the MacBeth Gallery in February 1908. Calling themselves The Eight and later dubbed the "Ashcan School" by critics, the group centered around their mentor Robert Henri and included George Bellows, Arthur B. Davies, Ernest Lawson, George Luks, Maurice Prendergast, Everett Shinn, and John Sloan. Nearly all of them lived close by and with varying degrees of frequency took the park as their subject.

The Square "Where Youth Lived and Reds Gathered"

However lively Glackens's park scenes may be, none capture the spirit of revolution that pulsed through Washington Square in the years just before World War I. The Greenwich Village area was fast gaining a reputation as a hotbed of youthful artists and intellectuals and a zone of tolerance for those who espoused progressive causes and wished to live unconventional lives. "New York had an ethical, where Paris had an aesthetic, Bohemia," claimed Max Eastman, editor of the socialist magazine *The Masses*. The muckraking journalist Lincoln Steffens, who moved to the Square following the death of his wife, was another witness to the era: "My 'home' was a room in Washington Square," he wrote in his *Autobiography,* "where youth lived and reds gathered, the young poets, and painters, playwrights, actors, and Bohemians, and labor leaders of a radical trend."

Nineteenth-century artists and writers around the Square were often of the same social milieu and political persuasion as their patrons—Morse and Hone, for example—and hewed to the traditions of society. By contrast, the radicals and writers of the early 1900s defined themselves as a distinct generation—a youth movement in revolt against the values of their parents and the past. Rejecting outworn social conventions, they formed alliances with European immigrants educated in Marxism, anarchism, and Russian literature. Their passionate challenging of government and industry ultimately shaped the dynamics and discourse of our time. Flocking to prewar Greenwich Village from other parts of the country, they were eager to embrace the cosmopolitanism of New York. Yet they favored "the Village," as it came to be known, because it was a quiet backwater that still retained many aspects of the small town life they'd left behind. "There was a quietness and quaintness, there were neighbors who knew one another, there was sauntering in the streets," Eastman recalled in his memoirs, *Enjoyment of Living.* Greenwich Village then had its corners

253

of affluence, Christine Stansell notes in *American Moderns,* but mostly it was a neighborhood down on its luck.

New arrivals readily embraced a "picturesque" poverty without reckoning on the impact their presence might have on the working-class Irish and Italian immigrants who were forced to live in the cheapest places to survive. In 1902, Mary Kingsbury Simkhovitch, a well-educated American-born social reformer, founded Greenwich House to improve the lives of the immigrants in the Village. Modeled on Jane Addams's Hull House in Chicago, the settlement house was located a few blocks from the Square. Simkhovitch and her colleagues found it "amusing and astounding to us who had fought against cellar lodgings as unhealthful, damp and unfit for human habitation, as they were, to see them revived as 'one room studios' and let often at six times the price of former rentals."

Bohemian newcomers constituted only a small percentage of the Village population, yet nonetheless their activities brought more attention to the area and bolstered its colorful reputation. Steffens recalled how astonished he had been to learn while on a trip out west that the place where he lived "was known out there. . . . Greenwich Village, which had been a simple fact, a neglected neighborhood of low rents, became the dwelling place of students, impecunious artists and down-and-out reds and the experimental laboratories for little theaters—this picturesque old quarter of the city was ridiculed and romanced into 'Greenwich Village,' a sort of Latin Quarter."

What distinguished Washington Square in these years was its aura of history and the European population along the south edge of the park. "Why has Washington Square a meaning, a fragrance, so to speak; while Washington Heights has none?" Djuna Barnes asked in 1916. Expanding on Howells's observations of the 1880s, Barnes noted: "Here on the North side are stately houses, inhabited by great fortunes . . . all those whose names rustle like silk petticoats, and on the other side congeries of houses and hovels passing into rabbit warrens where

Italians breed and swarm in the sun as in Naples, where vegetables and fruits are sold in the streets . . . and ice cream is made in the bedrooms and spaghetti on the cellar floor . . . Satin and motorcars on this side, squalor and pushcarts on that."

Where Life Was a Joy to a Broth of a Boy

The archetypal Greenwich Villager of this period was John Reed, a dashing young poet and journalist born in 1887 in Portland, Oregon. After graduating from Harvard and traveling in Europe, he shared quarters with three college classmates at 42 Washington Square, one of the old houses across from the southwest corner of the park. Walter Lippmann, another college friend, but far more conservative, would sometimes drop by. Reed's downstairs neighbor was Lincoln Steffens, one of the young man's inspirations and a friend of his father's. Steffens had met Reed's father, a U.S. marshal, while investigating a case of timber fraud in the West. As the journalist recorded in his *Autobiography,* the elder Reed had asked Steffens "to keep an eye on his boy, Jack, who, the father thought, was a poet." Steffens complied with pleasure, recounting how he liked it "when Jack, a big, growing, happy being, would slam into my room and wake me up to tell me about the 'most wonderful thing in the world' that he had seen, been, or done that night. Girls, plays, bums, I.W.W.'s, strikers—each experience was vivid in him. . . . Jack and his crazy young friends were indeed the most wonderful thing in the world." Reed encouraged Steffens to move to the Square after his wife died, thinking it would cheer him. Steffens in turn helped the younger man by introducing him to editors, publishers, and his muckraker friends.

One of Steffens's friends published Reed's first volume of poetry, entitled *A Day in Bohemia, or, Life Among the Artists,* which Reed dedicated to his mentor. His lighthearted verses about friends and activities in the "Quartier Latin" include the lengthy poem "Forty-two Washington Square" with its memorable lines:

But nobody questions your morals,
And nobody asks for the rent,—
There's no one to pry if we're tight, you and I,
Or demand how our evenings are spent.
The furniture's ancient but plenty,
The linen is spotless and fair,
O life is a joy to a broth of a boy
At Forty-two Washington Square!

Other lines of the poem, however, reveal Reed's emerging sensitivity to injustice and hint at the radicalization that would define his life:

There spawn the overworked and underpaid
Mute thousands;—packed in buildings badly made,—
In stinking squalor penned,—and overflowing
On sagging fire-escapes. . . .

While working as a reporter, Reed had become a radical supporter of labor. Early in 1913, workers at the silk mills of Paterson, New Jersey, were enduring a long walkout, which the New York papers, in collusion with one another, agreed not to cover. Reed went over to Paterson to get the strikers' stories and ended up in prison with some of the workers. After his release, he organized a huge fund-raising pageant at Madison Square Garden, accomplished with the financial backing of Mabel Dodge.

Dodge, a rich, attractive matron with a radiating personality and the courage of inexperience, as Lincoln Steffens wrote, held lively salons in her home at 23 Fifth Avenue. Against white walls hung with contemporary paintings, she encouraged loud discussions of then highly controversial subjects—trade unions, anarchism, birth control, the latest art, or the teachings of Freud and Jung. It was reputedly her idea to present a pageant to attract attention to the strike. Directed by Reed, with scenery painted by John Sloan, the sensational show featured a cast of fifteen hundred striking silk workers and was viewed by an audience of five thousand.

Two weeks after the performance, Reed sailed with Mrs. Dodge for Europe and they became lovers. Upon returning to New York, he moved into her Fifth Avenue mansion but was soon off to report on Pancho Villa in Mexico and then war in the Balkans. The young reporter regularly ended his dispatches with words that became a pacifist credo: "This is not our war." A few years later, Reed was back on the park, this time residing at number 43 Washington Square with Louise Bryant, a young woman he had met in Oregon, who later became his wife. Exempt from military duty because of poor health, Reed nevertheless found strength to travel with Louise to Russia and send back dispatches that only *The Masses* would publish.

The Masses, founded in 1911 by a Dutch-born Socialist, Piet Vlag, came under Max Eastman's direction in 1913. It soon developed into the prime vehicle for Village intellectuals—a clever publication of leftist leanings and impertinent humor. The managing editor, Floyd Dell, who lived for a while on the south side of the Square, listed the magazine's causes as "Fun, Truth, Beauty, Realism, Peace, Feminism and Revolution." Heavily illustrated with timely cartoons and satiric drawings, laced with poems as well as polemics, *The Masses* brought together an extraordinary group of writers and artists. Instead of paying its contributors, the magazine held open monthly meetings at which the contents of forthcoming issues were chosen by vote. This self-consciously democratic selection process was deemed too bourgeois by Hippolyte Havel, especially for poetry, which, he held, came from the soul. Havel, who sometimes played the fool in the group, was an avowed anarchist, passionate and well informed about avant-garde art, and a former lover of Emma Goldman. "Red Emma," as Goldman was known, embodied anarchism in the United States and was one of the most charismatic speakers on the subjects of civil liberties, sexual freedom, and other leftist causes. In addition to serving on the editorial board of the *Masses*, the Czech-born Havel wrote articles on art criticism for Goldman's journal *Mother Earth,* contributed to other publications, founding some of his own, and worked as a cook to support himself. The artist John Sloan was one of the regular contributors to *The Masses;* his wife Dolly acted as the publication's business manager. Sympathetic uptowners of means occasionally provided money, but often the magazine raised funds by organizing costume balls at Webster Hall on Eleventh Street.

Women's Rights

The Masses and the Village activists around it heartily endorsed the ideals of radical feminism. Max Eastman and his wife Ida Rauh, for example, listed their names individually on their mailbox, a shocking act for the time. Max, at the urging of his sister Crystal, briefly headed the Men's League for Woman Suffrage. Crystal Eastman, who held degrees in law and social work, was a leader in the women's rights movement and the allied cause of peace. In 1912, she had run the successful woman's suffrage campaign in Wisconsin; in 1915, she helped found the national Woman's Peace Party with Jane Addams of Chicago's Hull House. Eight years later, she co-authored the Equal Rights Amendment. For several years, the Eastman siblings, along with their respective spouses, friends, lovers, and servants shared a communal house in the Village and a country house in Croton-on-Hudson.

In the years before World War I, the suffrage movement was stepping up its efforts to win women the right to vote in New York State. Washington Square was often the launching site for mass demonstrations, an effective way to influence public opinion. By 1915, twelve states had already enfranchised women, and activity was intensifying in New York that year. One of the most extravagant parades took place on Saturday, October 23, 1915, two weeks before election day, when more than 25,000 participants assembled at the Square and marched up Fifth Avenue to 59th Street. Bridging class lines and religious, political and ethnic divisions, support for the suffrage movement united left-wing radicals, old-New-York society, labor unions, and simple working women. The parade was "a three-mile argument for equal rights," pronounced the *Sun* the next day. Although the event was judged to be a great success, the women of New York State did not get the vote until 1917; the Nineteenth Amendment securing universal suffrage was not passed until 1920.

The Masses flourished for only a few years. While the United States was drafting soldiers and preparing to enter the war in Europe, the radical publication continued to preach pacifism in defiance of the law. As a result, the Federal authorities revoked the magazine's mailing permit and banned it from being sold at subway newsstands, effectively strangling circulation. Funders withdrew support, and *The Masses* closed with a last issue in December 1917. The Justice Department charged Eastman, Dell, Reed, and some others with conspiracy and interfering with enlistment, but their trials in 1918 resulted in hung juries. Most of their left-wing friends experienced similar difficulties during the post-war "Red Scare." Some were imprisoned, and the foreign-born were deported. Emma Goldman was deported to Russia, her birthplace, but within a few years she denounced the totalitarian Soviet regime and was expelled. She spent the rest of her life wandering in Europe. Reed returned from Russia to stand trial with his friends. During what would be his last stay in the Village, he completed *Ten Days That Shook the World*, his major work on the Russian Revolution. Suspected for his communist sympathies and labeled a "Red," he and Louise returned to Russia, where he contracted typhus and died a few days before his thirty-third birthday in 1920. "He ceased to be the free soul that you (and I) remember," Lincoln Steffens wrote

Reed's mother. "He lived the life of a party communist at the end."[2] A hero to the Russians, Reed is buried in Moscow at the Kremlin wall. His story formed the basis of Warren Beatty's 1981 movie *Reds*.

The Liberal Club and the Provincetown Players

The arc of John Reed's life was unusually tragic. Yet even the briefest outline of his years on Washington Square suggests the tight web of affinities and relationships that bound together Village artists and activists early in the twentieth century. Art and politics often overlapped at the Liberal Club, 133 MacDougal Street, a few steps off the southwest corner of the Square. Originally located at Gramercy Park, the club moved to the Village in 1913 after its leader, Henrietta Rodman, spoke out on subjects that were too extreme for that neighborhood. A public schoolteacher and ardent feminist, she had incurred the locals' wrath by talking to her students about birth control. Rodman encouraged emancipated Liberal Club members to experience "free love" and pressed for racial integration in the group's membership.

At MacDougal Street, club members would take supper at Polly's Restaurant on the ground floor, run by Paula Halladay, an anarchist from Evanston, Illinois, and Hippolyte Havel, who wanted to recreate the cultural milieu he had experienced in Paris. After eating, the group would then troop upstairs for readings and discussions, art shows and amateur experimental theater. Regulars included Eastman, Steffens, Theodore Dreiser, Upton Sinclair, Vachel Lindsay, Sinclair Lewis, Sherwood Anderson, Louis Untermeyer, and the artists John Sloan and Marcel Duchamp. Club members frequently "borrowed" books from the Boni brothers' Washington Square Bookshop next door. (Albert and Charles Boni later founded the Modern Library series.) The back room of the Bonis' bookshop served as a small theater in 1914 for the first production of what became the Washington Square Players, a group dedicated to presenting noncommercial plays by American and

European authors to subscription audiences. Robert Edmund Jones, their first director, was a scenic artist who had designed the Paterson Strike Pageant with Reed. The company moved up to a little theater on Fifty-seventh Street in 1915.

Liberal Club members were also involved with the Provincetown Playhouse, the first theater in the country to commission and produce only American plays. George Cram "Jig" Cook and his wife Susan Glaspell had been eager to start a theater that would foster American talent. During their summers in Provincetown, Massachusetts, the Cooks established the Provincetown Players with friends from Greenwich Village. Looking about for a new play in the summer of 1916, they were recommended to Eugene O'Neill, who had left his "garbage flat," as he called his abode at 38 Washington Square, for Provincetown that season. The Cape Cod production of O'Neill's *Bound East for Cardiff* was so successful that, at Reed's suggestion, the Cooks decided to open a theater in New York.

They found space first at 139 MacDougal Street, next door to Polly's restaurant and the Liberal Club, and then took over an old dwelling a few doors down at 133 MacDougal. Playing to a small audience seated on simple benches, the Provincetown Players presented the work of several playwrights and made theater history for ten years. (In 1998, NYU renovated and reopened the Playhouse.) O'Neill soon gained recognition as a major dramatist, winning the Pulitzer Prize for *Beyond the Horizon* in 1920. His controversial play *All God's Chillun Got Wings* launched Paul Robeson on his career in 1924. O'Neill's affair with Louise Bryant formed the basis of *Strange Interlude,* and the saloon setting of *The Iceman Cometh* was modeled on a Sixth Avenue tavern a block from the Square where O'Neill and his friends congregated. The willowy red-headed poet Edna St. Vincent Millay appeared in a few roles at the Playhouse, and in 1927 Bette Davis made her debut there. One of the most popular actresses was Christine Ell, who managed the Players' dining hall on the second floor between her walk-on roles. She was also known to promenade through Washington Square with her leashed leopard cub.

World War I—The Arch Rebellion and the Alley Festa

Like most of his friends at the Liberal Club and *The Masses,* the Philadelphia-born artist John Sloan had socialist leanings and was strongly opposed to the United States's participation in World War I. A pacifist during the Spanish-American War, Sloan had hoped the socialist movement would be a "brake," as he put it, on nationalistic competition in the twentieth century. At the urging of one of his young art students, Sloan joined a group of rebels in staging a mock revolution to protest America's involvement in the European conflict, "one of my bohemian incidents, one of the very few," he confessed years later. The instigator was Gertrude Drick, according to local legend a "flamboyant Village poet" who preferred to be known as "Woe," so as to be able to announce "Woe is me." In addition to Sloan, Drick enlisted Charles Ellis, a painter, set designer, and actor with the Provincetown Players, and two other friends, Forrest Mann and Betty Turner. The fifth conspirator was Marcel Duchamp, the avant-garde French artist whose *Nude Descending a Staircase* had caused such a sensation at the Armory Show in 1913. Duchamp lived on West Tenth Street, about three blocks away from the Arch.

Drick had discovered one day that the door in the west pier of the Arch was open, and she instructed her friends how to enter and climb the spiral staircase to the roof. On a cold winter's night in January 1917, the rebels mounted to the top of Washington Arch and strung up some balloons. "Woe" then read aloud the document she and Ellis had prepared, declaring the secession of Greenwich Village from the America of big business and small minds. They called on President Wilson to extend protection to their domain as one of the small nations, the "Free and Independent Republic of Washington Square." One account mentions that they fired cap pistols. Sloan recalled that the group had hot water bottles to sit on, sandwiches, and thermos bottles of coffee or tea. The string of balloons left behind by the conspirators that night baffled neighbors and police who observed them hanging from the Arch the next morning. Three months later, the United States entered the war in Europe. Early in the summer of 1917, there were ceremonies in the Square to honor the visiting war delegations from Italy and Russia. In place of lighthearted balloons, the Arch was decorated with the flags and military insignia of America's new allies.

263

Sloan's *Arch Conspirators* is an elegy to the passing moment before the Great War. To Sloan, who had arrived in New York in 1902, Greenwich Village represented a spiritual haven, a sort of "liberal radical small town," he called it. Along with his dissident colleagues, he had believed in the possibility of transforming society, in a "revolution of consciousness" that would transcend any change in political rule. But his fierce engagement with such issues ended when the United States entered combat. Withdrawing from further political involvement, Sloan directed his attention to making art and forming the Society of Independent Artists with Glackens and Duchamp. (The French artist soon resigned from the Independents when the organizing committee, influenced by Glackens, refused by a narrow margin to exhibit his "ready-made" urinal, *Fountain,* in the first exhibition.) In the mid 1920s, he moved from Washington Place off the west side of the Square into the tower studio at the Judson Hotel on Washington Square South. When NYU began remodeling the building into a dormitory in the 1935, he reluctantly gave up his room in the Judson. Although the artist said he "begged the institution to let him stay, offering to teach, or take classes in Latin or geometry," Sloan had to leave and moved up to the Hotel Chelsea on West Twenty-third Street.

In addition to bohemians and radicals, the Village also hosted artists with more conventional politics. The sculptor Gertrude Vanderbilt Whitney, for instance, was a fervent patriot. Daughter of Cornelius

Vanderbilt II and wife of the very wealthy Harry Payne Whitney, Whitney resided in a mansion on Fifth Avenue. (Her great-grandfather was "Commodore" Cornelius Vanderbilt, whose fortune of $100 million had been doubled by his son William and was inherited by her father, the favorite grandson and principal heir.) Around 1906, she became more submerged in her artistic work and took a studio converted from one of the former stables in MacDougal Alley. The alley had been a private road servicing the houses along the west portion of Washington Square North.

At the outbreak of the war in Europe, Whitney quickly lent substantial support to the Allied cause by donating a million dollars of her own money to open a field hospital in France. She raised an additional $18,000 by holding two art exhibitions in December 1914, in the dwelling at 8 West Eighth Street attached to her studio. With the help of her able assistant Juliana Force, Whitney inaugurated a series of exhibitions to raise money for war victims, which also helped artists find patrons and gain visibility. Early in 1916, she gave John Sloan his first one-man show. He was forty-four and had never sold a painting. Although Whitney found Sloan's relentless talk of pacifism trying, she appreciated his talent nevertheless.

During the first week of June 1917, Whitney and a committee of artist and socialite friends staged the "Alley Festa," a street fair to raise money for the Red Cross and the American war effort. MacDougal Alley was transformed under red, white, and blue lights into a European fantasy, an ersatz townscape of bell towers, parapets, and balconies. There were Belgian, British, and Serbian Days and French and Italian Nights, each with coordinated food and entertainment. In her studio and adjoining balcony, Whitney ran a restaurant charging five dollars for a meal catered by Delmonico's, an elegant establishment on Fourteenth Street. One afternoon elephants and camels took passengers—not just children—for rides around Washington Square. On the closing night, a thousand people witnessed a pageant on the theme of allied nations welcoming Columbia, with Ethel Barrymore in the starring role. For the "Allies' Ball" following the pageant, several bands provided an uninterrupted flow of music, and patrons whirled on a dance floor that extended around from the mews to the front of 23 Washington Square North. The fair brought in more than $70,000 and sold over $540,000 in Liberty Bonds.

After the war, Whitney and Juliana Force continued to organize art exhibitions and help struggling American artists. When the Metropolitan Museum of Art turned down the offer of her collection of contemporary American art in 1930, Gloria Vanderbilt Whitney founded a new museum, which she housed in adjoining dwellings on Eighth Street. Blessed with a first-rate collection and an endowment to keep it going, the Whitney Museum of American Art opened in November 1931, with Juliana Force as director. It was the first such institution to focus exclusively on American work and one of the pioneers in presenting contemporary art. (The Museum of Modern Art, founded by three women and directed by Alfred Barr, had opened uptown two years earlier. It was preceded on a smaller scale by NYU's Gallery of Living Art, organized by Albert Gallatin from 1927 to 1943. At Gallatin's death, many works in the collection were donated to the Philadelphia Museum of Art.) After outgrowing the Eighth Street facility, in 1951, the Whitney moved uptown to a plot of land on 54th Street adjoining The Museum of Modern Art and then relocated in 1966 to its current home on Madison Avenue at 75th Street. Since 1967, art students and faculty of the Studio School have occupied the museum's first home on West Eighth Street.

"The Village is Young"

By the mid teens, increasing numbers of tourists were visiting the Village to "experience" the bohemian life downtown. Before the completion of the Seventh Avenue subway in 1918, they usually arrived by way of the Fifth Avenue bus to Washington Square, the last stop of the line. A number of little magazines, such as the *Quill,* with offices on West Fourth Street near the Square, cued visitors to the latest enticements of the neighborhood. Tourists disembarking near the south side of the Square would have encountered the Washington Square Restaurant, a second-floor establishment near John Reed's former lodging, where a patron could eat, dance, play chess, or sit by the fire. Run by an "impressively handsome woman" called "Romany Marie" Marchand, it offered something new: "a cafeteria where one may eat more cheaply and informally serving oneself," reported the *Quill* in its issue of November 1, 1917. Romany Marie, a former anarchist who had ushered at Emma Goldman's meetings, went on to run a number of successful enterprises that were popular with artists in the Village from the early 1900s through the 1940s. Her restaurant at 55 Grove Street was still going strong in 1947, when it advertised a dinner for $1.00, reduced from $1.50 to cooperate with President Harry Truman's request to lower prices.

Among the most popular places for those wanting a true "Village experience" was Bruno's Garret, located across from Judson Memorial Church on the corner of Thompson Street and Washington Square South. The rickety two-story house, razed in the 1940s, had originally served as the gravedigger's residence at the potter's field. In 1914, Guido Bruno moved in to the second floor of the old house and set up a printing operation, publishing the work of then unknown writers—Hart Crane and Djuna Barnes among others—in *Bruno's Weekly,* five cents a copy, or *Greenwich Village: A Fortnightly.* Bruno's instinct for discovering literary talent was outdone by his even stronger instinct for self-promotion. On the exterior of the Garret, Bruno posted his mission : "to get it written / to get it spoken / to get it down at any cost / at any hazard / it is for this only / that we are here." Inside, he transformed the space into a layman's fantasy of the artist's life—a messy place with gaudy decorations and half-finished Impressionist-style paintings on easels. He gave a number of artists' models and would-be poets and painters food and space to sleep; in return, they lived in the Garret and carried on the way uptowners thought crazy Villagers behaved. Bruno fed the Village mythology, reporting to the *Quill* that early one morning he had looked out from his window to see "radical people, exalted by the joy of life splashing wildly and gayly in the fountain." The swimmers were left alone by the police, who apparently regarded the group as "harmless nuts."[3] Such antics reinforced the Square's bohemian reputation and boosted the success of commercial ventures in the area.

Vague about his past and speaking with a mysterious accent, Bruno was in fact Curt Josef Kisch, who had emigrated from a village near Prague. Formerly an attendant in a hospital morgue, he was a happily married family man who commuted to work from Yonkers. As a result of a lawsuit in 1916, Bruno's presses were shut down and Grace Godwin took over the second floor. She transformed the Garret into Grace Godwin's—"a cheerful place for good coffee," according to the *Quill* of December 1917. Below Grace Godwin's, on the first floor of 58 Washington Square, was Rossi Brothers Confectioners, which offered ice cream, cigars, and cigarettes and was notorious for its willingness to sell tobacco products to women.

Late in the summer of 1916, construction began on the new IRT subway line running south from Times Square under Seventh Avenue. To build the subway and the station at Sheridan Square, the city demolished nine blocks of the Village, displacing hundreds of families and businesses. Scars from the cut endure in the odd angles of sheared-off buildings along Seventh Avenue below Twelfth Street. The new subway line pulled tourism from Washington Square west to Sheridan Square and ended the relative isolation of Greenwich Village. In a lament that would echo frequently over the next decades, residents feared that the Village would never be the same.

In "Washington Square," a song written in 1920 by Cole Porter and E. Ray Goetz with music by Melville Gideon, a couple muses on the attractions of Greenwich Village:

> Let's settle down on Washington Square
> We'll find a nice old studio there.
> . . . .
> We'll be democratic, dear,
> When we settle in an attic, dear,
> In Washington Square.

Young people living in the area identified older visitors seeking the novelty and excitement of the Village as "thrillage hounds," a term plucked from a line in a poem by the *Quill*'s editor, Bobby Edwards: "Way down south in Greenwich Village / where the spinsters come for thrillage. . . ." A writer in the *Quill* of February 1918 proclaimed: "The Village is young. It is boisterously young, defiantly young, inimitably young, and it has no patience with old age." Anticipating the cri de coeur of young people in the 1970s, these Villagers considered anyone over thirty to be old—"good people, but old."

A Chasm between the North and South Sides of the Park

In the years immediately following World War I, the chasm between the communities north and south of the park was symbolized by a flagpole erected by the Washington Square Association to honor the neighborhood's war dead. When Charles Lamb proposed the idea to the association, he recommended that the flagpole stand in the park on an axis with Fifth Avenue so that neighbors to the north could see it through the opening of the Arch. In that position, "Old Glory" would also be "a symbol to that great group of incoming, unknown people, south of Washington Square" and would make "strangers into true American citizens," he was quoted as saying in the Washington Square

Association's yearbook for 1919. Lamb and others seemed to have overlooked the fact that some of those "strangers" or their sons had readily gone off to war for their adopted country. On Sullivan Street, a block or so south of the Square, there hung a service flag with 175 stars signifying the number of young men in the immediate area who were in uniform. Some of them died in battle alongside the men from north of the park, yet the flagpole does not carry their names. For fifty years the memorial stood near the fountain, aligned with the Arch. After the park was renovated in 1970, the flagpole was relocated to a grassy plot slightly south and east of the Arch, where it remains today.

The insensitivity of residents on the north for their neighbors to the south deeply disturbed Reverend A. Ray Petty of the Judson Memorial Church. Invited to address the elite members of the Washington Square Association at their annual meeting in January 1921, the minister delivered a strong message. Babies were dying of malnutrition only a few hundred yards away, he said. "For the reason that we are so close to them and because we see only their frailties and only the dirt and the filth in which they exist, I think we are in danger of considering them as something other than people." Acknowledging that times were hard everywhere, Reverend Petty was particularly concerned about the young men in his district who had "gladly" gone to war for their new country. "They had always been a dago or a wop, but we took them out and put them there in khaki and they called our brothers and sons by their first names." Returning home after their first real taste of democracy, those soldiers saw their degradation and the squalor of their homes through new lenses and were angry to be "dagos and wops" again. Petty exhorted members of the Association to become involved, to use their talents to help those living south of the Square. "If we had a Chinese wall built across the Square, it wouldn't keep some of your people out any more effectively that you are out now. . . . Come on over into Macedonia and help us."[4]

Few members of the Washington Square Association ever become as involved with Judson Church as pastor Edward Judson and his successors had hoped they would. The organization's major interest was, and continues to be, the physical well-being of the park and neighborhood. Its purpose, as made clear in its founding mission statement, was "to maintain the present desireable character of the neighborhood, to receive complaints of householders and property owners, and to press those complaints upon the proper authorities; to take the necessary steps for improving the condition and appearances of the neighborhood and otherwise to render it attractive as a residential section."

Ever vigilant about businesses encroaching upon residential blocks, the association worked with the city's first zoning commission in 1914 to preserve Fifth Avenue and the intersecting side streets below Fourteenth Street for residential use. The group's success in this regard is appreciated today. Decades before landmark laws and the current tide of gentrification, the association also encouraged would-be homeowners to buy run-down houses and convert them into "desireable dwellings and apartments for those of modest income." Association yearbooks and minutes allude to letters, petitions, and continual lobbying efforts by members during Prohibition and the period of real estate development following World War I.

Prohibition

Passage of Prohibition—the Eighteenth Amendment—on July 2, 1919, was another source of discord among neighbors around the park. To the distinct annoyance of the more sedate residents, Prohibition seemed only to encourage the Village's rowdy inclinations. Among the first to take advantage of the ban on liquor were the owners of tea-rooms aimed at the tourist trade, who began offering alcoholic drinks during Prohibition. The *Quill* estimated that there were forty-three tea-rooms in the area in 1918. Then came cabarets featuring liquor and entertainment, run by outsiders trading on the Village's exotic reputation, but in the late 1920s, these were eclipsed by the nightclubs of

Harlem. By 1930, the most successful downtown business ventures—and the most ubiquitous—were speakeasies operated by Villagers. With its relaxed atmosphere and reputation for defying authority, the area was the easiest place to get a drink or buy bootleg liquor. Every sort of establishment—grocery, barbershop, cigar store—sold some kind of prohibited beverage. In her comprehensive study *Greenwich Village, 1920–1930,* Caroline Ware reports that there were thousands of liquor-producing establishments on local streets. It was not unusual to see truckloads of grapes unloading at tenements and stores, and most shopkeepers' hands were perpetually stained from underground wine-making activity. Although illegal, these operations had become almost as open as legitimate trade.

One of the most colorful figures of Prohibition was Barney Gallant, who achieved instant fame as the first New Yorker to be imprisoned for violating the Volstead Act in 1919. The Hungarian-born Gallant had been Eugene O'Neill's first roommate in New York and a member of the Liberal Club before it disbanded in 1919. He was the business manager of the Greenwich Village Theater and helped run the Greenwich Village Inn, both located on Sheridan Square. Gallant was said to have more friends than James J. Walker, the dapper, scandal-ridden Mayor, who was, of course, a friend of his as well. In the early 1920s, Gallant established Club Gallant at 40 Washington Square South, then moved it one block away to a house at 85 West Third Street where Edgar Allen Poe and his wife had lived for several months in 1844–45. Gallant opened another establishment on the Square in 1930—the exclusive Speako de Luxe at 19 Washington Square North, next door to the house built by Henry James's grandmother.

While partygoers were enjoying Gallant's hospitality, the Washington Square Association was pressing for stricter enforcement of violations, citing the noise and "the vicious and sometimes criminal element which was a constant menace to the peace and prosperity of the neighborhood." The association's yearbook for 1922 reports that for its "courageous attack on the vice situation and its stand for decent and wholesome citizenship, the Association has won public credit and applause." Meanwhile, other Villagers were calling for the repeal of Prohibition and staging marches around Washington Square.

Development Intrudes

The nuisance of speakeasies proved to be relatively short-lived—Prohibition came to an end on January 1, 1934. But around the same time, there arose a more permanent threat to the character of the park as owners or heirs of private residences began to sell and lease property to real estate developers. By the 1920s, the Washington Square district was reemerging as a choice place to live. Rents went up and in a familiar pattern of New York real estate, those of more modest means— the artists, writers, and European shopkeepers whose presence was intrinsic to the area's appeal—were being driven out. Working from his office at 40 Washington Square, Vincent Pepe, one of the shrewdest Village landlords, cleverly promoted the Village as a desirable address and converted blocks of run-down tenements into attractive accommodation, boosting rents by as much as 140 percent. "Rents have been multiplying . . . it is alleged, by the competition of bourgeois people who know nothing of art, but like to wear flowing ties and live in the midst of temptations," the *New York Times* observed on September 19, 1922. "Greenwich Village Too Costly for Artists to Live There: Values Increased So That Only Those Who Can Write Fluently in Checkbooks Can Afford It," a *Christian Science Monitor* headline proclaimed on August 29, 1927.

Development around the Square capitalized on the area's charm but was more fundamentally propelled by an acute housing shortage in the city and the promise of a fiscal incentive. For a short period, from 1921 to 1924, New York City exempted newly constructed units from all taxation for ten years. As property became available around Washington

Square, developers rushed in to erect tall apartment houses similar to the successful high-rise residences uptown on Fifth, Park, and West End Avenues, and Central Park West. The first such building on lower Fifth Avenue opened on the northeast corner of Ninth Street in 1921. Its thirteen stories replaced a Greek Revival house at 23 Fifth Avenue, formerly the home of the Civil War general Daniel Sickles, and more recently the scene of Mabel Dodge's salons.

A year later, in April 1922, three Greek Revival houses at 14, 15, and 16 Washington Square on the west side of Fifth Avenue were partially demolished in order to be converted into a five-story apartment house. The homes were part of the Rhinelander estate, which held most of the property along the park from Fifth Avenue to MacDougal Street. No. 14 at the corner, the home of William Rhinelander Stewart's maiden aunts, Julia and Serena Rhinelander, had been vacant since Serena's death in 1914. Maynicke and Franke, the architectural firm working for the Rhinelander Real Estate Company, preserved most of the red-brick shells of the buildings and reused other old materials— marble flooring, iron balconies—in a manner that anticipated the adaptive reuse more common to the later twentieth century. The imposing stone stoops of the three houses were removed, but the distinctive granite doorway with two Corinthian columns from the corner Rhinelander house was reused at the central entrance of the low-rise apartment building. The Rhinelander Company spent about $257,000 on renovating and expected the apartments to be ready for tenants within the year.[5] Two stables behind the houses were converted into multiple dwellings, a few of which were rented by cultural organizations. The garden with its small central fountain was reserved for the use of tenants and closed off from Fifth Avenue by the original iron fence on the property.

Six years later, in 1928, in what was the largest individual transaction on Washington Square to date, the Rhinelanders leased their apartment property to Mr. A. E. Lefcourt, a developer of office build-

273

ings in midtown. Lefcourt planned to demolish the Rhinelander apartment block, along with the adjoining houses at 17 and 18 Washington Square North and the converted stables on Fifth, in order to erect a huge apartment house or apartment-hotel. The deal was of particular interest to the real estate community at the time because it signaled confidence in the Square's residential stability and its potential for development. If realized, the tall building would have been the first significant break in the row of ninety-year-old houses around the park.[6]

Lefcourt's project never advanced, either because of changed plans or a financial reversal, but he later joined a syndicate incorporated as Two Fifth Avenue, which closed a deal for a one-hundred-year lease on the property. The syndicate's plans were to build two matching thirty-story apartment houses, each composed of eighteen full floors with setback towers adding twelve more stories. The total cost was estimated to be $10,000,000. Architects and builders had been selected and existing tenants vacated, but a short time later, financial difficulties caused the project to be abandoned.[7] The Rhinelanders refurbished the apartments, found new tenants, and held on to the property until the idea of Two Fifth Avenue resurfaced again.

Growth on the West

Unfortunately, the restraint of the five-story Rhinelander Apartments on the north was not matched on the west side of Washington Square. There beginning in 1925, a series of tall apartment houses were sprouting over the remains of stately old homes. First to go was 32 Washington Square West on the north corner of Washington Place, a handsome Italianate townhouse with a front garden built by James W. Alsop in 1850–51. The four-story dwelling, the kind of home that had contributed to Washington Square's reputation for quiet elegance, was distinguished by floor-length windows opening out onto balconies adorned with wrought-iron railings. Despite its historic pedigree, the house was torn down and replaced in 1925 by a classically styled, fifteen-story red-brick apartment house built as a cooperative by Deutsch & Schneider. As described in the real estate section of the *New York Times* of May 1, 1932, each apartment unit offered four exposures and an "atmosphere like a charming small country house . . . all outside rooms."

No matter how charming the accommodations at 32 Washington Square, that first skyscraper directly on the park galvanized residents into action. Members of the Washington Square Association and the Fifth Avenue Association formed a Joint Committee for the Saving of Washington Square and in 1926 proceeded to petition the Board of Estimate to modify zoning ordinances. They recommended limiting the height of any future building on the Square to one-and-a-half times the width of the streets bounding it. Given the fifty-foot width of streets around the park, that would mean a maximum of seventy-five feet, about the height of the five-story, high-ceilinged houses that had been there for nearly a century. Stricter zoning, it was hoped, would limit future growth. "It is a trifle late to talk of 'saving' Washington Square," noted the *New York Times* in April 1926. "However, the open area is there, with all its varied associations, and it would be a pity if a parallelogram of skyscrapers should convert it into a sort of hole between towering cliffs."

The farsighted recommendations of the Joint Committee for the Saving of Washington Square were not heeded. Within a few years, the west side of the park was banked with buildings that more than doubled the recommended height. These and other new buildings in the vicinity appeared "monstrous" to Edmund Wilson, then editor of the *New Republic,* who lived at 1 University Place, across from the northeast corner of the park. "They loom over the village like mountains, and they have already changed its proportions. . . . The whole village seems now merely a base for these cubic apartment buildings," he wrote angrily (*New Republic,* October 12, 1927).

In 1926–27, a sixteen-story apartment house at 29 Washington

Square was erected across from the northwest side of the park. The massive structure on two lots replaced a six-and-a-half-story multiple residence, the "Washington," built in the 1890s, which in turn had supplanted an older house that had at one time belonged to the architect James Renwick. The architectural firm of Gronenberg & Leuchtag enriched the simple and subdued brick exterior of No. 29 with neo-Gothic details around the main door, horizontal banding in the midsection, and arches at the top story. Real estate ads touted the benefits of the residence, which featured housekeeping apartments of four to eight rooms and one to three baths, log-burning fireplaces, and "everything modern." A decade later, Eleanor Roosevelt planned to settle there with President Franklin Delano Roosevelt after his final term ended. She knew the neighborhood well, because from 1933 to 1942, she had kept a modest apartment on the top floor of a house at 20 West Eleventh Street, where her friends Esther Lape and Elizabeth Read lived. The fifteenth-floor apartment at 29 Washington Square appealed to her because the absence of steps from sidewalk to elevator made it easily accessible for the president's wheelchair. But President Roosevelt visited the apartment only one time. After his death in 1944, Mrs. Roosevelt lived there alone until 1949.

Following on the heels of construction at the Square's northwest corner, excavation began in November 1928 at the southern end of the block for a third large apartment house—37 Washington Square, a site previously occupied by three older dwellings. Gronenberg and Leuchtag, the architects of No. 29, enlivened the brick façade of No. 37 with similar Italian-Gothic details—arcaded windows, a stone parapet set on low arches, and colorful terra-cotta tile trim. Advertisements boasted of the apartments' modern conveniences—electric refrigeration, incinerators, kitchen exhaust fans, and enclosed showers. Keeping in step with its neighbors, the Holley Hotel situated at the midpoint of Washington Square West expanded the adjoining Holley Chambers into a sixteen-story apartment hotel in 1929.

Rapid development along the west side of the park inevitably destroyed some precious relics of the past. Yet over time, the four residential buildings along Washington Square West gained respect as standard-bearers of the 1920s style. Their dark brick exteriors and consistent cornice lines present a unified and harmonious street front. Balancing the tall loft buildings on the east side of the Square, together they form an imposing west wall for the great outdoor room that is Washington Square Park.

By the spring of 1932, the Sunday real estate section of the *New York Times* was advertising a dozen apartment houses on and around Washington Square. Only one was located on the south side of the park at 71 Washington Square, close to the eastern corner. Intended for middle-class tenants, it was, one ad discreetly stated, a residence "for people who without being extravagant have requirements developed through years of living in accord with their tastes and culture." On the blocks north of the park, one realtor estimated, at least thirty-eight buildings and six large apartment hotels had gone up in recent years. Most of them are still standing. The tallest among them and closest to the Square is One Fifth Avenue, a twenty-nine-story apartment-hotel that replaced four houses at 1, 3, 5, and 7 Fifth Avenue. It was developed in 1927 by Joseph Siegel and designed by Helmle Corbett & Harrison working with Sugarman & Berger, who specialized in apartment buildings. Compared to the more classically inspired styles favored on the west side of the park and along lower Fifth Avenue, One Fifth is jazz—its Art Deco setbacks and shaded masonry trim syncopated by Gothic Revival arcades, buttresses, and gargoyles. "There is a real kick in this super-castle, yet this is thoroughly modern architecture," Lewis Mumford wrote in the *New Yorker* of October 1, 1927. Although not immediately on the park—the building stands behind the Row and Washington Mews—its soaring towers have become an indelible element of Washington Square.

Depression

Withstanding the onslaught of development, Prohibition, and the uncertainties of the Depression, the Washington Square vicinity survived into the 1930s as a stable neighborhood made up of an affluent mixture of artists, professionals, and academics. When a 1937 Works Project Administration Guide emphasized the Village's bohemian atmosphere of "free verse, free lives, free world," local burghers objected to the characterization. They cited instead the precinct's forty-three churches in the one-and-a-third mile area, its four thousand flowering window boxes, the heavy attendance at community sings, and the highest rate of home ownership anywhere in the city. Furthermore, Greenwich Village's eight savings banks accounted for 10 percent of the deposits in savings banks in New York State, and 7 percent of savings bank deposits in the United States as a whole, the neighborhood paper, the *Villager,* noted on February 18, 1937. Harry Hopkins, head of the WPA in Washington, soon apologized to the community.

The park, however, was not faring well with city resources stretched to meet substantial welfare needs. Heavily used and sporadically tended, Washington Square's lawns were brown, its trees were withering, and the fountain was not flowing because the basin leaked so badly. Grass planted optimistically in the spring rarely thrived because of the "energetic small boys and unleashed dogs on the lawns," the Washington Square Association noted. (As a partial remedy, schoolchildren were assigned to monitor their peers.) Newspapers littered the park "from one end to the other" on pleasant days. "The only time Washington Park is clean is when it rains," a letter to the *New York Times* griped on March 21, 1930. Furthermore, paving was so badly cracked as to pose a danger to pedestrians. A similar problem had arisen thirty-five years earlier, when William Rhinelander Stewart had complained to Parks Commissioner David King about the condition of the asphalt paths, "so bad in many places that language is not adequate to describe it."[8] Finally, in 1931, acknowledging that walks needed to be completely repaved, the Parks Department applied 40,000 square feet of asphalt and 160 cubic yards of concrete to park paths.

By the spring of 1936, with the Depression deepening, parks throughout the city were suffering from increased vandalism and panhandling. Two hundred patrolmen were assigned to guard the public greens, and six additional watchmen on overlapping tours of duty were stationed at Washington Square to provide twenty-four hour protection.[9] Nonetheless, a busy schedule of activities in the park continued unabated that year. Hopeful poets displayed their verses on a fence next to the House of Genius during an outdoor poetry exhibition. The annual May Day parade led by Norman Thomas, socialist candidate for president in every election from 1928 to 1948, assembled in the Square before heading uptown. At the citywide American Ballad Contest held in the park in August, two barbershop quartets from the Village won first and second place. And on Labor Day, 1936, for the second year in a row, a band organized under the Federal Music Project played for a folk-dancing demonstration at the fountain, attracting three thousand spectators. A few weeks later, on the last day of the Washington Square Outdoor Art Exhibit, there was a great community sing. Most of these events, like the Square's semi-annual outdoor art exhibition begun in 1932, were related to federally sponsored programs designed to lift morale—or in the case of the art show, to increase artists' incomes—during the Depression years.

The consequences of such intensive park use made some Villagers uneasy. Early in 1938, it was announced that the official start of the World's Fair would lead off from Washington Square, and that after a review of troops in the park, a cavalcade of dozens of floats and forty-eight automobiles would pass under the Arch. In response to the community's concern that the anticipated crowds would ruin the park's fragile lawns, the parade through the Square was cancelled.[10] Rundown though it may have been, the park engendered a fierce loyalty among its users in the 1930s, a loyalty that would be severely tested as NYU, real estate developers, and Robert Moses, the city's ultimate "power broker," tried to impose their wills on Washington Square.

Robert Moses' Plans

Immediately following the inauguration of Republican Mayor Fiorello La Guardia on January 1, 1934, Robert Moses was installed as New York's parks commissioner. With his legendary vigor, Commissioner Moses spent the year attending to run-down parks throughout the city. He repaired the fountain in Washington Square, making it into a wading pool with steps, and fixed the leaking roof of the Arch, using New Deal funding and relief workers. One year later, however, Village residents were astonished to discover that Moses was preparing a comprehensive redesign of the Square. The *Villager,* a local weekly founded in 1933, broke the story on March 14, 1935: "Official plans for the complete remodeling of Washington Square Park will shortly be made public."

Officials declined to discuss the proposed makeover, but a fairly complete diagram somehow gleaned from the Parks Department indicated some radical changes. The plan, drawn by the landscape architect Mitchell Rapuano, called for symmetrically arranged grass plots, new benches, rough pavement to discourage roller skating, and groves of young trees to compensate for the older ones that would have to be removed. Traffic, which for years had followed a route down Fifth Avenue, under the Arch and through the park, would instead be diverted around the Square in a one-way circle around the green. The fountain, entirely redone only the summer before, was now to be torn out and replaced by a long rectangular reflector pool set directly south of the Arch and realigned with the monument and Fifth Avenue.

Within days the community was bristling with outrage, calling the plan an atrocity. The proposal would convert the Square "into an island of din surrounded by a racetrack," commented one irate resident in the *Villager*. John Sloan worried that buses driving around the Square would be "an encircling menace to the lives of children." And he objected to the Park Department's "pseudo-Europeanizing" of the park with formal patterns of paths and lawns and pool. "What is the matter with the Park Commissioner?" John Goodrum Miller of 71 Washington Square demanded in the *Villager* two weeks after the announcement. "Does he not know what Washington Square stands for? Would he put bowling alleys in the Parthenon, a swimming tank on Bunker Hill or a gymnasium in the Lincoln memorial?"

What really alarmed neighbors was not only the possible loss of the Square's old trees and irregular pathways, but the prospect of heavy traffic at their doorsteps. As details of the $2,000,000 plan emerged, it appeared that the streets encircling the park were to be widened to accommodate the increased flow of cars and buses around the park. The Washington Square Association immediately adopted a resolution opposing the traffic changes and moved to create a special committee to discuss improvements for the park with Moses. "Do something quickly," urged Gilbert Hodges of 29 Washington Square. "Commissioner Moses works fast. . . . He is hard to stop when he gets his chin up."[11]

Robert Moses' rise to power had begun in 1924 when Governor Alfred E. Smith appointed him president of the State Parks Council and commissioner of parks for Long Island. Within a few years, Moses managed to complete Jones Beach and the Northern and Southern State Parkways. He himself never drove—a private car and driver chauffeured him everywhere—and yet before his career ended forty-four years later, he had built all of the existing major highways, parkways, and expressways of metropolitan New York, with the exception of the East River Drive. He completed all the tunnels and bridges that link New York islands with the mainland, built most of the public and private housing projects, created Lincoln Center, and constructed hundreds of new parks and playgrounds in and out of the city. Although civil service rules prevented people from holding several public offices at the same time, Moses circumvented such restrictions, eventually heading twelve offices and operating through an authority whose records were never made public. As Robert Caro chronicles in his 1975 book *The Power Broker: Robert Moses and the Fall of New York,* Moses at the peak of his career had absolute power over every building project in the city. No contract could be granted without his approval. Brilliant, ruthless, and possessed of an iron will, he could be patronizing and mean-spirited—and he never forgot a slight.

In proposing a redesign for Washington Square before consulting the local population, Moses unwittingly launched a movement of tenacious civic activism. For three decades, the interrelated issues of the park's redesign and traffic in and around the Square plagued the neighborhood. Ultimately, Greenwich Village was the only community ever to vanquish Moses. But the seeds of distrust he planted have tinged most dealings between the city and the Village ever since.

A group of Village residents preparing to challenge Moses organized a "Save Washington Square Committee" to unify efforts of the Washington Square Association, the Greenwich Village Association, and dozens of other neighborhood groups opposed to the city's plans for the park. The Greenwich Village Association, with a broad membership that drew from all parts of the Village, invited Moses to speak at its annual meeting in May, but he declined to appear because of "pressing office duties." Moses as a rule never attended open meetings. Instead, he sent a letter to Mary Simkhovitch—the longtime director of Greenwich House and a nationally respected housing reformer he had come to know—to be read at the public gathering and printed in the *Villager* of May 23, 1935:

> You will be glad to hear that the reconstruction of Washington Square Park is going to be left to posterity. . . . We plan only to restore and improve the square now, without changing its present

basic character and design. There are all sorts of people around Washington Square, and they are full of ideas. There is no other section in the city where there are so many ideas per person, and where ideas are so tenaciously maintained. Reconciling the points of view . . . is too much for me. The filling in of Orchard Beach in the Bronx, the development of Jones Beach or of Marine Park in Brooklyn, and the building of the Triborough and Henry Hudson Bridges, are child's play in comparison.

Moses' retreat was temporary. Although he agreed to recondition Washington Square as it was—to patch walks, repair the boundary fence, reseed lawns and cultivate shrubbery—the promised face-lift never happened.[12] "So much money is being spent for trees and shrubs for all New York City, while Washington Square is so neglected," wrote an aggravated local to the *New York Times*, April 6, 1938. "Surely Commissioner Moses might give us a few loads of sod or just some grass seed. One of the benches ought to be placed in the Museum of the City of New York as an antique. The walks in the park are so broken, I doubt if a solid square foot could be found." At last, in the spring of 1939, Moses had forty new benches installed on the east side of the Square, to the surprise of NYU students, who until then had been accustomed to perching on the old iron rail fence along the boundary of the park.

In the summer of 1939, four years after his first round at Washington Square, Parks Commissioner Moses reintroduced his old plan for the Square, slightly modified but still featuring a broad circumference roadway. This time, the design called for an ornamental lily pond centered directly south of the Arch and flanked by symmetrically arranged play areas and public toilets. The WPA would provide at least $500,000 of the estimated total cost of $638,000, and work was scheduled to begin in October. The Washington Square Association and its allies at New York University objected. One of the sharpest opponents was

Henry H. Curran, a former borough president and deputy mayor, and a local resident. Curran said the plan resembled a "bathmat," an epithet that stuck through all subsequent discussions. But this time Moses did not yield. Remarking on "the strange assortment of human beings who live around the Square," he threatened the Washington Square Association that if controversy over the plan did not cease by November 1, the Parks Department would put the Square's renovation "at the bottom of the list of projects." In response, locals accused him of being "dictatorial" and "high-handed." After expressing strong disapproval of the plan, however, association members voted by a narrow margin (19 to 18) to accept it as "the only practicable solution."[13]

Other Village groups remained firm in their opposition and protests continued. NYU students organized a rally in November, with John Sloan as a featured speaker. The university mainly objected to the encircling double roadway on grounds that it would endanger the 32,000 students pouring in and out of classes at all hours.[14] Meanwhile, the Volunteer Committee for the Improvement of Washington Square, led by Pierce Trowbridge Wetter of 24 Washington Square North, was gathering signatures for petitions and meeting with city officials in an attempt to block the Board of Estimate from approving Moses' plan. With assistance from Robert C. Weinberg, a local architect, the committee also developed an alternative plan. Their scheme provided one-way traffic lanes around and through the park, and a pedestrian crossing along the entire east side near NYU.[15] Substantially less expensive to implement than the Rogers plan, the committee's scheme received the support of several civic groups, including the Citizens Union.

At the end of February 1940, Moses pulled back. Mayor La Guardia reassured the protesting groups that the proposed improvement for the Square was "so remote a plan there seems no need to worry about it."[16] But Commissioner Moses did construct three urgently needed play areas in the park in 1941, with the help of the WPA. A survey conducted by the Parks Department had determined that in addition to the hundreds of preschool children living around Washington Square, there were 4,500 pupils attending six nearby elementary schools, none of which had adequate playgrounds. Nor did the Square have any designated play spaces. Accordingly, Moses built one playground with slides, swings and jungle gyms on the south side of the park, and provided two sand pits and play equipment for younger children on the north. The areas were fenced in, provided with benches, and landscaped.[17]

World War II put a halt to work in the park. On June 19, 1945, a month after the peace treaty with Germany had been signed, General Dwight D. Eisenhower passed through Washington Square on a triumphal tour of the city. In honor of "Eisenhower Day" buntings and flags hung from buildings throughout the Village. When a great squadron of motorcycle police led the cavalcade onto Washington Square South, the general stood erect in his car. Hundreds of spectators, many of whom had sons, daughters, husbands, and sweethearts who had served under Eisenhower, waved and called out their individual welcomes. North of the Arch, local Girl Scout and Boy Scout troops massed their colors and received a personal salute from the commander.

Following the war, the Parks Department resumed its efforts to redo Washington Square and in 1947, sought to implement the so-called Rogers plan, named after Borough President Hugo E. Rogers, who introduced it. A modification of Moses' first scheme, it proposed to reroute traffic around the Arch and to provide for straighter roads through the park. But it also called for removing the fountain and adding a "turn-out" area in the central section of the park to accommodate eight to ten buses at a time.[18] Controversy swirled once again, forcing the Rogers plan to be shelved. Park redesign was once more put on hold pending the question of roads in and around the park. The issue of traffic would take another fifteen years to resolve, and along the way, there were other challenges for the community to overcome.

RADICALS AND REAL ESTATE

Saving the Row

While Moses continued to tinker with plans for the Square, developers were greedily eying the aged dwellings sitting on the valuable property along the park's perimeter. Rumors spread that Sailors' Snug Harbor might not renew the leases expiring in 1936 on the original Row
houses, and there was talk about building tall apartments on the property. Such fears were partially allayed when NYU leased 4 and 6 Washington Square North for long-term use. No. 5 had already been acquired by the university and remodeled as the chancellor's residence
in 1940. After considering overtures from developers and real estate
agents for a number of years, the trustees of Sailors' Snug Harbor announced in April 1937 that "to lease 'the row' for modern apartment
buildings would be to break faith with the original owners."[19] Locals
heaved a sigh of relief.

Sailors' Snug Harbor agreed to preserve the exteriors of the brick
Row houses while thoroughly modernizing the interiors to bring in
higher rentals commensurate with the property values. To meet the
requirements of "present-day families of the better sort," modern
plumbing and oil-fired heating were installed. Some of the houses
were to be divided into two- and three-room suites. Others could be
rented whole for $6,000 to $10,000 a year. It was even suggested that
the city should designate one of the houses as the official mayoral residence.[20] (Gracie Mansion was not designated as the mayor's home
until 1942.)

Although a number of the Row houses were already vacant, plans
were not filed until February 1939, by which time all the leases for No.
7 to No. 13 had been surrendered. The project extended to Washington Mews, the alley directly behind the Row, where former stables on
the north side had been converted into comfortable dwellings in 1916.
On the south side of the mews, Sailors' Snug Harbor now tucked in
some additional rental property—a line of two-story houses separated

from the Row by a garden. The small scale of the buildings, the gardens and the cobblestone alley all figured in the Mews's quality of "quiet charm," advertised in the *New York Times* of February 11, 1939.

Public Park or Private Campus?

After the war, veterans returning to school under the GI Bill were swelling the ranks of NYU students and taxing the school's facilities. To ease the space crunch, the university actively sought to acquire property around the Square as it came up for sale. Its acquisitiveness alarmed tenants who stood to lose their homes in the school's takeovers, and objections to NYU's expansionism rapidly spread through the neighborhood. The first place to come under scrutiny was the easternmost section of the Row. In October 1946, NYU announced that it had acquired 1, 2, and 3 Washington Square North and would take over the premises as soon as tenants were out. The university planned to use two of the Row houses for veterans' affairs and the third for religious-social groups: the Newman Club, the YMCA, and the Menorah Society.

Artist occupants of 3 Washington Square, stunned to receive eviction notices for the end of the year, protested vigorously. They were devoted to their walk-up studios with high ceilings and perfect light. Such attributes compensated for the hardships they stoically endured, such as hauling up their own coal for the fireplaces that were their sole source of heat until 1959, when heating was installed. Bathrooms, too, were communal. Edward Hopper had moved into a studio at 3 Washington Square in 1913. After his marriage to Josephine Nivison in 1924, he and his wife moved into a larger apartment on the fourth floor facing the park, where they shared a bathroom with neighbors until 1941. At a hearing before the Office of Price Administration in February 1947, another old-timer, F. W. Stokes, testified that he had lived in the house for nearly half a century. The eighty-eight-year-old artist calculated that he had paid out nearly $45,000 for his studio by then and said that he expected to spend his remaining years there. Students, too, pleaded with the university to let the artists remain in their studios. NYU lost, not out of consideration for tenants but for technical reasons of law, and the artists of No. 3 were allowed to stay.[21]

The success of residents battling NYU on the north side of the park was not matched on the south. Washington Square South is intersected by three streets to form four short blocks. On the easternmost block stood 71 Washington Square, the only tall apartment house on that side of the park. Along the park to the west, the row of old dwellings included the so-called "House of Genius" and the grave digger's home that later became Bruno's Garret. Judson Church dominated the third block between Thompson and Sullivan Streets, followed by the westernmost block of early nineteenth-century houses extending to MacDougal Street. Within a few years, this streetscape would present a very different face.

In the fall of 1947, attention shifted to two sections of Washington Square South. Anthony Campagna, a well-known local builder, had quietly bought up the frontage between Thompson Street and West Broadway in 1945 and filed plans for a twelve-story, 302-unit apartment house to be constructed as soon as lots were cleared.[22] The boardinghouses on his chosen block, dilapidated and draped with fire escapes, were "rickety, ratty and unsanitary," recalled a former lodger, but they were treasured for their illustrious history. Extending the appellation of Branchard's "House of Genius," this stretch of low-scale buildings became known collectively as "Genius Row." Its threatened loss outraged the community.

Bishop William T. Manning, the retired bishop of the Episcopal Diocese of New York and a resident of 8 Washington Mews, hatched a plan to save the block by converting the houses into a "living art center" with studios, galleries, classrooms, and homes for artists and writers. Passionate about preserving the Square's cultural heritage, Manning set out to raise funds for the project. He assembled a committee, which included Henry Curran, John Sloan, and Carl Van Doren, and won the endorsement of City Planning Commissioner Robert F. Wagner Jr. Edward Hopper, Thornton Wilder, Lewis Mumford, and Eugene O'Neill, among others, heartily supported the idea. Campagna offered to sell the property to Manning's committee, but it was unable to raise the money in time.

On Saint Patrick's Day, 1948, the easternmost house of Genius Row came down. As if to strengthen the claim that genius had truly dwelt in these rooms, the wrecking crew discovered short poems scribbled on walls of the ground floor and murals painted in quarters upstairs. Still hopeful of saving the remaining three houses, Manning persevered in his fund-raising, cheered by the Supreme Court's reversal of the eviction order served on occupants in the remaining houses. But at the end of June, after another option to buy expired, the bishop admitted defeat: no angels had come forward to save the Square.[23] Demolition on the remaining houses began immediately. Plans for the apartment house specified that the structure would be of modified Georgian design, seven to fourteen stories high, arranged in setbacks. There would be 240 apartments of from one to five rooms and some terraces. The *Villager* of July 1, 1948, reassured its readers regarding Anthony Campagna's intentions: "Knowing him as this community does, it can be assured that the new building will help maintain the highest traditions of this residential neighborhood."

Two weeks later on July 16, the front page of the *New York Times* issued a thunderbolt: Campagna had sold his property to New York University. "In a surprise purchase reported to be in keeping with its long-range expansion and building plans for the blocks facing Washington Square," the university had acquired Genius Row and, with the exception of one small parcel, the entire block between Washington Square and West Third Street. Campagna explained that NYU had been "feeling his pulse" about his willingness to sell ever since he bought the property in 1945. At the end of June, however, "well-known

289

public officials," whom Campagna declined to identify, had made a strong plea for him to turn the block over to NYU. The university re-opened negotiations and quickly closed the deal on July 7. One of the unidentified "public officials" was understood to be Robert Moses, acting in his capacity as city construction coordinator.

Campagna acknowledged that he and his family were making a "substantial sacrifice" in selling the block, but said that they "were motivated by their interest in educational matters. . . . Neither I nor my sons . . . would stand in the way of something that will be of more enduring value to the public than our project." The price to be paid by NYU was the appraised valuation refigured by a realty company, plus an additional sum to cover some of the builder's accrued expenses. News of the deal set neighbors howling and prompted the City Rent Commission to investigate for possible violations. NYU's sly purchase raised local residents' worst fears that the school intended to "usurp" the Square at what they felt to be the expense of "public interest."[24] The next year, Campagna announced that he would use the thousand tons of steel ordered for his thwarted project on Washington Square South to construct a fifteen-story apartment house in St. Louis.[25] After Genius Row was razed, the land stood empty. In an attempt to soothe community relations, NYU temporarily converted the lots into a park area with grass, cross walks and benches. On the corner of Thompson Street across from the Judson, the school built a tennis court over the spot where the grave digger's house had stood.

The Law Center

In September 1947, around the same time that Campagna had filed plans to build an apartment house on the site of Genius Row, NYU announced its intention to build a Law Center somewhere along the south side of the park. Refusing to identify the exact location, Vice-Chancellor Leroy Kimball stated only that the projected structure would cover an entire square block and would conform to the architectural character of the surroundings. Almost immediately, it became evident that the only possible site was the westernmost block between MacDougal and Sullivan Streets, running south from Washington Square to West Third Street. That property, owned by Columbia University, was "under contract for sale" said a representative in September 1947, and leases would not be renewed. The lots in question included 42 Washington Square, the address celebrated in Jack Reed's verse.

The three hundred tenants living on the block, joined by artists, publishers, and neighborhood and church groups, immediately formed a committee to block the proposed law school building. They collected ten thousand signatures and petitioned city administrators to invoke legal protection for "public monuments, historical and traditional spots and artistic sites." Their cause was supported by an eclectic group of prominent citizens, including Eleanor Roosevelt, the statesman Elihu Root, The Museum of Modern Art's director, Alfred Barr, and the jazz musician Teddy Wilson. City Councilman Joseph Sharkey asserted that NYU was "definitely breaking the spirit of the law by attempting to evict people. Moreover, it is wrong to preempt Washington Square Park as a campus." But NYU Chancellor Harry W. Chase, relying on the advice of Parks Commissioner Robert Moses, remained silent. Moses believed the community was acting "irresponsibly" and advised university officials to "keep still about the whole thing rather than try to concoct any elaborate defense."[26]

A year before the Law Center plans were announced, the Washington Square Association had released a comprehensive survey of Greenwich Village by one of its members, the architect and city planner Arthur C. Holden. Intended as a guide for future development, the 1946 study had designated three sides of the park to be preserved as residential areas. Holden recommended that NYU's growth be limited to sections east and south of Washington Square. The university had contributed money to help pay for the report, and some NYU personnel were members of the Washington Square Association. Thus, to many in the community, the university's subsequent proposal for a law center on the Square and its purchase of land from Columbia were a measure of the school's disregard for its neighbors. The outcries continued through the fall and winter of 1947–48. "The university indicated little desire to work out its problems within the framework of larger plans for this vital area of New York City," complained the *Villager*. "Nor, for that matter, have the Planning Commission and Mr. Robert Moses.[27]

"What good are thousands of more lawyers if the essence of decent community living has been destroyed in one of the few residential parts of the city?" queried Morris Ernst, a neighbor. "The Square itself will eventually become the campus of N.Y.U. unless the residents of Greenwich Village do something about it," another letter to the *New York Times* warned. Former Borough President Henry Curran added to the protests: "The proposed Law Center would inevitably turn the western half of Washington Sq. into a campus. . . . With the easterly half already under that kind of blight, the whole square would be stolen from the public to whom it belongs and made an adjunct of an institution." Another local resident concisely summed up the neighborhood's view: "A public park is not intended as a private campus."[28]

In June 1948, New York University purchased the parcel along the park from MacDougal to Sullivan Street south to West Third Street from Columbia University. About 310 people, a number of them families, resided in the twenty-two houses on the site. At the end of October, occupants received a formal notice from the law school's dean, Russell Niles, requesting that they vacate their homes by December 31, 1948, two months away. The university offered the services of its real estate agent to help tenants find new quarters and granted a two-month concession on rent, hoping to encourage them to move voluntarily. Residents mobilized to resist eviction, hiring a lawyer to represent them, and raising funds for legal fees by tithing themselves 25 percent of their monthly rents. After meeting with Dean Niles, their lawyer reported that the university was "in no mood to negotiate" and wanted the Law Center completed by October 1950.[29]

Neighborhood groups solidly banded together in what they regarded as a crucial battle to protect the Square from NYU's grasp. Edward Hopper wrote to the *Villager* in February 1949, complimenting the paper for defending Washington Square in the face of NYU's aggression. "Any further infiltration . . . will ruin a fine old section of New York City, and everyone in the city should be aroused to defend it." That month, in response to all this criticism, a member of the university's debating team requested the radio station WOR to broadcast a debate: "Resolved: That Expansion on Washington Square Is in the Interest of the Public." Peter M. Toczek represented NYU; Otho K. DeVilbiss, secretary of Washington Square Neighbors, spoke for the opposition. At the end of the program, the station invited listeners to vote on the issue by sending in postcards. Within a few days, WOR's tally stood at 1,598 in favor of Washington Square Neighbors, 125 for New York University.[30] Barely two months later, on April 1, 1949, the university signed a lease with Sailors' Snug Harbor, extending its hold on the north side of the Square to include all the houses of the Row for 203 years.

On the south side of the park, legal tactics had slowed the eviction process, but despite the tenants' efforts, demolition began in August. The Law Center's cornerstone was laid on January 31, 1950. As work progressed, water began to seep into the excavation. A news photographer on the scene captured a view that appeared in the papers, and WPIX relayed the scene to thousands of homes with televisions. Evicted occupants and other local residents may have experienced some secret pleasure in the long-buried Minetta Water extracting sweet revenge on their behalf.

Shortly before the Law Center officially opened as Vanderbilt Hall in September 1951, the neighborhood was invited to a preview inspection and housewarming. The five-story brick and limestone-trimmed building by the firm of Eggers & Higgins, in collaboration with the university architect, Fiske Kimball, was designed around an open court, with an arcade along the park façade. To one critic, it suggested "more nearly Independence Hall in Philadelphia than the Brick Row across the Square." Setting aside months of rancor and minor stylistic quibbles, the general reaction was positive, or at least resigned. "It is safe to say that the ensemble does the Square no dishonour," the *New York Times* concluded on September 26, 1951.

Through the 1950s, NYU's presence quietly spread along the west side of the park. First the university acquired the two large apartment buildings on the north and south corners of Washington Square West (No. 29 and No. 37) to accommodate high-ranking university faculty and administrators. Then, in 1956, the Law Center Foundation used a gift of a million dollars from the Charles Hayden Foundation to construct a residence hall for the law students that would incorporate the Holley Hotel and Chambers at No. 33, midway along Washington Square West. Remodeled by the architects who designed the law school, the building was renamed Hayden Hall. Plans called for a swimming pool in the basement, but Minetta Brook interfered once more. In order not to disturb the waters of the stream, the pool was limited to a depth of four feet. The shallow pool is gone now, and since 1986, Hayden has been a dormitory for undergraduates.

A vestige of Minetta lives on, however, in the form of a two-foot tall bronze statue of Pan by Gutzon Borglum standing in a small room off the entry vestibule of Hayden Hall. The bronze, previously in the lobby of the Holley Hotel, was the centerpiece of a fountain fed by Minetta's waters. Some indication of the interest this work generated may be gleaned from the fact that the statue's dedication ceremony on December 3, 1930, was carried over seventy-four radio stations of the recently founded Columbia Broadcasting System. Not long after sculpting the delicate Pan, Borglum set to work on the colossal sculpture project for which he became famous—the Four Faces carved into Mount Rushmore in South Dakota.

High Rise on the North

No sooner had NYU begun constructing the Law Center on Washington Square South than a private developer announced the purchase of property on Washington Square North. In January 1950, a syndicate headed by Samuel Rudin acquired the Rhinelander holdings comprising the Rhinelander Apartments and two lots facing the park, plus a collection of residences along Fifth Avenue north to Eighth Street. Rudin expected to develop the site immediately into a large apartment house of no more than twelve stories, with terraces, landscaped roof gardens, and a parking garage. The high rise was to be designed by Emery Roth & Sons in "Colonial style," to harmonize with the neighborhood's historic architecture. "We recognize and respect the sentiment of the neighborhood with respect to preservation of the old-time atmosphere," Rudin assured the community.[31]

Five years earlier, Joseph G. Siegel had tried to acquire the property from the Rhinelander Estate for a similar purpose. Siegel, who had built One Fifth Avenue and was involved in the 1922 conversion of the Rhinelander Apartments, had proposed a twenty-eight-story apartment house for the site, with luxurious amenities he detailed in a *New Yorker* interview of January 1945. Wreckers were slated to start demolition for the $7,000,000 project the following November, but Siegel's plans were somehow squelched.

The most impressive house remaining on the property was the white limestone mansion at 8 Fifth Avenue, built in 1856 by John Taylor Johnston. No longer functioning as a single-family residence, the hundred-year-old house was partially occupied by NYU's Center for Safety Education. Next to it, at 4 Fifth Avenue, stood Johnston's former stable, shared by three organizations—the Voice Center Club, the Greenwich Village Church, and the Clay Club, where the sculptor Isamu

Noguchi had a studio. Slightly back from the street was the carriage house that had serviced 14 Washington Square. Renumbered 2 Fifth Avenue, it functioned as a residence for NYU's Chancellor Henry Chase in the late 1930s and was the home of the Theatre Collective when the novelist Dawn Powell ate supper there on New Year's Eve, 1934. "Any organization's dream," she noted in her diary. The carriage house also held the Engineering Women's Club, a group formed at the time of Herbert Hoover's presidential campaign. (Hoover had been dubbed the "Great Engineer" in 1928.) In addition to the organizations, about thirty families inhabited the various buildings.

Reaction to Rudin's plans was swift. As a boy, Hamilton Fish Armstrong had looked out on the 1896 "sound money" parade passing through the Arch. Now editor of the journal *Foreign Affairs*, he urged action: "A large apartment on the corner would throw the Washington Arch out of scale and make it look like a meaningless toy." He and a group of his friends hoped that public-spirited citizens might acquire the land and save the dwellings. "It is unthinkable that for the lack of a few hundred thousand dollars, New York is to lose these houses which are the only remaining monument of the life of Old New York." NYU, too, voiced concern that a taller building would "alter the architectural atmosphere" of the north side of the Square.[32]

New York Senator Herbert H. Lehman and Representative Frederic R. Coudert Jr. introduced bills in Congress to permit the federal government to accept the Rhinelander House and the Engineering Women's Club as historic property. But Samuel Rudin objected, arguing that the Rhinelander House was not an authentic piece of history—the three original Greek Revival houses on the site had been sacrificed in its making—but "a tenement that deserved to be torn down long ago."[33] Furthermore, the next two houses at 17 and 18 Washington Square North had been recently torn down because of building violations. Their lots stood empty except when used as exhibition space during the outdoor art shows on the Square. Opposition to Rudin's plan led the City Planning Commission to seek amendments for certain zoning regulations that would limit future residential buildings on the Square to a height approximating that of the existing row houses on Washington Square North. Amending the zoning laws was a slow and tedious process. Meanwhile, Rudin was legally within his rights, following an earlier regulation that allowed the height of a new building on the Square to reach twelve stories.

The civic agencies and planning groups struggling to save Washington Square finally reached a compromise with the developer in the spring of 1950. Rudin agreed to build the section of the apartment house occupying the five lots closest to the park at a height consistent with the cornice line of the old houses remaining on Washington Square. Two higher sections would rise to the rear. For several months, architects from Emery Roth worked with Harvey Wiley Corbett, an architect representing the Municipal Art Society, and Arthur Holden, author of the Washington Square Association's planning survey, to refine the compromise design scheme.[34] After viewing the final plans early in 1951, many neighbors considered the victory a small one. Yet only a year later, the Greenwich Village Chamber of Commerce honored Samuel Rudin for his "cooperation in maintaining the cornice line of the adjacent Washington Square North mansions" and for using red brick on the low section to conform to the Row.[35]

By taking advantage of municipal regulations that granted extra height in exchange for open courtyard space, Rudin was actually able to make the building nineteen stories high in the sections set farthest back from the park. The main core of the building rises fourteen stories, with five additional "setback" floors arranged in two towers. Julian Roth of Emory Roth & Sons designed the low, five-story section along the Square in a 1950s version of red-brick "Georgian" style to harmonize with the houses of the Row. The rest of the building received a more modern treatment, with gray glazed brick on the exterior. Interest in the building was greater than in any other apartment

RADICALS AND REAL ESTATE

house he had built, said Rudin, and applications for apartments out-numbered the available space.[36] Among the first tenants was the Hungarian-born photographer André Kertész, who resided at Two Fifth Avenue until 1985. Many of his well-known images of Washington Square were shot from his twelfth-floor terrace.

Moses Redux

Early in 1952, a front-page story in the *New York Times* informed its readers that the Parks Department had allocated funds to redo Washington Square Park. The renovations would follow the 1947 Rogers plan, which eliminated the fountain and created two straight north-south roads through the park. One road would be widened an extra eight feet to allow for bus parking. Playground facilities and a roller-skating area would be located south of the Arch between the roads. An aide to Commissioner Moses said the proposed changes would "improve the park along both ornamental and functional lines," and the Municipal Art Commission had already given its tentative approval. But parents and residents around the Square reacted with alarm when they realized that children would have to cross lanes of traffic to reach playgrounds surrounded by cars and buses. Shirley Hayes knew the park well from her time spent watching her four sons play there. She quickly organized the Washington Square Park Committee and with the help of another neighborhood activist, Edith Lyons, roused the neighbors. Within a month, four thousand people had signed petitions objecting to the Parks Department plan.[37] But defeating the current design was not enough. Hayes was determined to eliminate all traffic through the Square forever.

What seems obvious in retrospect was radical then. Impressed by the Village's opposition, Borough President Robert F. Wagner withdrew the Parks Department's plan in early June and agreed to discuss alternatives. Fifth Avenue buses could make the turnaround at the Arch, Hayes proposed, and other vehicles could circle the green, as they do at Gramercy Park. Closing the roads within the park would allow for much-needed play space.[38] It soon became apparent, however, that roadways through Washington Square were only one piece of a grander scheme to "beautify" Greenwich Village, and that behind that scheme was Robert Moses. The battle for eliminating traffic in the park was thus inextricably linked to Moses' larger vision for the downtown area.

Urban Renewal and a Library on the Square

Following World War II, the government initiated programs to address both the acute housing shortage and the deterioration of many inner cities. The goal was to clear out antiquated tenements in slum districts and replace them with high-rise housing projects. Under Title I of the National Housing Act of 1949, property for urban renewal could be acquired by the city and sold to private developers at reduced rates. As an incentive, the federal government would pay two-thirds of the loss incurred by the city in the sale of such property, and the city would assume one-third of the loss. The developer, or "sponsor," building on the land would pay all the construction costs, providing that workable redevelopment plans were approved by the community. Title I was never intended to allow private developers to exploit valuable property at high cost to the city and federal government. Nor was it meant to permit sound buildings to be demolished in order to satisfy private interests.

Park Commissioner Robert Moses, in addition to his other titles, was chairman of the mayor's Slum Clearance Committee. In 1949, he had tried to clear out a good part of the west Village but was stopped by the brilliantly organized community resistance led by Jane Jacobs. (Several years later Jacobs wrote *The Death and Life of Great American Cities* decrying such renewal projects, now a classic in urban studies.) Moses then turned his eye to the "South Village," authorizing a study for two housing projects in the area in March 1953. If completed, the first project would have destroyed the nineteenth-century cast-iron lofts in the area now known as Soho. The district was saved by a crusade launched by the historian and preservationist Margot Gayle, who was among the first to call attention to the historic and aesthetic value of cast-iron architecture. The second of Moses' projects, the Washington Square Southeast Redevelopment, focused on streets fanning out from the southeast corner of the Square, the old "French quarter," home to many of the city's European waiters and maître d's. There, Moses wanted to clear out narrow streets crowded with century-old housing, small businesses, and commercial lofts to construct three superblocks with nine fourteen-story apartment houses.

To secure the Title I redevelopment southeast of the Square, Moses enlisted NYU as a partner. Under Chancellor Henry T. Heald (the title of president was used after 1956), the university was then engaged in an intensive self-study to determine its future directions. With 38,000 enrolled students, NYU was eager to develop into an elite private university of national and international significance. In order to attain this goal, it would have to consolidate its programs and find space for constructing dormitories, classrooms, laboratories, and a library to supplement or replace its inadequate and obsolete facilities. Letters and memos preserved in NYU's archives indicate that Moses assured the university of the land it needed for expanding its facilities on Washington Square in return for the administration's support of his plans for the redevelopment project and roadway through the park. Eager to obtain land and recognizing the city's urgent need for housing, NYU backed the Title I proposal.[39]

Anticipating the public's hostility toward NYU's expansion, Moses counseled Chancellor Heald to overlook or ignore local opposition and to place the university's interests ahead of good relations with neighbors. And indeed, Village residents vehemently protested "Operation Eyewash," as they called the proposed redevelopment. After public hearings in September and October of 1953, the City Planning Commission agreed with the community and rejected both the Washington Square Southeast Redevelopment plan and Moses' speedway through the park. The Manhattan Borough President's Community Planning Board concurred. But in November 1954, the more powerful citywide Board of Estimate gave its approval to the $29,000,000 program, and the city took title of the land on November 19, 1954.

The following summer under Title I provisions, the Washington Square Development Corporation purchased the six-block, fourteen-acre parcel southeast of the Square for $5.2 million and began to build the high-rise housing blocks of Washington Square Village. New York University acquired three acres of property abutting the Square for $1.2 million and continued to raise money for the library and student center slated for Washington Square South. Loeb Student Center opened in 1959 on the west side of La Guardia Place, over the ghosts of Genius Row. Designed by Harrison & Abramovitz, Loeb was built in a modern style typical of the 1950s. Forty years later, it would come down to make way for a much larger student center, expected to open in 2002.

Building the library on Washington Square South was more problematic, because it came at a time when town-gown relations were at their lowest point. In 1960, the development corporation offered to sell the southern portion of its land to NYU for the original purchase price. By the mid 1960s, the university had purchased Washington Square Village, the high-rise apartment blocks built under Title I, to house faculty and married students. NYU was also constructing three new apartment towers designed by I. M. Pei, now known as the Silver Towers, on the southernmost acres. Although one of the new towers was designated as middle-income housing, the other two were reserved exclusively for the university. Further stoking the community's aggravation, Chancellor Heald's successor, Carroll Newsom, had promised that NYU would construct an experimental elementary school next to the towers, but it never happened. Instead, the university built Coles Gymnasium on the site.

Bobst Library, named for its major donor, Elmer Holmes Bobst, was not completed until 1972, after extended rancorous debate within the community. Neighbors questioned the legality under the Title I Slum Clearance Act of tearing down the modern, well-kept apartment house at 71 Washington Square—no slum—to build a library for a private university. They were troubled at the zoning changes and variances granted by the city and murmurings about deals made with Moses and other city officials.

When library plans by the architects Philip Johnson and Richard Foster were revealed to the public, neighbors were enraged. Railing against NYU's apparent insensitivity to the setting on a historic park, they objected to the library's immense size: the building would fill a full block, plus an extra forty feet of city land granted to the university by a municipal variance. (The library's bulky width and height could have been pared down with no loss of usable space, were it not for Johnson's 100-foot atrium rising twelve stories through the center.) Most disturbing to the community was that Bobst would tower over the Square and block light from the normally sunny, southern part of the park where children played. Led by Jane Jacobs and Democratic District Leaders Edward Koch and Carol Greitzer, dedicated residents conducted a shadow study to demonstrate the effect of the shadows Bobst would cast on the park in different seasons, but with no luck. The Elmer Holmes Bobst Library was constructed as planned. Standing on the east side of La Guardia Place, Bobst's fortresslike, twelve-story exterior faced in red sandstone mimics some of the classic elements of nearby commercial buildings. It dominates the Square by its sheer bulk and casts shadows over what had been the sunny south side of the park.

Around the time that Bobst was completed, shrinking enrollment and serious financial problems forced NYU to sell its McKim, Mead & White University Heights campus. At the beginning of the fall semester of 1973, the university brought all its undergraduates back to Washington Square. The new Bobst Library and the Loeb Student Center on the south side of the park formed the heart of New York University's distinctly downtown campus.

No More Traffic

After the bout over the Title I redevelopment in 1955, the community's focus returned to the issues of park redesign and roads through the Square. Moses, like Boss Tweed nearly a century before him, understood that improved traffic flow leading to a Fifth Avenue South address would enhance property values south of the Square. To him, the road was an essential piece of the Washington Square Southeast redevelopment, and he took an active role in promoting the schemes he favored for the park. The modified Rogers plan with a playground isolated by lanes of traffic was replaced by Borough President Hulan Jack's proposal, endorsed by Moses, for a depressed four-lane highway with a footbridge linking the two sides of the park. Villagers disparagingly nicknamed the plan "the Big Ditch." The Parks Department suggested yet another solution: a tunnel from Eighth Street to West Third Street, which would pass under the park. There was no mention of the old bones that might be encountered in the process of excavating. Moses then proposed a four-lane highway divided by a center mall planted with trees. In November 1957, Shirley Hayes and the Washington Square Committee bombarded Hulan Jack and Mayor Robert Wagner with 16,000 cards and letters expressing their opposition.

The *Village Voice*, an irreverent paper established in 1954, wryly noted at the time, "Whatever satisfaction Hulan Jack gets out of being Borough President . . . must certainly be modified by the fact that he has to look ahead to many more meetings with Villagers on the subject of traffic lanes through Washington Square."[40] Defying Moses, the borough president backed a plan for a two-lane road that would be only thirty-six feet wide. Moses called it "ridiculously narrow" and pressed for his extra twelve feet. An adequate road, he said, was part of the agreement with the developers of the Washington Square South apartments, who "were formally, officially, and reliably promised under the Slum Clearance Act . . . a Fifth Avenue address."[41]

Early in 1958, the Joint Emergency Committee to Close Washington Square Park to Traffic emerged under the leadership of Raymond Rubinow, an enigmatic figure who lived on Gramercy Park and described himself as a "foundation consultant" and civic activist. Rubinow assembled an impressive group of New Yorkers for his committee—Eleanor Roosevelt; Margaret Mead; Jane Jacobs, Norman Redlich, a NYU law professor; the *Village Voice*'s publisher, Edwin Fanchon; Mary Nichols; and several others. Jacobs was an astute pragmatist and, according to her peers, one of the best community organizers around. Mary Nichols kept the subject of traffic before the public through her hard-hitting articles in the *Voice*. Lewis Mumford, a longtime foe of Moses' approach, lent his support as well. "The attack on Washington Square by the Parks Dept. is a piece of unqualified vandalism. . . . The notion that Fifth Avenue must be made to plow through Washington Square to justify the change of West Broadway's name to Fifth Avenue is nonsensical," he argued at one hearing.[42] Eleanor Roosevelt agreed, writing in her *New York Post* column *My Day* for March 23, 1958: "I consider it would be far better to close the square to traffic and make the people drive around it . . . than to accept the reasons given by Robert Moses, Commissioner of the Parks Dept., to ruin the atmosphere of the square."

Employing shrewd tactics, the Joint Emergency Committee worked closely with other Village groups and used the press and political rivalries to great advantage. Redlich, later dean of NYU law school, recalled that rallies and other events calling attention to the traffic issue were scheduled on the weekends, not only to attract bigger crowds but also to make the papers on Monday, generally a slow news day. Carefully timed press releases to New York's eleven daily papers drew competing reporters, who invariably showed up for fear of missing a scoop.

Moses was feeling the pressure in the spring of 1958. Norman Vincent Peale, the influential pastor of the Marble Collegiate Church, wrote to the *New York Times* in April protesting the wider highway. "Little parks and squares, especially those possessing a holdover of the flavor and charm of the past, are good for the nerves—and perhaps for the soul. . . . Let us give sober thought to the preservation of Washington Square Park as an island of quietness in this hectic city." At a hearing before the City Planning Commission in May, Morris Ernst, a resident of the Square, claimed New Yorkers had a right to know whether there had been a "fix or clandestine talks" that committed the city to widening the road through the park. Ernst questioned Moses' relationship with the developers who were expecting their frontage on West Broadway to gain a Fifth Avenue South address and be connected to Fifth by a large roadway through Washington Square.

During a radio interview a few days later in May, Moses hinted at a strategic retreat as a means of attaining ultimate victory. "There is something to be said . . . for letting an unreasonable opposition have its way; find out by experience that it doesn't work. . . . How can you choke off all traffic in Washington Square? It is preposterous."[43] In July 1958, the City Planning Commission voted in favor of Hulan Jack's proposal for a two-lane road, thirty-six feet wide. But Moses, never one to give up easily, brashly asserted in his minority opinion that his four-lane semi-depressed roadway "will be accepted when drummed-up local hysteria subsides, mudslinging ends and common sense and goodwill prevail."[44]

During the mid 1950s, a reform group calling themselves the Village Independent Democrats (VID) were challenging the Tammany organization for control of the party. Led by Carol Greitzer, a future City Council member, and Edward Koch, later mayor from 1977 to

305

1989, the VID worked closely with Rubinow's Joint Emergency Committee to close the park to traffic. A VID poll released in March 1958 revealed that two-thirds of Greenwich Village voters disapproved of both Moses' and Jack's plans; 58 percent favored closing the park to traffic.[45] Because it was an election year, all the candidates for office—Republicans and Democrats alike—were supporting the park closing, hoping to win Villagers' votes that fall. Greitzer believes that the rival political factions actually energized people. The head of Tammany was Carmine DeSapio, officially the New York County Democratic leader and a powerful figure throughout the state. Redlich, a member of the Joint Emergency Committee and a reform Democrat, was appointed as a liaison to DeSapio. If the Tammany leader was convinced that most Villagers wanted the park closed, he would go along. And because Borough Commissioner Hulan Jack owed his political life to DeSapio, he too would fall in line. Some VID and Joint Committee members objected to consorting with DeSapio in this way. Although it proved effective, the tactic caused deep personal rifts among the group.

Prodded by the Tammany leader, the Board of Estimate scheduled a public hearing on Thursday, September 18. Rubinow's committee organized a rally in front of City Hall to take place before the hearing and presented Carmine DeSapio with a petition on a huge scroll weighing almost twenty pounds, signed with 30,000 names. About 150 people showed up sporting green "Save the Square" buttons and carrying pink, white and yellow "Parks are for People" parasols. During the hearing, DeSapio dramatically passed the petition on to the board and argued long and eloquently for closing the road. Representatives of the Washington Square Chamber of Commerce, NYU, and the Washington Square Association spoke in favor of the two-lane road. Mayor Wagner listened intently. The board postponed action on the proposal until the following month.[46]

On October 23, 1958, Borough President Hulan Jack, heeding De-

Sapio, requested the Board of Estimate to direct the traffic commissioner to keep all vehicles—except buses and emergency traffic—out of Washington Square Park. The trial period, expected to run for thirty to sixty days, began a week later. Ten-foot signs announcing the closing were placed at the northern and southern entrances to the park. Police directed traffic and helped confused drivers find alternate routes. Contrary to Moses' dire predictions, there was little congestion and no chaos.

To celebrate the hard-won victory, the Joint Emergency Committee staged a "Grand Closing" ceremony a week later on Saturday, November 1, 1958. "Square Warriors" and their children helped "tie up the Square with ribbons—not cars" and pushed a sedan labeled "last car through Washington Square" through the Arch. All the politicians up for election the following week made speeches and mingled with supporters. At the end of the afternoon, the crowd adjourned for a cocktail party and free champagne punch at the Fifth Avenue Hotel. Five months later, in April 1959, Washington Square was permanently closed to all but emergency traffic. Buses were restricted to a turn-around at the Arch or rerouted around the Square. After seven years of dogged fighting, Shirley Hayes's idea of a traffic-free Washington Square was a reality. "If Mrs. Hayes wrote the script," the *Voice* declared on April 15, "it was Ray Rubinow . . . who managed to pin down city officials and make them listen to it."

The community gathered for a final celebration at a gala masquerade party held June 12, 1959. Allan Churchill, author of *The Improper Bohemians,* presented silver keys to eleven designated "Square Savers:" DeSapio and Jack; Rubinow and Joint Committee members Jacobs, Redlich, Edith Lyons, George Popkin, Nathan Scheinman, and Stanley Tankel; *Villager* publisher Merle Bryan Williamson, and VID co-leader candidate Gwen Worth. A thousand costumed revelers paraded and danced to live music. The highlight of the evening came after midnight, when a group of Square Savers rushed to the stage to

seize a life-size cardboard effigy of an automobile that had been constructed by the stage crew of the Phoenix Theater. Ignoring an outbreak of rain, they ignited the cardboard sports car and watched it
burn, a symbol of the elimination of cars from Washington Square. For
the first time since the Parks Department took over the park in 1870,
Washington Square was traffic-free.

To those involved in the struggle, closing the Square to traffic represented a heroic victory—a double triumph of people over cars and
people over politicians. But to Gilbert Millstein, the situation presented an engaging paradox, noted in his book *New York: True North*
(1964). In the section of the city thought of as a first refuge of the
avant-garde—home to radicals and icon-smashers—the battles to save
the park were led by individuals of unimpeachable bourgeois respectability and fought not for the purpose of changing but of preserving. Looking back from our vantage point nearly a half-century
later, these respectable Villagers restored the integrity of the nineteenth-century parade ground to the twentieth-century park and did
indeed preserve a piece of history. But in doing so, they made it possible for the Square to change once again and renew itself for the
future.

Epilogue
Washington Square Today

*W*ashington Square at the beginning of the twenty-first century is thriving. Its pathways are full of pedestrians, its playgrounds are brimming with children, and its benches are well occupied. Clusters of young people sit on the low concrete rim encircling the central plaza; dozens more lounge around the fountain basin. In the chess area, players hunch over their games, fingers poised on timers. Mounted police pass by, the clip-clop of their horses evoking an earlier century in the park. Rarely does noise from surrounding streets intrude.

With the first hint of spring, picnickers spread out on the grassy areas and art students take out their sketch pads. Classes meet under the trees. In summer, sun-starved city dwellers stretch out on folding chairs and blankets on the lawn on the southwest side of the park. On hot days, when the fountain's jets send plumes of water skyward, it is likely that someone will splash in the water. In winter, whenever snow coats the city, sleds appear, snowmen grow, and snowball fights break out. Year-round, early-morning joggers and walkers pace the park's outer perimeter walk, an informal track a half-mile in length, while mutts and rare breeds mingle in the dog run, established in 1994 across from Judson Memorial Church. (A dog run had been instituted a few years earlier in the northwest section of the park, but early-morning barking disturbed residents, and so the run was relocated.) Dog owners, a forceful advocacy group in the park, have planted roses and other flowers along the exterior of the fence in an effort to make the graveled enclosure more palatable to those who do not own dogs.

The park closes at 11:30 P.M.—an announcement of the fact is intoned over a loudspeaker—and reopens at 6:30 A.M. During the night, to ensure general security and to limit homeless people from sleeping on park grounds, playgrounds and public toilets are locked and police barriers block entrances to the park. A few homeless men and women do climb over the low railings to sleep in the Square, but more seek shelter on the neighborhood streets.

On weekends and mild days throughout much of the year, locals are easily outnumbered by tourists from faraway places and visitors from elsewhere in the city, all of whom come to observe or participate in the spirited life of the Square. Jamming musicians, jugglers, fire-eaters, international performers, and buskers of every persuasion vie for attention in and around the fountain basin. Washington Square is now more densely used, per square foot, than any other park in the city. Heavy use takes a toll. Lawns turn to dust; garbage overflows. On Sunday evenings, the debris spills over the numerous garbage cans and wafts out to the surrounding sidewalks. By Monday morning, park workers and municipal sanitation crews have temporarily returned the place to a tidier state.

Neighbors in the vicinity have come to accept the Square's crowded, carnival-like atmosphere as a condition to be enjoyed, endured, or ignored. But when the first beatniks and bongo drums appeared in the late 1950s, many nearby residents were uneasy. There was a sense that the park was being taken over permanently by "outsiders," whose spontaneous performances were not entirely welcome. (One of the original "beat" personalities was Allen Ginsberg, who gave readings of his works in the park.) The 1961 folksingers' revolt in Washington

Square—the very words might provoke smiles nowadays—was an early signal of this shift in park use.

Folksingers had been meeting in the park on warm Sundays for many years, and as the popularity of their music grew, so did their audiences. After traffic was banned through the center of the park, the area around the fountain became a more congenial place for large groups to assemble. Noise was escalating. Early in April 1961, Parks Commissioner Newbold Morris banned folksinging in Washington Square, stating that "unnecessary noises, musical or otherwise, must not be allowed to conflict with other persons' right to a little peace and quiet." The musicians and their followers protested, there were scuffles with police, and fistfights broke out; ten people were arrested. Further demonstrations over the next weeks involved thousands of people. While many Villagers and New Yorkers at large viewed Morris's decree as an infringement of civil rights, a number of local residents supported the ban. It was not the singing they objected to, they said, but the fact that the music attracted crowds from all over the metropolitan district, "creating an overcrowded, unsanitary, disorderly condition."

Visitors had been flocking to the Village and passing through Washington Square for decades. Mocked in a previous era as "thrillage hounds" and disciplined for unruly behavior during Prohibition, outsiders were generally tolerated because they were good for the local economy, and their boisterous presence was usually temporary. Rebellious youths were nothing new either, but the 1960s generation seemed different. It was not necessarily the folksingers but the beatniks and hippies—long-haired and unkempt, hanging out in packs—that made some locals uneasy. The ban on singing was lifted a month later, and musicians returned to the park. People who frequented the Square in those days reminisce about hearing Bob Dylan, Joan Baez, and other folk icons at the outset of their careers strumming near the fountain.

EPILOGUE

If remembered at all today, the ban on singing in the park only made city officials look foolish. Nonetheless, the folksingers' protest, contemporary with the incipient civil rights movement, raised some fundamental questions with regard to public space: How do we determine what is permissible? Whose rights are paramount? And whose park is it after all? These issues are just as relevant today as Washington Square continues to wrestle with ongoing challenges.

Drugs first came into the park around the same time as the folksingers were gathering at the fountain. In a 1964 article in the *New York Times* analyzing the unique sociology of Washington Square, Gay Talese observed how each of the park's distinct populations staked out its own territory—the secret to their successful co-existence. Families and kids, motorcycle "cats," Frisbee-tossing students, old marrieds and "squares" each had their particular turf. The walk between the Holley statue and the chess area in the southwest corner was designated "junkie row." Through the 1960s and 1970s, drug dealers aggressively expanded their turf in the park. Head shops selling drug paraphernalia opened on nearby streets, bolstering the Square's reputation as an easy place to find narcotics. Dozens of the stores survived until Mayor Rudolph Giuliani's controversial crusade on "quality of life" infractions closed them down in the mid 1990s.

Reports of earlier grievances—tramps in the park of the 1890s, or vandalism in the 1930s—convey a level of annoyance or disgust, but never intimate that physical safety was threatened. In the early 1970s, Washington Square was a dangerous place. In 1973, Oscar Newman, a professor of city planning at NYU, said the screams of people being mugged in the park often reached the windows of his bedroom at 29 Washington Square. Newman, the author of *Defensible Space,* a book on the use of design strategies to limit crime, proposed that a seven-foot wrought iron fence, compatible in design with the historic railings along the Row, be erected around the park to combat muggings, vagrancy, and vandalism. The fence, an expensive and to many a dubious proposition, was never built. (Fencing is not popular among Village egalitarians.) Shortly afterward, New York City was facing a devastating fiscal crisis. Municipal budgets were slashed, and families who could afford to move—more often white than black—left in droves. It was a bleak period for Gotham, as it was for urban centers around the nation.

As the "white flight" during these years might suggest, Washington Square was not immune to the racial tensions reverberating across the country. On an evening in September 1976, the lethal combination of drugs, race, and mistaken identity led to a tragic fatality in the park. A gang of young white men and boys armed with clubs and chains swept through the park looking for a dealer who had sold one of them oregano instead of marijuana. Warned of the impending attack, black pushers fled, but one young man, a native of the Dominican Republic and a member of his nation's volleyball team, was struck down by a club from behind and died a week later from the blows. A writer for the *Village Voice* who lived around the park laid the blame squarely on his neighbors' doorsteps. "The community of Greenwich Village permitted a blatantly criminal situation to flourish in Washington Square, and that situation generated a blatantly criminal response. The people who created the cause cannot duck the responsibility for the effect." This was a painful challenge to a district that prided itself on its liberal values.

A decade after New York's fiscal crisis, the economy picked up, and New York began to rejuvenate. Real estate values rebounded, and there was mounting pressure on municipal authorities to clean up parks and restore security. In the mid 1990s, the Giuliani administration assigned extra police to the Square, where they have continued to make frequent drug sweeps and conduct "sting" operations aimed at buyers as well as pushers. In addition, over a dozen surveillance cameras were installed around the Square to provide police with a taped record of any questionable activities. The cameras have remained in place, as has a police van permanently stationed on the south side of the park. Police maintain that the tapes are destroyed promptly after review, but some locals consider the cameras to be a violation of privacy and strenuously object to the heavy police presence on the Square. Although more muted than before, vestiges of drug dealing stubbornly remain despite all the enforcement measures. During crackdowns, dealers seep out to adjacent streets. When things quiet down, they stealthily return to offer "smokes" to prospective customers, while the usual park activities swirl around them.

The Square's physical appearance today is the outcome of a 1970 renovation planned entirely by and for the community in a unique process that might only have happened in the Village. With roads through the Square closed—except for the bus turnaround—at the end of 1958, the park site regained a physical integrity that had been lacking since Boss Tweed's redesign a century earlier. Streets within the park were officially "de-mapped" in 1959; three years later, the ground occupied by the roads was transferred from the Department of Transportation to the Parks Department. The transfer had the effect of increasing park land by three-quarters of an acre, from 8.26 to 9.749 acres. After buses were prohibited from using the park as a turnaround terminal in 1963, Washington Square, traffic-free at last, was ready for its long-awaited rehabilitation.

With the promise of an uninterrupted expanse came the opportunity to rethink what the Square should be. Writing in *Death and Life of Great American Cities* in 1961, Jane Jacobs declared that the park, beloved and valued over so many years, was one of the most successful in the United States, stimulating passionate attachment among widely differing income, occupational, and cultural groups. She urged that Washington Square be treated tenderly and the reasons for its popularity studied and applied to the field of planning. However, the Parks Department under Commissioner Morris proposed a formal, symmetrical design, which would have required, among other changes, moving the fountain in line with the Arch. The plan was roundly rejected by Villagers and blasted by architectural critics for its tired vision and deadly clichés.

Over a period of months that stretched to years, the local Community Planning Board No. 2, chaired by Anthony Dapolito, worked with representatives of local organizations to reach some consensus about the Square's future. (District planning boards made up of local residents had recently been formed as a way providing direct liaison with the borough president's office and other city agencies.) At the board's recommendation, Dapolito appointed a committee of nine Village architects, who, working with the Parks Department, agreed to redo the Square according to guidelines hammered out by the community. Robert Nichols, a landscape architect, coordinated the team effort. In the four decades since undertaking the redesign process, Dapolito has remained on the community board, currently serving as head of the Parks committee. Dapolito, the proprietor of Vesuvius Bakery in the South Village, where he grew up—nowadays regarded as an extension of Soho—is the city's longest-serving community board member and affectionately, if unofficially, acknowledged as the "mayor" of Greenwich Village.

The refurbished Square—those involved preferred to call it a restoration rather than a redesign—maintained the gently curving walks and lawns of the historic park, but introduced other features that affected how the park would be used. Although some elements have been altered or added—like the dog run— the 1970 scheme has for the most part remained intact. Play spaces were carefully planned for each age group from young toddler to teenager, and set on the elevated, brick-paved section near the "teen plaza" on the south side of the park, there are even courts for petanque, a game similar to bocce. The playgrounds of 1970 on the north side of the park, designed for younger children, were replaced in 1995. An "adventure" playground intended for older children near the southwest corner has now all but disappeared. Its wooden play equipment, deemed unsafe by later safety standards, was dismantled a few years ago. The only remnants of that play area are three prominent "mounds," artificial asphalt-covered hills, which have deteriorated but manage to attract occasional skateboarders or toddlers trying to master their first hill. Whenever there is talk of removing the mounds, nostalgic supporters speak out on their behalf. In recent years, the mounds area has functioned as a set for informal productions of Shakespeare plays, presented free for several weeks each summer. A more formal stage area is formed by the raised podium southeast of the fountain, overlooking the plaza around the Garibaldi monument. Frequently used for concerts and performances, it serves as the setting for the Washington Square Music Festival's outdoor summer concerts, coordinated since 1977 by the daughter of the woman who started the music series in 1959.

The greatest change brought about by the 1970 community renovation was the opening up of the central area around the fountain to create a large sunken plaza. Ringed by shade trees, the plaza is accessible on four sides by a series of shallow steps, now paved over into ramps, that lead to a broad encircling walkway. Low concrete walls under the shade trees along the plaza's rim provide perches for sitting or watching people or performers in the circle. Secondary circular plazas in each corner of the park and at the Holley and Garibaldi monuments attract smaller gatherings. These open spaces were intended to make the Square safer by allowing for greater visibility as people walked through the park, day or evening. In practice, however, the dimensions of the main sunken plaza create an arena that encourages large crowds to congregate. Despite many signs around the park prohibiting bicycle riding and skateboarding, the central expanse of paving around the fountain, with ramps on four sides, is too enticing for some to resist.

Barely a dozen years after the community refurbished the park, there was talk of redoing the Square, of "correcting" features viewed as the unfortunate result of design by committee. Village leaders, proud of the park and the process by which it was accomplished and always leery of municipal interference, rejected the idea of a makeover. Now more than two decades later, while there may be agreement about the need for enhancing the landscape or replacing mismatched benches and mixed styles of lighting fixtures, little public money is available, especially since the disaster of September 11. At the beginning of 2002, however, the community board began discussing the idea of a comprehensive restoration of the park, a subject on which the community has many opinions.

In the minds of many locals, the greatest threat to Washington Square is NYU's growth along the south side of the park. The university's latest building projects on the Square—a new student center and an expansion to the law school—revived feuding over park "ownership" and reignited long-smoldering town-gown antagonisms. Not since the building of Bobst Library in the late 1960s had the community been at such loggerheads with the school.

The first of the expansion projects is located on the corner where Loeb had stood for forty years before being demolished in 1999. Over the ruins of the former student center rises the university's new, twelve-story Helen and Martin Kimmel Center for University Life and Skirball Center for the Performing Arts. Designed by Kevin Roche John Dinkeloo & Associates, the Kimmel Center was designed to match the height and scale of Bobst Library and harmonize with the university's Main Building and other loft buildings along the east side of the Square, now all NYU facilities. Although it fits the footprint of the defunct Loeb Student Center, the Kimmel Center is more massive. Critics are disturbed that the new building towers over the park, blocks the sun, and closes in the Square. Since the landmarked district ends at the park, buildings along Washington Square South can rise as high as zoning will allow, which is twelve stories. The new campus center also houses the 1,000-seat theater of the Skirball Performing Arts Center, which opponents fear will cause severe traffic congestion around the park. But in June 2000, a state supreme court judge dismissed a community lawsuit seeking to bar the university from further construction until an environmental impact study could be made and lifted the temporary restraining order halting work at the site. As of this writing, construction moves ahead on the Kimmel Center, which is due to be completed before the end of 2002.

Separated by just over a quarter of a century, the Bobst Library and the Kimmel buildings highlight NYU's transition from a commuter school to a major residential urban research university. The Kimmel Center proclaims the resounding success of the institution's transformation. New York University is now the largest private university in the country and one of the top-ranked institutions of higher education in the United States and throughout the world. Admission to the college and graduate schools has become highly selective, and student life around Washington Square is flourishing. Since the current boundaries of the campus stretch well beyond the Square, the university has introduced nonpolluting "trolleys," run on compressed natural gas and painted a vivid violet, the school color, to shuttle around students and faculty.

The second NYU project affecting the south side of the Square is not technically on the park, but involves the smaller houses around and behind Judson Memorial Church. Early in 2000, the law school announced its purchase of houses a block south of the park on West Third Street, and along Thompson Street, where the church owned a row of buildings that it could no longer afford to keep up. Judson was promised the space it needed in the law school's new building, and in return, NYU gained contiguous property, so that the arrangement seemed fair.

But the community immediately leapt at the law school's plan on three counts. First, NYU's eleven-story structure on the block was to rise directly behind the bell tower of the Judson Memorial Church, competing with the silhouette of the historic, nationally landmarked structure. Second, the unified row houses along Thompson Street, used by the Judson for church programs, were of architectural significance because they had been designed in the 1890s by McKim, Mead & White as part of the church complex. And, third, one of the small, shabby red-brick houses around the corner at 85 West Third Street (then called Amity Street) had been the home of Edgar Allan Poe and his wife for about six months in the winter of 1844–45. Despite the fact that nothing was left of the original interior from Poe's time, the house's association with the writer galvanized fierce and widespread opposition to its demolition. An alliance of determined local residents, preservationists, Poe scholars, and others joined battle, and the university, led by John Sexton, dean of the law school, agreed to compromise. (Sexton takes over as NYU's president in the fall of 2002.) Taking into account the community's major objections, the architectural firm Kohn Pedersen Fox Associates redesigned the law school's addition to incorporate the façades of the historic houses and reduce the height of the tall sections behind Judson tower. By broadening the bulk of the building to fill the full half-block along West Third Street, the architects maintained the same the square footage for the school. While the university's accommodation may signal improved relations in the future, the law school's expansion and the new student center undeniably change the south side of the Square.

New York University and Washington Square are closely bound by a shared history and location. Every year in May, the Square is awash in purple gowns and banners as NYU holds its graduation ceremonies in the park. Trumpets blare from the top of the Arch, and for that day, Washington Square is truly the university's quad and the Arch its symbol. Hours later, the folding chairs are gone, bleachers have been broken down, and the usual mix of park patrons drifts back in. Approximately 50,000 students attend the school in some capacity, and a good portion of them live in the vicinity. Their impact on the local economy and local street life is obviously significant, but the community rarely complains about student pranks or disturbances. In fact, most residents acknowledge that they enjoy living around an academic center. It is usually the administration that is the butt of bad feelings.

Over the past twenty years, the school has made a concerted effort to improve its image in the community. To keep channels of communication open and address issues of mutual concern, the Office of Community Relations, established years ago to work with the neighborhood, holds regularly scheduled meetings with representatives of community groups. Members of the university's administration sit on the boards of local organizations and community board committees. NYU makes its concerts, lectures, films, and other programs available to the public, opens the library and sports center to residents (on a limited basis) and generously provides facilities for community-sponsored activities. For many years, the university has organized annual clean-up days in Washington Square, provided funds for extra park personnel and projects, and run summer programs for children. Every year on Halloween, NYU bagpipers lead costumed youngsters on a march around the Square. At Christmas, a school brass group accompanies carolers at the Arch. In conjunction with the forthcoming restoration of the Washington Arch, NYU established an endowment in 2001 to provide funds for the monument's perpetual maintenance. While fully appreciating the university's generosity and numerous services to the community, neighbors remain ambivalent about NYU's intentions. Years and years of battling the university superpower have left a residue of distrust and disappointment that is tough to dissolve.

For one hundred and seventy-five years, Washington Square Park has managed to work well as a public green space. During all that time, it has rarely been in very good condition. The park was already run-down in the 1850s, a little over twenty years after it began functioning as a parade ground and fashionable square. The state of the park had slipped enough after its rebirth in 1870 to trouble residents at the time the Arch was built in the 1890s. Throughout the 1930s and on into the rest of the twentieth century, locals were continuously registering the same tiresome complaints to the Parks Department. Badly cracked and patched pavements were hazardous; the Arch needed care; litter was not picked up; trees and lawns required attention. Today, landscape experts would point to the critical need for soil restoration, long-term tree care, a sprinkler system, and restorative work on the Arch and fountain. But there are more plantings and mature trees in the park than ever before; the old hanging elm has weathered another precarious century. Flowers are blooming, the grass is mostly green, and the park gets by.

As amply demonstrated in the preceding chapters, Washington Square is no fossilized relic of the past. Its continuous and vigorous use, coupled with its ability to absorb change, exemplifies a more fluid attitude toward preservation. In his book *The Same Ax Twice: Restoration and Renewal in a Throwaway Age,* Howard Mansfield describes the fate of two objects. One old axe, its original parts intact and worn to a lovely patina, hangs on a wall as a treasured memento. Another axe of similar vintage is still in use, but its worn-out blades and handles have been replaced a few times over. Although the second tool retains none of its original elements, it functions as it was intended to, and thus remains essentially the same axe. The Square is a bit like that second axe.

Washington Square may never be a perfectly manicured park. It is too heavily used for that. Besides, park devotees would argue that such perfection would be contrary to the nature of the Square, that a certain urban grittiness is invigorating and essential to its appeal—and its beauty. A glance at the fountain, the Arch, and the buildings around the Square suggests its venerable past. A look at people in the park confirms the city's energy and diversity, keys to New York's healthy future. In the evolution of the site over the years—its multiple roles, the making of its monuments, and the efforts of loyal citizens to guard its welfare—Washington Square has been a remarkable laboratory for testing the principles of democracy. It is a fitting emblem of a city and a nation where anything is possible.

Notes

ONE From Potter's Field to Parade Ground

1. *Skinny Island: More Tales of Manhattan* is the title of a collection of short stories by Louis Auchincloss (Boston: Houghton Mifflin, 1987), but I was not aware of this at the time of writing.

2. For documents pertaining to freed Africans, see I. N. Phelps Stokes, *The Iconography of Manhattan Island, 1498–1909* (New York, 1926), 4: 73–106, 6: 1643–44. See also Christopher Moore, "Land of the Blacks," *Seaport* 3, no. 1 (Fall–Winter 1995): 8–13.

3. *Minutes of the Common Council of the City of New York, 1784–1831* (New York, 1917), April 10, 1797, 2: 336. The Council's *Minutes* are henceforth cited as *MCC*.

4. New York City Municipal Archives, Real Estate Records, TR 392 and 600; L274, P222, Apr. 10, 1797.

5. The petition from residents regarding the burial ground is acknowledged in *MCC*, April 24, 1797, 2: 339, and is quoted at length in Stokes, *Iconography*, 4: 1340.

6. *MCC*, May 15, 1797, 2: 348–49. New York City Municipal Archives, Common Council Papers, 1797–98, M.N. #6818.

7. *MCC*, May 29, 1797, 2: 351.

8. Ibid.; *MCC*, Aug. 7, 1797, 2: 374; Feb. 18, 1799, 2: 512; Apr. 6, 1801, 2: 725.

9. *MCC*, June 30, 1800, 2: 641.

10. *MCC*, Aug. 10, 1807, 4: 522; Aug. 17, 1807, 4: 525. The African Zion Methodist Episcopal Church used this burial ground until 1827 and then founded a new cemetery on lots owned by the church in Seneca Village, an African American settlement located between West 81st and 86th Streets on land that later became Central Park.

11. *MCC*, Sept. 5, 1808, 5: 25.

12. N. S. Olds, "The Stroller," *Villager*, Oct. 13, 1949, 16. The story also appears in Rufus Rockwell Wilson, *New York in Literature* (New York, 1947). Tragically, Hamilton's son Philip, at age twenty, had died three years before his father in a duel at Weehauken.

13. Peter Nielson, *Recollections of a Six Years' Residence in the United States of America* (Glasgow, 1833), quoted in Bayrd Still, *Mirror for Gotham: New York Seen by Contemporaries from Dutch Days to the Present* (1956; reprinted, New York, 1994), 103–4.

14. Complaints about potter's field, *MCC*, Sept. 6, 1819, 10: 53; interments, May 29, 1820, 10: 168; corpses Aug. 7, 1820, 10: 254–55; potter's field nearly filled, Dec. 20, 1824, 14: 211; decision to close, Jan. 31, 1825, 14: 307.

15. C. S. Francis & Co., *A Picture of New York in 1848* (New York, 1848), 85. From Bayrd Still Papers, NYU Archives, box 7, folder on burial grounds.

16. *New York Times*, Aug. 2 and 3, 1965.

17. *MCC*, Jan. 3, 1826, 15: 150; Jan. 16, 1826, 15: 160; Feb. 27, 15: 233–34.

18. *MCC*, Dec 18, 1826, 15: 748.

19. *MCC*, Jan. 27, 1827, 16: 48–49; Nov. 5. 1827, 16: 578.

20. *Evening Post*, April 20, 1829. Reference from Bayrd Still Papers, NYU Archives. "Talk on New York 1829," for the New-York Historical Society, 1979.

21. George Combe, *Notes on the United States of North America, during a Phrenological Visit in 1838–1839–1840* (3 vols.; Edinburgh, 1841), 23.

22. Gerald J. Barry, *The Sailors' Snug Harbor: A History, 1801–2001* (New York, 2000), 51. Luther Harris, "Washington Square," *Seaport*, Spring 1999, 30–32. Hone was familiar with Hudson Square, a private development predating Washington Square, on land owned by Trinity Church near the Hudson River. As a member of the Trinity vestry, Hone would have appreciated the income generated for the church from this project.

23. *New York Morning Herald,* May 19, 1835. The tale of Rip Van Winkle was published with "The Legend of Sleepy Hollow" in a collection of Washington Irving's stories in 1820. Irving, who often used the pen name Diedrich Knockerbocker, lived in Colonnade Row on Astor Place in the 1830s. The first issue of the *Morning Herald,* published by James Gordon Bennet, came out on May 6, 1835.

24. *New York Times,* June 6, 1881, 2.

25. NYU Archives, Exhibition on the University Building, April 1999.

26. The indestructible ailanthus is the tree in Betty Smith's novel *A Tree Grows in Brooklyn* (1943), of which two movie versions appeared. The Chinese call it the tree of heaven. But its foliage has a horrible smell when crushed.

27. *Evening Post,* May 11 and 14, 1849.

TWO   A New City Park Takes Shape

1. Mariana Griswold Van Rensselaer, "Fifth Avenue," *Century Magazine,* Nov. 1893, 5.

2. Ibid.; Arthur Barnes, "Washington Square," *Harper's Weekly,* July 14, 1894, 660–61.

3. The *New York Times,* May 18, 1871, noted that 110,000 ballots had been cast by 80,000 voters, out of a total population of 944,129.

4. *New York Times,* June 5, 1888, 8.

5. The New-York Historical Society, Department of Prints, Photographs, and Architecture, McKim, Mead & White Papers: Washington Arch correspondence file. Hereafter referred to as McKim, Mead & White Arch file.

6. McKim, Mead & White Arch file and *Harper's Weekly,* May 4, 1889, 343.

7. *Harper's Weekly,* May 11, 1889, 375.

8. Ibid., 378.

9. *Sun,* April 30, 1889, 1.

10. The *Evening Telegram, Springfield Republican,* and *Boston Transcript* endorsed the *Commercial Advertiser's* proposal, quoted in the *Commercial Advertiser,* May 3, 1889. The *World,* May 5, 1889, pronounced that although both the *Sun* and the *Tribune* were claiming credit for suggesting the permanent arch, "the honor belongs to the *Commercial Advertiser.*" Excerpts printed in the *Commercial Advertiser,* May 6, 1889.

11. *Chicago Herald,* May 7, 1889, quoted in the *Commercial Advertiser,* May 10, 1889; *Mail and Express,* May 13, printed in the *Commercial Advertiser,* May 15, 1889.

12. Letter from Robert De Forest to Stanford White, May 13, 1889, McKim, Mead & White Arch file. Information regarding the qualities of marble from conversations with Katherine Burns Ottavino, stone conservator and partner in A. Ottavino Corp., June and Nov. 1998.

13. Letter from William Stewart to Stanford White, May 5, 1892, The New-York Historical Society, New York City Misc. MSS: Washington Arch Papers, hereafter referred to as WAP, box 3, folder 1.

14. Letter from Stewart to White, December 7, 1891, McKim, Mead & White Arch file; letter from White to Stewart, Dec. 8, 1891, WAP, box 2, folder 2.

15. Letter from Stewart to White, April 16, 1891, McKim, Mead & White Arch file.

16. Letter from Stewart to White, Feb. 23, 1892, McKim, Mead & White Arch file; letter from White to Stewart, Feb. 25, 1892, WAP, box 2 folder 2.

17. *Sun,* Oct. 13, 1892, 2.

18. Letter from Stewart to White, Oct. 13, 1892, McKim, Mead & White Arch file.

19. Letter from Stewart to White, June 5, 1893, WAP, box 3, folder 1.

20. Letter from White to MacMonnies, Nov. 8, 1893, McKim, Mead & White Arch file.

21. Letter from Stewart to White, Jan. 8, 1894, WAP, box 3, folder 1. Press Release Jan.–Feb. 1895, WAP, box 3, folder 1. MacMonnies ultimately achieved wide recognition for his sculptural work on another arch—the Soldiers' and Sailors' Monument at the entrance to Prospect Park in Brooklyn, for which he designed the quadriga, 1898, and the army and navy groups, completed in 1904. And Stewart, a prodigious fund-raiser, was soon at work raising money to complete President Ulysses S. Grant's Tomb, begun in 1885 but not finished until 1897.

22. Michael Kammer, "Richard Watson Gilder and the New York Tenement House Commission of 1894," *Bulletin of the New York Public Library,* June 6, 1962, 364–82. The bill led to sweeping changes with regard to light, air, fire controls, sanitation, plumbing, and legal density in tenement hous-

ing, and it also earmarked $3 million for building new small parks on the lower East Side. Robert De Forest, another committee member, was also active in this area. He served as the first commissioner of the city's Tenement House Department under Mayor Seth Low, and was appointed chairman of New York State's Tenement Housing Committee by Roosevelt. Married to Emily Johnston, granddaughter of John Johnston, he lived for many years in the Johnston family house at 7 Washington Square North and, like his father-in-law, John Taylor Johnston, served as president of the Metropolitan Museum of Art.

23. The statement appeared in the *New York Mirror*, July 13, 1839, where it is attributed to the correspondent of the *Baltimore Transcript*, writing from New York. It goes on: "Never was the organ of destructiveness more prominently developed among any people than among the New Yorkers. No sooner has a splendid pile of buildings been erected . . . than a new whim arises, the work of demolition commences."

24. Joan Jacobs Brumberg, *A Mission for Life: The Story of the Family of Adironam Judson* (New York, 1980), 181–82. Brumberg quotes from an article written by Judson, "The Church and Its Social Aspect," *Annals of the American Academy of Political and Social Science* 30 (July–Dec. 1907): 4, and from Judson's introduction to Charles Hatch Sears, *The Redemption of the City* (Philadelphia, 1907), x.

25. Municipal Archives, lease between Memorial Baptist Church as landlord and James Knott, tenant of "The Judson," April 18, 1891.

26. NYU Archives, Judson Hall file.

27. NYU Archives, University Building file.

28. *New York Times,* Oct. 31, 1896, 8; Nov. 1, 1896, 1 and 3.

29. *New York Times,* Oct. 1, 1899, 3.

30. Letter from Stewart to White, Sept. 27, 1893, WAP, box 3, folder 1.

31. *New York Times,* May 27, 1916, 5; May 30, 5.

32. NYHS Arch file. Press Release by Stewart, "A New Statue of Washington for the Washington Arch"; also in *New York Times,* Feb. 22, 1918, 11. Stewart had alerted White to potential water problems in the summer of 1892. In spite of extensive waterproofing completed the previous March, he saw water falling from a pipe at the keystone and noted that after every rain there was trouble. McKim, Mead & White Arch file, Stewart to White, July 5, 1892.

33. From conversations with Katherine Burns Ottavino, June and November 1998. Ms. Ottavino conducted the 1998 stabilization work on the Arch and closely documented the findings.

34. *New York Times,* Jan. 18, 1909, 8.

35. NYU Archives, Washington Square Association, Yearbook for 1910, 15.

36. Leon Stein, *The Triangle Fire* (Philadelphia, 1962), 94. The *World,* which carried extensive coverage of the fire, reported that police at the morgue where bodies were laid out chased off more than forty pickpockets searching for jewelry or hidden purses (*World,* Mar. 26, 1911, 3).

37. Rosey Safran, "The Washington Place Fire," *Independent* 70, no. 3255 (April 20, 1911): 840–41. Saffran was interviewed by a representative of the *Independent* shortly after the fire. The article was reprinted in *ILGWU News History,* 1910–11, 6.

38. From remarks by Frances Perkins at the fiftieth anniversary commemoration of the fire, Mar. 25. 1961. Her speech was printed in full in *Congress Bi-Weekly: A Review of Jewish Interests* 3, n. 30 (Feb. 4, 1963). Excerpts from her talk also appear in Stein, *Triangle Fire.*

39. Stein, *Triangle Fire,* 207.

THREE   Radicals and Real Estate

1. Gelett Burgess, "East Side, West Side, All Around the Square," *Villager,* June 4, 1936, 12.

2. *The Letters of Lincoln Steffens* (New York, 1938), 2: 921, quoted in David Caute, *The Fellow-Travellers: A Postscript to the Enlightenment* (New York: Macmillan, 1973), 216.

3. *Quill,* Dec. 1, 1917, 22, quoting an earlier Bruno contribution.

4. NYU Archives, Washington Square Association Yearbook for 1921, 30–34.

5. *New York Times,* Apr. 30, 1922, sec. 2, 3.

6. *New York Times,* Oct. 3, 1928, 53, and Oct. 7, 1928, sec. 12, 1.

7. *New York Times,* Oct. 15, 1930, 25; May 1, 1932, sec. 12, 1–2.

8. Letter from William Stewart to David King, May 7, 1895, McKim, Mead & White Arch file.

9. *Villager,* Mar. 19 and May 14, 1936

10. *Villager,* Feb. 24–Apr. 28, 1938.

11. *New York Times,* Apr. 4, 1935, 23. *Villager,* Apr. 4, 1935, 8.

12. *New York Times,* Apr. 8, 1936, 25.

13. *New York Times,* Oct. 9, 1939, 21; Oct. 11, 1939, 29; Jan. 5, 1940, 21.

14. *New York Times,* Nov. 5, 1939, 48.

15. *New York Times,* Jan. 24, 1940, 1.

16. *New York Times,* Feb. 29, 1940, 21.

17. *New York Times,* June 4, 1941, and Nov. 24, 1941.

18. *Villager,* Sept. 8, 1949.

19. *Herald Tribune,* April 4, 1937, real estate section. In the mid 1930s, 1 Washington Square North was valued at about $15,000, as was the double house (No. 12–13) on the Fifth Avenue corner, but their lots were worth $90,000 and $260,000, respectively.

20. *Villager,* April 4, 1937, 6.

21. *New York Times,* Feb. 4, 1947, 27; Feb. 20, 12; May 17, 1947, 17.

22. *Villager,* Sept. 11, 1947, 1 and 6; Dec. 18, 1947, 20.

23. *Villager,* March 16, 1848, 1. *New York Times,* May 1, 1948, 13; June 28, 1948, 21.

24. *New York Times,* July 16, 1948, 21.

25. *Villager,* Oct. 27, 1949, 17.

26. *New York Times,* Sept. 29, 1947, 8; *Villager,* Sept. 18, 1947, 1; *Herald Tribune,* Oct. 19, 1947, real estate section, 1.

27. *Villager,* Nov. 4, 1948, 1; Feb. 10, 1949, 1; Feb. 16, 1949, 1.

28. *New York Times,* Sept. 11, 1947, 29; *Villager,* Sept. 18, 1947; Sept. 25, 1947; Feb. 26, 1948.

29. *Villager,* Nov. 4, 1948; Feb. 17, 1949, 16.

30. *Villager,* Feb. 10, 1949, 1.

31. *New York Times,* Jan. 4, 1950, 1.

32. *Villager,* Jan. 19, 1950, 16; Mar. 30, 1950, 1.

33. *Villager,* Apr. 4, 1950, 16.

34. *New York Times,* Mar. 4, 1951, 72. Anticipating the Landmarks Preservation Commission formed in 1965, the Municipal Art Society was then compiling a list of historic buildings to be considered for preservation.

35. *Villager,* Feb. 14, 1952, 1.

36. *New York Times,* Oct. 14, 1951, sec. 8, 1.

37. *New York Times,* Feb. 17, 1952, 1; *Villager,* Apr. 3, 1952, 1; May 29, 1952, 1.

38. *New York Times,* June 4, 1952.

329

39. Jonathan S. Freedman, "What Public? New York University, New York City, Public Relations and the Case of the Washington Square Southeast Redevelopment Project" (term paper, 1993, NYU Archives, Manuscript Collection 121.34). Freedman quotes extensively from correspondence between Moses and Heald regarding the redevelopment project and NYU's attitude toward the community. These papers are preserved in the NYU Archives Record Group 3.0.6, box 12.

40. *Village Voice,* Nov. 6, 1957.

41. Moses issued a statement regarding Washington Square on Dec. 24, 1957, reprinted in full in the *Village Voice,* Jan. 1, 1958, 1. His fixation on imposing a Fifth Avenue address on what was then a decidedly inelegant part of town attracted enough attention to be spoofed in a *New Yorker* column, " Talk of the Town," Apr. 4, 1959: "Can you imagine what it will be like when all those bars-and-grills and hardware joints have Bob Moses' Fifth Avenue addresses?"

42. *New York Post,* Mar. 8, 1958.

43. Robert Moses, interview, CBS radio program, *Let's Find Out,* quoted in *New York Times,* May 19, 1958, 27.

44. *New York Times,* July 17, 1958, 32.

45. *New York Post,* Mar. 8, 1958.

46. *New York Times,* Sept. 19, 1958, 1; *Villager,* Sept. 25, 1958.

Bibliographic Essay

No listing of sources can be complete in a project of this type, where detours are numerous and discoveries often serendipitous. What follows is a selective bibliography indicating the most relevant sources.

To unravel the Square's multilayered history, I scoured the New York City Municipal Archives and Records Center, the major repository for all such data, for property transactions—leases and deeds of sales—relating to the blocks and parcels around Washington Square. Early census records are available at the United States Census Office. Drawings and plans of New York City parks before 1934 are found in the Municipal Archives, but maps and plans after 1934 are housed in the Map File at the New York City Parks and Recreation Olmsted Center at Flushing Meadow. Photographs of the park after 1934 are located in the Photo Archives, Central Park Arsenal. The Board of Commissioners of the Department of Public Parks's *Annual Report* for the years ending 1871–74, the *Annual Reports* of the Department of Parks of the City of New York (New York, 1898–1934), and Borough of Manhattan *Annual Reports* after 1916 detail the projects, expenditures, and progress of work on individual parks.

Prime sources relating to the Arch are used courtesy of the New-York Historical Society. Material may be found in the McKim, Mead & White Papers: Washington Arch correspondence file, Department of Prints, Photographs, and Architecture, and under New York City Misc. MSS: Washington Arch Papers. The New York Public Library Center for the Humanities holds one of the few existing copies of *The History of the Washington Arch in Washington Square, New York* (New York, 1896). Family records are kept in the New York Public Library's Irma and Paul Millstein Division of United States History, Local History & Genealogy. For historic prints, the best sources are Columbia University's Avery Architectural and Fine Arts Library, the Metropolitan Museum of Art, the Museum of the City of New York, the New-York Historical Society, the New York Public Library's Miriam and Ira D. Wallach Division of Art, Prints and Photographs, New York University's Office of University Archives, the Tamiment Institute Library, and the Seymour B. Durst Old York Library at the Graduate Center of the City University of New York.

New York University's Office of University Archives has extensive material relating to Washington Square. Building files contain records on nearly every structure located along the perimeter of the Square, and the collection of prints and photographs is arranged by street and subject. The Office of University Archives also holds the Washington Square Association papers, with yearbooks and related material from 1906 on, as well as Bayrd Still's papers on Washington Square history, with information accumulated by this urban scholar over a lifetime—bibliography, notes on readings, lectures, and references to prime sources—a boon to any scholar in this field.

Throughout this project, I turned to I. N. Phelps Stokes's *The Iconography of Manhattan Island, 1498–1909* (6 vols.; New York, 1926, reprinted 1967), an indispensable finding aid and treasure trove of New York's history. Abundant references to Washington Square in magazines and newspapers of the nineteenth and twentieth centuries report events and relay attitudes and opinions. Among the most useful papers and periodicals are the *Century Magazine, Commercial Advertiser, Frank Leslie's Illustrated Newspaper, Harper's New Monthly Magazine, Harper's Weekly, Herald, New York Herald Tribune, New Yorker, New York Evening Post, New York Times, Scribner's, Sun, New York Tribune, Villager,* and *Village Voice.* Specific articles are cited in the text or notes only when quoted directly.

My research on the Square was greatly eased by the timely publication of several outstanding books on New York's history, which provided information as well as bibliographic cues: *The Encyclopedia of New York City,* edited by Kenneth Jackson (New Haven, 1995); Edwin G. Burrows and Mike Wallace, *Gotham: A History of New York City to 1898* (New York,

332

1999); and *New York: An Illustrated History* by Ric Burns and James Sanders with Lisa Ades (New York, 1999). I owe a special debt to Elizabeth Blackmar and Roy Rosenzweig's *The Park and the People* (New York, 1992), a study of Central Park that proved to be an exemplary and inspiring model. Jane Jacobs's *The Death and Life of Great American Cities* (New York, 1961) indelibly shaped my thinking about New York—and about all cities— many years ago.

Books about Greenwich Village abound. *Around the Square, 1830–1890: Essays on Life, Letters, and Architecture in Greenwich Village*, edited by Mindy Cantor (New York, 1982) suggested the potential breadth of Washington Square as a subject to me. Its essays were incorporated into and supplemented in *Greenwich Village: Culture and Counterculture*, edited by Rick Beard and Leslie Cohen Berlowitz and published for the Museum of the City of New York (New Brunswick, N.J., 1993). Many of the earlier guides are useful as well for what they reveal of their own times, as well as relating stories about the past. Among these, I would note especially Alice Chapin's *Greenwich Village* (New York, 1917), one of the first guides for tourists to the Village; Henry Collins Brown's *Fifth Avenue Old and New, 1824–1924* (New York, 1924) and *Glimpses of Old New York* (New York, 1916); and Charles Dickens's *American Notes* (London, 1842, reprinted 1957), with humorous but unsparing observations about the city at the time of his visit in 1842. Descriptions of the early parade ground can be found in Asa Greene's *Glance at Old New York* (New York, 1837), and there are also references to the Square in Thomas Janvier's *In Old New York* (New York, 1894, reprinted 2000); *King's Handbook of New York City* (New York, 1893, rev. ed., 1972); *Nelson's Guide to the City of New York and Its Neighborhood* (Edinburgh, 1859); Robert Shackleton's *The Book of New York* (Philadelphia, 1928); Frederick Van Wyck's *Recollections of an Old New Yorker* (New York, 1932); and E. Idell Zeisloft's *The New Metropolis, 1600–1900* (New York, 1899), which is noteworthy for historic nineteenth-century photographs. The *National Cyclopedia of American Biography* (New York, 1891–1984) is useful for information on nineteenth-century figures. In a more recent vein, Lloyd Morris's *Incredible New York* (New York, 1951) and Kate Simon's *Fifth Avenue: A Very Social History* (New York, 1978), are generally good for social history.

The *Villager,* a local Greenwich Village newspaper, which regularly pub-

333

lished columns on local history, published *The Villager Guide to Greenwich Village* (New York, 1959). *The Greenwich Village Guide,* edited by Clementine Wheeler (New York, 1947), offers information on the historic Village and a directory to 1940s attractions. Henry W. Lanier's *Greenwich Village Today and Yesterday,* with photographs by Berenice Abbott (New York, 1949), is prized for Abbott's 1930s and 1940s pictures of the park and local streets. André Kertész's *Washington Square* (New York, 1975) displays the photographer's images of the park from 1946 to 1971. Among later books on the Village and Square are Edmund Delaney's *New York's Greenwich Village* (Barre, Mass., 1967); Delaney and Charles Lockwood's *Greenwich Village A Photographic Guide,* with photographs by George Roos (New York, 1984); Carole Klein's *Gramercy Park: An American Bloomsbury* (Baltimore, 1987); Terry Miller's *Greenwich Village and How It Got That Way* (New York, 1990); and Gilbert Millstein's *New York: True North* (New York, 1964). All these worthy publications enriched my knowledge and helped me conceive the form and tone of this book.

Bruce Weber's *Homage to the Square: Picturing Washington Square, 1890–1965,* an exhibition catalog of the Berry-Hill Galleries (New York, 2001), is a thorough, well-documented survey of art and artists connected to the Square. Norval White and Elliot Wilensky's *AIA Guide to New York City* (4th ed., New York, 2000) is handy for checking architectural references. John Kouwenhoven's *The Columbia Historical Portrait of New York: An Essay in Graphic History* (New York, 1972) is a unique, well-organized annotated compendium of historic images. Christopher Gray's articles over the past decade or so in the *New York Times*, although not cited individually here, present detailed information about the city's historic buildings and streetscapes.

ONE   From Potter's Field to Parade Ground

Christopher Moore's "Land of the Blacks," *Seaport* 3, no. 1 (Fall–Winter 1995): 8–13, is a seminal study of the land grants and freed slaves of New Amsterdam. Specific references to the potter's field and parade ground are to be found in the *Minutes of the Common Council of the City of New York, 1784–1831* (New York, 1917). The history and architectural merit of every building in the historic district of Greenwich Village is described in detail in the New York City Landmarks Commission's *The Greenwich Village Historic District Designation Report* (New York, 1969), an exhaustive report prepared for the purpose of winning landmark status for the area, which happened in good measure because of this Herculean labor. See also Robert C. Weinberg, "Brief Historical Review of Houses on the North Side of Washington Square" (an unpublished report dated March 1963 in the New York University Archives). Several essays in Beard and Berlowitz's *Greenwich Village: Culture and Counterculture* deal specifically with the early years of Washington Square: see Thomas Bender, "Washington Square in the Growing City," 27–35; Carol Ruth Berkin, "Washington Square: A Woman's World," 134–41; Thelma Wills Foote, "CrossRoads or Settlement? The Black Freedmen's Community in Historic Greenwich Village, 1644–1855," 120–33; Sarah Bradford Landau, "Greek and Gothic Side by Side: Architecture in the Village," 68–82; and Bayrd Still, "The Washington Square Neighborhood, 1830–1855," 111–19.

For more information on the Row, see Gerald J. Barry's *The Sailors' Snug Harbor: A History, 1801–2001* (New York, 2000) on the historic ties between Snug Harbor and Washington Square; and Luther Harris's "How Sailors 'Built' Washington Square" in *Seaport* (Spring 1999), 28–35. See also Talbot Hamlin's *Greek Revival Architecture in America* (New York, 1944); Charles Lockwood's *The New York Row House, 1783–1929* (New York, 1972); and Donald J. Olsen's *The Growth of Victorian London* (New York, 1976). Two student papers on the subject are on file in the New York University Archives: Marlene Schiffman, "Washington Square Park as a Parade Ground, 1826–1851" (unpublished paper prepared for Introduction to Public History II, 1998); and Laura Helene Schoenbaum, "Manhattan's Washington Square Park: Its History, Evolution, and Prospects for Change" (M.A. thesis, Cornell University, 1988).

For specific aspects of New York's history, see Charles E. Rosenberg's *The Cholera Years: The United States in 1832, 1849 and 1866* (Chicago, 1962); Ira Rosenwaike's *Population History of New York City* (Syracuse, N.Y., 1972); and Edward Spann's *New Metropolis: New York City, 1840–1857* (New York, 1981) and "The Greatest Grid: The New York Plan of 1811," in *Two Centuries of American Planning*, edited by Daniel Schaffer (Baltimore, 1988). Thomas Bender's *New York Intellect: A History of*

335

Intellectual Life in New York City from 1750 to the Beginnings of Our Own Time (New York, 1987) was most useful for discussions of the founding of New York University and the relationships among artists, writers and patrons. Colonel Eammons Clark's *History of the Seventh Regiment of New York 1806–1889* (2 vols.; New York, 1890) describes the regiment's development and how it functioned—its use of the parade ground, role in local riots and service in the Civil War.

A number of sources are important for understanding the dynamics of class and race as played out on Washington Square before the Civil War. See Ivar Bernstein's riveting study *The New York City Draft Riots* (New York, 1990); Daniel J. Walkowitz, "The Artisans and Builders of Nineteenth-Century New York: The Case of the 1834 Stonecutters' Riot," in Beard and Berlowitz's *Greenwich Village: Culture and Counterculture*, 199–211. Both Sean Wilentz's *Chants Democratic: New York City and the Rise of the American Working Class, 1788–1850* (New York, 1984) and James Weldon Johnson's *Black Manhattan* (New York, 1930, reprinted, 1991) are illuminating studies that have become classics.

On art around the Square in this period, in addition to sources listed above, see Annette Blaugrund's *The Tenth Street Studio Building* (Southampton, N.Y., 1997); Neil Harris's *The Artist in American Society: The Formative Years, 1700–1860* (New York, 1966); and Catherine Voorsanger and John K. Howat's *Art and the Empire City, New York, 1825–1861* (New Haven, 2000). On individual artists, see Nicholai Cikovsky Jr. and Franklin Kelly's *Winslow Homer* (New York, 1990); *Alexander Jackson Davis—American Architect, 1803–1892*, edited by Amelia Peck (New York, 1992); Jacob Landy's *The Architecture of Minard Lafever* (New York, 1970); *Samuel F. B. Morse: His Letters and Journals, Edited by his Son, Edwin Lind Morse* (Boston, 1914; reprinted 1972); Samuel Prime's *The Life of Samuel F. B. Morse* (New York, 1875); and Paul J. Staiti's *Samuel F. B. Morse* (Cambridge, 1980).

Writers living in the area are discussed in Susan Edmiston and Linda Cirino's *Literary New York* (Boston, 1976), an extremely useful and well-documented volume, which covers the twentieth century as well. Literary and artistic life around the Square is discussed in two essays in *Greenwich Village: Culture and Counterculture:* Paul R. Baker, "Cultural Moorings

336

in the Nineteenth Century Village," 283–89, and Denis Donoghue, "The Jamesian House of Fiction," 302–7. Also helpful are Arthur Bartlett Maurice's *New York in Fiction* (New York, 1901) and Leon Edel's *Henry James: A Life* (5 vols.; Philadelphia, 1953–72), the definitive biography. Several of Henry James's works refer to the Square, notably *A Small Boy and Others* (New York, 1913); his *Autobiography* (New York, 1956), and his novel *Washington Square* (London, 1880, reprinted, 1986). See also Theodore Winthrop's *Cecil Dreeme* (Boston, 1861).

For personal reminiscences about early New York and life on the Square, see D. Maitland Armstrong's *Day before Yesterday, 1836–1918* (New York, 1920), written by a lawyer, diplomat, and artist who grew up near the Square and worked on projects with Stanford White; Emily Johnston De Forest's *John Johnston, Merchant* (New York, 1909), by the daughter of James Taylor Johnston about her paternal grandfather, the Row's founder, and id., *James Colles, 1788–1883: Life and Letters* (New York, 1926), about De Forest's maternal grandfather, both rich in period detail. *The Diary of Philip Hone, 1828–1851*, edited by Allan Nevins (2 vols.; New York, 1927), and *The Diary of George Templeton Strong*, edited by Allan Nevins and Milton Halsey Thomas (4 vols.; New York, 1952), are essential to any study of the city. The diaries of Edward Neufville Tailer, Jr. (1830–1917), 57 volumes dating from 1846 to 1917, preserved in the Manuscript Collection of the New-York Historical Society, are full of period detail and in the later years include news clippings and other items pasted on the pages. For a further sampling of firsthand impressions, see Bayrd Still's *Mirror for Gotham: New York Seen by Contemporaries from Dutch Days to the Present* (1956, reprinted New York, 1994).

The most complete discussion of New York University's history and its relation to the Square from the 1830s to the 1990s may be found in Thomas J. Frusciano and Marilyn H. Pettit's *New York University and the City* (New Brunswick, N.J., 1997). On the earlier years, see *New York University, 1832–1932*, edited by Theodore Francis Jones (New York, 1933), and Leroy Kimball, "The Old University Building and the Society's Years on Washington Square," *New-York Historical Society Quarterly* 32, no. 3 (July 1948): 149–219.

TWO   A New City Park Takes Shape

For information on Boss Tweed and the renovation of Washington Square
in the 1870s, I consulted the Department of Public Parks *Annual Reports*
for the years ending 1871–74, contemporary newspapers, and the following sources: Oliver Allen, *The Tiger: The Rise and Fall of Tammany Hall*
(Reading, Mass., 1993); William Alan Bales, *Tiger in the Streets* (Cornwall,
N.Y., 1962); and Alexander Callow Jr., *The Tweed Ring* (New York, 1966).
Rosenzweig and Blackmar's *The Park and the People* was extremely helpful for clarifying the politics and identifying the key figures, many of whom
were involved with Washington Square. Witold Rybszyinski's *A Clearing in
the Distance: Frederick Law Olmsted and America* (New York, 1999) enhanced my appreciation for Olmsted and also shed light on Ignaz Pilat, who
was responsible for the Square's redesign.

On the subject of public sculpture, see Michele Bogart's *Public Sculpture and the Civic Ideal in New York City, 1890–1930* (Chicago, 1989), and
Margot Gayle and Michele Cohen, *The Art Commission and the Municipal Art Society's Guide to Outdoor Sculpture* (New York, 1988). For information on particular sculptors, see also Wayne Craven's *Sculpture in America*
(Newark, Del., 1984); Lewis I. Sharp's *John Quincy Ward, Dean of American Sculpture* (Cranbury, N.J., 1985; and the Whitney Museum of American Art's *Two Hundred Years of American Sculpture* (New York, 1976).

The Centennial and the building of the Arch in Washington Square are
treated in two publications of the period: Clarence Winthrop Bowen, *The
History of the Centennial Celebration of the Inauguration of George Washington as the First President of the United States* (New York, 1892), and *The
History of the Washington Arch in Washington Square, New York, including the Ceremonies of Laying the Cornerstone and the Dedication* (New
York, 1896). The latter, with chapters by William Rhinelander Stewart,
Richard Gilder, and others, conveys the large sentiments and small details
that went into this great undertaking. The William Rhinelander Stewart papers and the McKim, Mead & White files on the Washington Arch, both located at the New-York Historical Society, together form a correspondence
that should delight anyone interested in the subject or period. Accounts in
contemporary newspapers and magazines provide a wealth of material, re-
course to which had to be limited given the scope of this book.

338

For further information on Stanford White, see Paul Baker's *Stanny* (New York, 1989); Leland M. Roth's *McKim, Mead & White, Architects* (New York, 1983); Richard Guy Wilson's *McKim, Mead & White, Architects* (New York, 1983); Robert Stern, Thomas Mellins, and David Fishman's *New York, 1880: New York Architecture and Urbanism in the Gilded Age* (New York, 1999); and Robert Stern, Gregory Gilmartin, and John Montague Massengale's *New York, 1900: Metropolitan Architecture and Urbanism, 1890–1915* (New York, 1983). Beth Sitterly, "The Washington Square Arch: A Case Study in the Cleaning of Marble at the Turn of the Century" (M.A. thesis, Columbia University, 1998), recounts the development of the Arch and its sculpture, with emphasis on the different marbles employed and the challenges of conservation. Also useful for discussions of art and architecture in this era are William H. Gerdts's *Impressionist New York* (New York, 1994), on images of urban life; Mary Smart's *A Flight with Fame: The Life and Art of Frederick MacMonnies (1863–1937)* (Madison, Conn., 1996); John Taurenac's *Elegant New York: The Builders and the Buildings, 1885–1915* (New York, 1985); and Bruce Weber's *Homage to the Square*, cited above.

The social and economic conditions of the period after the Civil War are fully examined in Eric Foner's *Reconstruction America's Unfinished Revolution, 1863–1877* (New York, 1988). The classic study of poverty and the plight of children in New York, Jacob A. Riis's *How the Other Half Lives* (New York, 1890, reprinted, 1971), describes conditions close to Washington Square. Michael G. Kammen, "Gilder and the New York Tenement House Commission of 1894," *Bulletin of the New York Public Library*, June 1962, 364–82, details the contributions of Richard Watson Gilder apart from his editorship of *Century Magazine* and his involvement with the Arch. See also two essays in Beard and Berlowitz's *Greenwich Village: Culture and Counterculture*: Mindy Cantor, "Washington Arch and the Changing Neighborhood," 83–92, and Josphine Gattuso Hendin, "Italian Neighbors," 142–50. From a more personal point of view, Hamilton Fish Armstrong's *Those Days* (New York, 1963) describes life around the Square at the turn of the century. Armstrong's father was D. Maitland Armstrong, whose memoir is noted above.

For material relating to the "second growth" around the Square in the 1890s, see Frusciano and Pettit, *New York University and the City*, on the construction of NYU's Main Building, and Joan Jacobs Brumberg's *A Mission for Life: The Story of the Family of Adironam Judson* (New York, 1980) on the building of Judson Memorial Church. Ron Chernow, *Titan: The Life of John D. Rockefeller, Sr.* (New York, 1998), throws more light on Judson's patron. Henry James's *The American Scene* (1907; reprinted, Bloomington Ind., 1968) records James's comments on the Arch and the Square in the early 1900s.

The following sampling of writings informs our thinking about the late-nineteenth-century Square. H. C. Bunner's *Midge* (New York, 1886) is a popular novelette by the editor of *Punch* about life on Washington Square South and the adjacent "French quarter." William Dean Howells's *A Hazard of New Fortunes* (New York, 1890, reprinted 1994) presents a sweeping view of the contemporary city, with specific descriptions of the park. Mark Twain and Charles Dudley Warner's *The Gilded Age: A Tale of Today* (Connecticut, 1874), is a broad satire of the post–Civil War era and Boss Tweed; Albert Bigelow Paine's *Mark Twain: A Biography* (New York, 1912) refers to Twain's meeting Robert Louis Stevenson. Edith Wharton's *The Age of Innocence* (New York, 1920, reprinted 1996) and the novellas in *Old New York* (New York, 1924, reprinted 1995) characterize the social set associated with Washington Square. Wharton's *A Backward Glance* (London, 1934) is her autobiography. More biographical material is found in Shari Benstock's *No Gifts From Chance: A Biography of Edith Wharton* (New York, 1994). See also a welcome new addition: *The Greenwich Village Reader: Fiction, Poetry and Reminiscences 1872–2002*, edited by June Skinner Sawyers (New York, 2001).

Among books dealing with the Triangle Fire, I found Leon Stein's *The Triangle Fire* (Philadelphia, 1962) to be most thorough and compelling. Newspapers from the time of the Triangle strike in the fall of 1909 and again in the days after the fire on March 25, 1911, are filled with harrowing stories and pictures.

THREE   Radicals and Real Estate

For information on the bohemian scene in New York, the most recent study is Christine Stansell's *American Moderns: Bohemian New York and the Creation of a New Century* (New York, 2000), an outstanding updated treatment of the subject. Notable earlier accounts are Albert Parry's *Garrets and Pretenders: A History of Bohemianism in America* (New York, 1933, reprinted 1960), for the nineteenth century, and Allen Churchill's *The Improper Bohemians* (New York, 1959), which focuses on the twentieth. Leslie Fishbein's *Rebels in Bohemia: The Radicals of "The Masses," 1911–1917* (Chapel Hill, N.C., 1982) examines the socialist publication *The Masses* and those involved with it. See also Edmiston and Cirino, *Literary New York* (cited above) for discussions of these and other writers living in the Village.

The period before World War I is described by several artists, writers, and radicals living around the Square: Djuna Barnes, *Greenwich Village As It Is* (1915, reprinted, New York, 1978); Willa Cather, "Coming Aphrodite," in *Youth and Bright Medusa* (New York, 1920, reprinted 1961); Edith Lewis, *Willa Cather Living* (New York, 1953), a biography of the author written by her companion; Floyd Dell, *Homecoming* (New York, 1933); and Max Eastman, *Enjoyment of Living* (New York, 1948). John Reed, *The Day in Bohemia: or, Life among the Artists* (New York, 1913) records his impressions in rhyme. *John Sloan's New York Scene, from the Diaries, Notes, and Correspondence, 1906–1913*, edited by Bruce St. John (New York, 1965) and *The Autobiography of Lincoln Steffens* (New York, 1931) are lively accounts of the prewar era by important participants on the scene. John Reed's lover Mabel Dodge Luhan's protracted memoir *Intimate Memories* (4 vols.; New York, 1933–36) is most relevant for volume 3, *Movers and Shakers*, about her salons at 23 Fifth Avenue and the Paterson Strike Pageant. Winifred L. Frazer's *Mabel Dodge Luhan* (Boston, 1984) covers similar material in biographical form. Harold S. Wilson's *McClure's Magazine and the Muckrakers* (Princeton, N.J., 1970) explores the pioneering journalism of the magazine and its writers.

On discussions of the political activism of this era and the interrelationship between art and politics, see Allen Antliff's *Anarchist Modernism: Art, Politics, and the First American Avant-garde* (Chicago, 2001), a fascinating and provocative study. See also Blanche Wiesen Cooke, "The Radical Women of Greenwich Village: From Crystal Eastman to Eleanor Roosevelt," 243–58, and Leslie Fishbein, "The Culture of Contradiction: The Greenwich Village Rebellion," 212–28, in Beard and Berlowitz's *Greenwich*

Village: Culture and Counterculture. Ronald Schaffer, "The New York City Woman Suffrage Party 1909–1919," in *New York History* 43, 1 (1962): 269–87, documents the progress of the suffrage movement with reference to activities around Washington Square. Issues of *The Masses* (1911–17), the Washington Square Association Yearbooks (1906–31 in the NYU Archives) and, on a more frivolous note, *The Quill* (1917–28), suggest the widely varying interests of Greenwich Village neighbors.

For specific artists working on the Square in the early 1900s, see William Gerdts's *William Glackens,* with an essay by Jorge H. Santis (New York, 1936); Ira Glackens's *William Glackens and the Ashcan Group* (New York, 1957); Will Hicock Low's *A Painter's Progress* (New York, 1977); John Loughery's *John Sloan, Painter and Rebel* (New York, 1995); Bernard B. Perlman's *Revolutionaries of Realism: The Letters of John Sloan and Robert Henri* (Princeton, N.J., 1997); and Helen Farr Sloan's *John Sloan: New York Etchings (1905–1949)* (New York, 1978). Gloria Vanderbilt Whitney and efforts on behalf of the progressive artists she befriended are discussed in Avis Berman's *Rebels on Eighth Street: Juliana Force and the Whitney Museum of American Art* (New York, 1990). For artists of mid century, refer to Irving Sandler, *The New York School* (New York, 1978).

Caroline Ware's *Greenwich Village, 1920–1930: A Comment on American Civilization in the Post-War Years* (New York, 1935, reprinted, 1977, 1994) is a sociological study of the different populations in the Village during Prohibition. For further information on the Village following World War I, note Daniel Aaron, "Disturbers of the Peace: Radicals in Greenwich Village, 1920–1930," 229–42; Brooks McNamara, "'Something Glorious': Greenwich Village and the Theater," 308–19; and Jan Ramirez, "The Tourist Trade Takes Hold," 371–92, in Beard and Berlowitz's *Greenwich Village: Culture and Counterculture.* On or by writers around the Square in 1920s and 1930s, see Thomas Clark Pollock and Oscar Cargill's *Thomas Wolfe at Washington Square* (New York, 1954), Edmund Wilson's *The Twenties,* edited by Leon Edel (New York, 1975); and Dawn Powell's *The Diaries of Dawn Powell,* edited by Tim Page (South Royalton, Vt., 1995).

Robert A. Caro's *The Power Broker: Robert Moses and the Fall of New York* (New York, 1975), the authoritative study of Moses, says little about his projects around the Square. Moses himself is more forthcoming but brief on the subject in his book *Working for the People: Promise and Performance in Public Service* (New York, 1956). See also Roberta Gratz's *The Living City* (Washington, D.C., 1989); Jane Jacobs's *Death and Life of Great American Cities;* and Jonathan S. Freedman, "What Public? New York University, New York City, Public Relations and the Case of the Washington Square Southeast Redevelopment Project" (NYU Archives MC 121. 34), which traces the evolution and implications of NYU's relationship with Moses through memos and correspondence preserved in the University Archives. Frusciano and Pettit's *New York University and the City* (cited above) addresses the subject as well. Joan Marans Dim and Nancy Murphy Cricco's *The Miracle on Washington Square: New York University* (Lanham, Md., 2001) celebrates the university at the turn of the twenty-first century. Robert A. M. Stern, Gregory Gilmartin, and Thomas Mellins's *New York, 1930: Architecture and Urbanism between the Two World Wars* (New York, 1988) and Robert A. M. Stern, Thomas Mellins, and David Fishman's *New York, 1960: Architecture and Urbanism between the Second World War and the Bicentennial* (New York, 1995, 2d ed., 1997) place the Square's development in the context of mid-twentieth-century architecture. The story of closing the park to traffic emerges from scores of articles in New York newspapers. In addition to scouring the *New York Times* index and issues of the *Villager* and *Village Voice,* I was fortunate to receive a set of clippings, correspondence, and related material, "Greenwich Village . . . The Sixties . . . The Fight for Preservation," compiled by Carol Greitzer for the lecture series in honor of Mary Perot Nichols at New York University, November 1996.

343

Index

Numbers in *italics* denote illustrations.

349

351

353

About the Author

Emily Kies Folpe was graduated from Bryn Mawr College and received her M.A. and Ph.D. in art history from Columbia University. She has worked at The Museum of Modern Art, New York, as educator and coordinator of public programs and has taught art history at Sarah Lawrence College and other institutions. Ms. Folpe is currently an independent scholar, lecturing at the Metropolitan Museum of Art and teaching at New York University's School of Continuing and Professional Studies. She lives with her husband on Washington Square.

Other Books in the Series

A Land Between, Owens Valley, California
Rebecca Fish Ewan

Spaces between Buildings
Larry R. Ford

Medicine Moves to the Mall
David Charles Sloane and Beverlie Conant Sloane

The Redrock Chronicles: Saving Wild Utah
T. H. Watkins